Microsoft® POWERPOINT® 97

Step by Step

Other titles in the *Step by Step* series:

*Microsoft Access 97 Step by Step

*Microsoft Excel 97 Step by Step

*Microsoft Excel 97 Step by Step, Advanced Topics

*Microsoft FrontPage 97 Step by Step

 Microsoft Internet Explorer 3.0 Step by Step

 Microsoft Office 97 Integration Step by Step

*Microsoft Outlook 97 Step by Step

 Microsoft Team Manager 97 Step by Step

 Microsoft Windows 95 Step by Step

 Microsoft Windows NT Workstation version 4.0 Step by Step

*Microsoft Word 97 Step by Step

*Microsoft Word 97 Step by Step, Advanced Topics

Step by Step books are available for the Microsoft Office 95 programs.

*These books are approved courseware for Certified Microsoft User (CMOU) exams. For more details about the CMOU program, see page xvii.

Microsoft®

POWERPOINT® 97

Step by Step

Perspection

Microsoft *Press*

PUBLISHED BY
Microsoft Press
A Division of Microsoft Corporation
One Microsoft Way
Redmond, Washington 98052-6399

Library of Congress Cataloging-in-Publication Data
Microsoft PowerPoint 97 step-by-step / Perspection, Inc.
      p.   cm.
    Includes index.
    ISBN 1-57231-315-3
     1. Computer graphics.   2. Microsoft PowerPoint for Windows.
    I. Perspection, Inc.
    T385.M522 1997
    006.6'869--dc21   96-38987
                                               CIP

Printed and bound in the United States of America.

1 2 3 4 5 6 7 8 9 Rand-T 2 1 0 9 8 7

Distributed to the book trade in Canada by Macmillan of Canada, a division of Canada
Publishing Corporation.

A CIP catalogue record for this book is available from the British Library.

Microsoft Press books are available through booksellers and distributors worldwide. For
further information about international editions, contact your local Microsoft Corporation
office. Or contact Microsoft Press International directly at fax (206) 936-7329.

Macintosh, and TrueType are registered trademarks of Apple Computer, Inc. Microsoft,
Microsoft Press, MS-DOS, PowerPoint, and Windows are registered trademarks of Microsoft
Corporation. Other product and company names mentioned herein may be the trade-
marks of their respective owners.

Companies, names, and/or data used in screens and sample output are fictitious unless
otherwise noted.

For Perspection, Inc.
Managing Editor: David W. Beskeen
Author: Steven M. Johnson
Production Editor: Gary Bedard
Copy Editor: Pam Mayne
Technical Editor: Holly J. Todd
Indexer: Marc Savage Indexing

For Microsoft Press
Acquisitions Editor: Casey D. Doyle
Project Editor: Maureen Williams Zimmerman

Perspection, Inc. & Microsoft Press

Microsoft PowerPoint 97 Step by Step has been created by the professional trainers and writers at Perspection, Inc., to the exacting standards you've come to expect from Microsoft Press. Together, we are pleased to present this self-paced training guide, which you can use individually or as part of a class.

Perspection, Inc. is a technology training company committed to providing information to help people communicate, make decisions, and solve problems. Perspection creates software training books, and designs and develops interactive multimedia applications for Windows-based and Macintosh personal computers.

Microsoft PowerPoint 97 Step by Step incorporates Perspection's training expertise to ensure that you'll receive the maximum return on your training time. You'll focus on the skills that increase productivity the most while working at your own pace and convenience.

Microsoft Press is the independent—and independent-minded—book publishing division of Microsoft Corporation. The leading publisher of information on Microsoft software, Microsoft Press is dedicated to providing the highest quality computer books and multimedia training and reference tools that make using Microsoft software easier, more enjoyable, and more productive.

IMPORTANT—READ CAREFULLY BEFORE OPENING SOFTWARE PACKET(S). By opening the sealed packet(s) containing the software, you indicate your acceptance of the following Microsoft License Agreement.

MICROSOFT LICENSE AGREEMENT

(Book Companion Disks)

This is a legal agreement between you (either an individual or an entity) and Microsoft Corporation. By opening the sealed software packet(s) you are agreeing to be bound by the terms of this agreement. If you do not agree to the terms of this agreement, promptly return the unopened software packet(s) and any accompanying written materials to the place you obtained them for a full refund.

MICROSOFT SOFTWARE LICENSE

1. GRANT OF LICENSE. Microsoft grants to you the right to use one copy of the Microsoft software program included with this book (the "SOFTWARE") on a single terminal connected to a single computer. The SOFTWARE is in "use" on a computer when it is loaded into the temporary memory (i.e., RAM) or installed into the permanent memory (e.g., hard disk, CD-ROM, or other storage device) of that computer. You may not network the SOFTWARE or otherwise use it on more than one computer or computer terminal at the same time. For the files and materials referenced in this book which may be obtained from the Internet, Microsoft grants to you the right to use the materials in connection with the book. If you are a member of a corporation or business, you may reproduce the materials and distribute them within your business for internal business purposes in connection with the book. You may not reproduce the materials for further distribution.

2. COPYRIGHT. The SOFTWARE is owned by Microsoft or its suppliers and is protected by United States copyright laws and international treaty provisions. Therefore, you must treat the SOFTWARE like any other copyrighted material (e.g., a book or musical recording) except that you may either (a) make one copy of the SOFTWARE solely for backup or archival purposes, or (b) transfer the SOFTWARE to a single hard disk provided you keep the original solely for backup or archival purposes. You may not copy the written materials accompanying the SOFTWARE.

3. OTHER RESTRICTIONS. You may not rent or lease the SOFTWARE, but you may transfer the SOFTWARE and accompanying written materials on a permanent basis provided you retain no copies and the recipient agrees to the terms of this Agreement. You may not reverse engineer, decompile, or disassemble the SOFTWARE. If the SOFTWARE is an update or has been updated, any transfer must include the most recent update and all prior versions.

4. DUAL MEDIA SOFTWARE. If the SOFTWARE package contains both 3.5" and 5.25" disks, then you may use only the disks appropriate for your single-user computer. You may not use the other disks on another computer or loan, rent, lease, or transfer them to another user except as part of the permanent transfer (as provided above) of all SOFTWARE and written materials.

5. SAMPLE CODE. If the SOFTWARE includes Sample Code, then Microsoft grants you a royalty-free right to reproduce and distribute the sample code of the SOFTWARE provided that you: (a) distribute the sample code only in conjunction with and as a part of your software product; (b) do not use Microsoft's or its authors' names, logos, or trademarks to market your software product; (c) include the copyright notice that appears on the SOFTWARE on your product label and as a part of the sign-on message for your software product; and (d) agree to indemnify, hold harmless, and defend Microsoft and its authors from and against any claims or lawsuits, including attorneys' fees, that arise or result from the use or distribution of your software product.

DISCLAIMER OF WARRANTY

The SOFTWARE (including instructions for its use) is provided "AS IS" WITHOUT WARRANTY OF ANY KIND. MICROSOFT FURTHER DISCLAIMS ALL IMPLIED WARRANTIES INCLUDING WITHOUT LIMITATION ANY IMPLIED WARRANTIES OF MERCHANTABILITY OR OF FITNESS FOR A PARTICULAR PURPOSE. THE ENTIRE RISK ARISING OUT OF THE USE OR PERFORMANCE OF THE SOFTWARE AND DOCUMENTATION REMAINS WITH YOU.

IN NO EVENT SHALL MICROSOFT, ITS AUTHORS, OR ANYONE ELSE INVOLVED IN THE CREATION, PRODUCTION, OR DELIVERY OF THE SOFTWARE BE LIABLE FOR ANY DAMAGES WHATSOEVER (INCLUDING, WITHOUT LIMITATION, DAMAGES FOR LOSS OF BUSINESS PROFITS, BUSINESS INTERRUPTION, LOSS OF BUSINESS INFORMATION, OR OTHER PECUNIARY LOSS) ARISING OUT OF THE USE OF OR INABILITY TO USE THE SOFTWARE OR DOCUMENTATION, EVEN IF MICROSOFT HAS BEEN ADVISED OF THE POSSIBILITY OF SUCH DAMAGES. BECAUSE SOME STATES/COUNTRIES DO NOT ALLOW THE EXCLUSION OR LIMITATION OF LIABILITY FOR CONSEQUENTIAL OR INCIDENTAL DAMAGES, THE ABOVE LIMITATION MAY NOT APPLY TO YOU.

U.S. GOVERNMENT RESTRICTED RIGHTS

The SOFTWARE and documentation are provided with RESTRICTED RIGHTS. Use, duplication, or disclosure by the Government is subject to restrictions as set forth in subparagraph (c)(1)(ii) of The Rights in Technical Data and Computer Software clause at DFARS 252.227-7013 or subparagraphs (c)(1) and (2) of the Commercial Computer Software — Restricted Rights 48 CFR 52.227-19, as applicable. Manufacturer is Microsoft Corporation, One Microsoft Way, Redmond, WA 98052-6399.

If you acquired this product in the United States, this Agreement is governed by the laws of the State of Washington. Should you have any questions concerning this Agreement, or if you desire to contact Microsoft Press for any reason, please write: Microsoft Press, One Microsoft Way, Redmond, WA 98052-6399.

Table of Contents

Table of Contents

Table of Contents

Saving a presentation,
see Lesson 1, page 18

Changing text in Outline
view, see Lesson 1, page 10

Moving around a
presentation,
see Lesson 1,
page 8

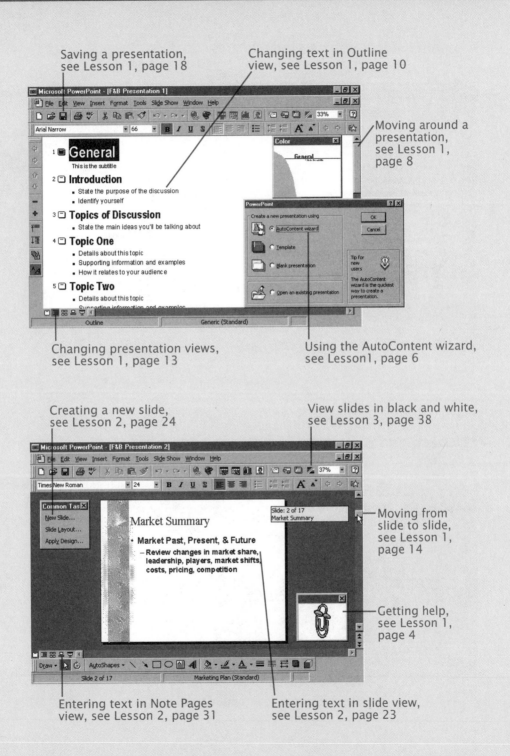

Changing presentation views,
see Lesson 1, page 13

Using the AutoContent wizard,
see Lesson1, page 6

Creating a new slide,
see Lesson 2, page 24

View slides in black and white,
see Lesson 3, page 38

Moving from
slide to slide,
see Lesson 1,
page 14

Getting help,
see Lesson 1,
page 4

Entering text in Note Pages
view, see Lesson 2, page 31

Entering text in slide view,
see Lesson 2, page 23

*Quick*Look Guide

Opening an existing presentation, see Lesson 3, page 36

Formatting text in Outline view, see Lesson 4, page 66

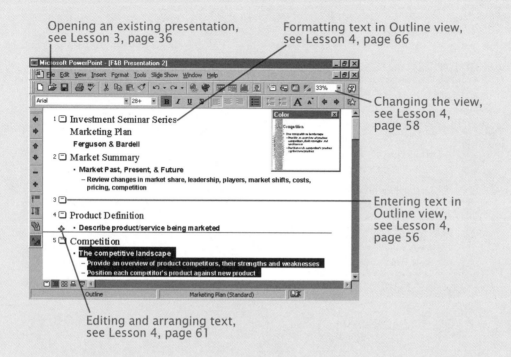

Changing the view, see Lesson 4, page 58

Entering text in Outline view, see Lesson 4, page 56

Editing and arranging text, see Lesson 4, page 61

Check spelling, see Lesson 5, page 82

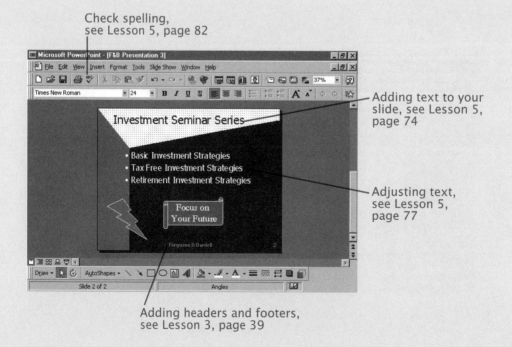

Adding text to your slide, see Lesson 5, page 74

Adjusting text, see Lesson 5, page 77

Adding headers and footers, see Lesson 3, page 39

Adjusting text indent markers,
see Lesson 6, page 105

Applying templates,
see Lesson 6, page 96

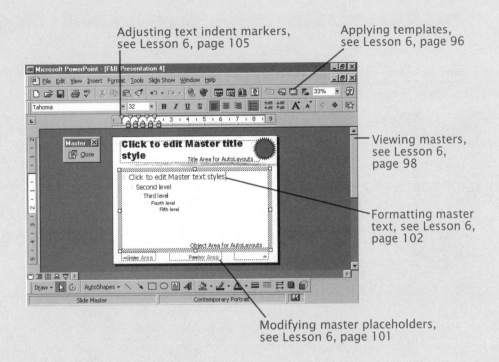

Viewing masters,
see Lesson 6,
page 98

Formatting master
text, see Lesson 6,
page 102

Modifying master placeholders,
see Lesson 6, page 101

Adding a background,
see Lesson 7, page 120

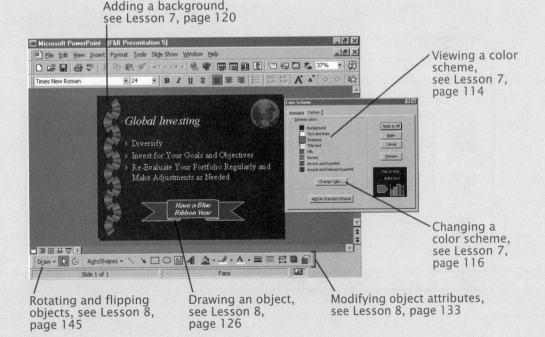

Viewing a color
scheme,
see Lesson 7,
page 114

Changing a
color scheme,
see Lesson 7,
page 116

Rotating and flipping
objects, see Lesson 8,
page 145

Drawing an object,
see Lesson 8,
page 126

Modifying object attributes,
see Lesson 8, page 133

Formatting a chart,
see Lesson 10, page 192

Inserting a Microsoft Word
table, see Lesson 9, page 162

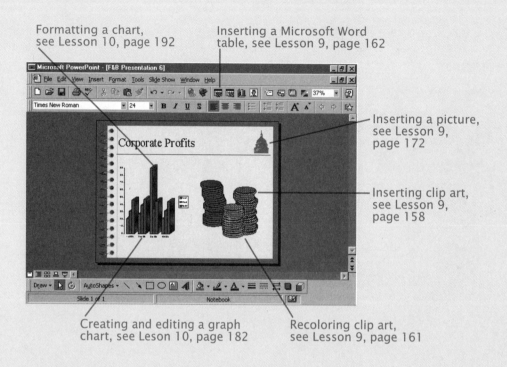

Inserting a picture,
see Lesson 9,
page 172

Inserting clip art,
see Lesson 9,
page 158

Creating and editing a graph
chart, see Leson 10, page 182

Recoloring clip art,
see Lesson 9, page 161

Inserting comments,
see Lesson 14, page 254

Creating hyperlinks,
see Lesson 13, page 240

Animating slide
text, see Lesson 11,
page 211

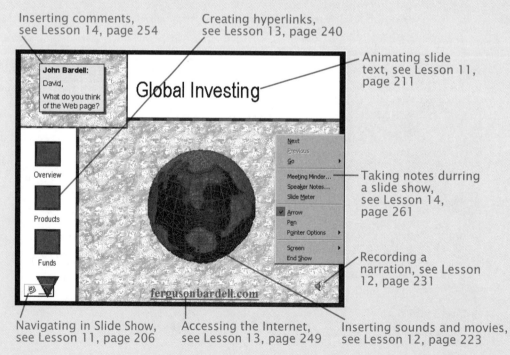

Taking notes durring
a slide show,
see Lesson 14,
page 261

Recording a
narration, see Lesson
12, page 231

Navigating in Slide Show,
see Lesson 11, page 206

Accessing the Internet,
see Lesson 13, page 249

Inserting sounds and movies,
see Lesson 12, page 223

Finding Your Best Starting Point

Microsoft PowerPoint, the leader in presentation graphics software, has all the tools you'll need to create professional, compelling presentations quickly and easily. *Microsoft PowerPoint 97 Step by Step* shows you how to use Microsoft PowerPoint to simplify your work and increase your productivity.

 IMPORTANT This book is designed for use with Microsoft PowerPoint 97 for the Windows 95 and Windows NT version 4.0 operating systems. To find out what software you're running, you can check the product package or you can start the software, click the Help menu at the top of the screen, and click About Microsoft PowerPoint. If your software is not compatible with this book, a Step by Step book for your software is probably available. Many of the Step by Step titles are listed on the second page of this book. If the book you want isn't listed, please visit our World Wide Web site at http://www.microsoft.com/mspress/ or call 1-800-MSPRESS for more information.

Finding Your Best Starting Point in this Book

This book is designed for readers learning Microsoft PowerPoint for the first time, and for more experienced readers who want to learn and use the new features in Microsoft PowerPoint. Use the following table to determine your best path through the book.

If you are	Follow these steps

New...

to computers

to graphical computer programs

to Windows 95 or Windows NT

to PowerPoint

1 Install the practice files as described in "Installing and Using the Practice Files."

2 Become acquainted with the Windows 95 or Windows NT operating system and how to use the online Help system by working through Appendix A, "If You're New to Windows or PowerPoint."

3 Learn basic skills for using Microsoft PowerPoint by working sequentially through Lessons 1 through 3. Then, you can work through Lessons 4 through 14 in any order.

If you are	Follow these steps

Switching...

from Lotus Freelance

from Harvard Graphics

1 Install the practice files as described in "Installing and Using the Practice Files."

2 Learn basic skills for using Microsoft PowerPoint by working sequentially through Lessons 1 through 3. Then, you can work through Lessons 4 through 14 in any order.

If you are	Follow these steps

Upgrading...

from PowerPoint for Windows 95

1 Learn about the new features in this version of the program that are covered in this book by reading through the following section, "New Features in PowerPoint 97."

2 Install the practice files as described in "Installing and Using the Practice Files."

3 Complete the lessons that cover the topics you need. You can use the table of contents and the *Quick*Look Guide to locate information about general topics. You can use the index to find information about a specific topic or feature from PowerPoint 97.

If you are	Follow these steps

Referencing...

this book after working through the lessons

1 Use the index to locate information about specific topics, and use the table of contents and the *Quick*Look Guide to locate information about general topics.

2 Read the Lesson Summary at the end of each lesson for a brief review of the major tasks in the lesson. The Lesson Summary topics are listed in the same order as they are presented in the lesson.

Certified Microsoft Office User Program

The Certified Microsoft Office User (CMOU) program is designed for business professionals and students who use Microsoft Office 97 products in their daily work. The program enables participants to showcase their skill level to potential employers. It benefits accountants, administrators, executive assistants, program managers, sales representatives, students, and many others. To receive certified user credentials for a software program, candidates must pass a hands-on exam in which they use the program to complete real-world tasks.

The CMOU program offers two levels of certification: Proficient and Expert. The following table indicates the levels available for each Microsoft Office 97 program.

Software	Proficient level	Expert level
Microsoft Word 97	✔	✔
Microsoft Excel 97	✔	✔
Microsoft Access 97		✔
Microsoft PowerPoint 97		✔
Microsoft Outlook 97		✔
Microsoft FrontPage 97		✔

Microsoft Press offers the following books in the *Step by Step* series as approved courseware for the CMOU exams:

Proficient level:

Microsoft Word 97 Step by Step, by Catapult, Inc. ISBN: 1-57231-313-7

Microsoft Excel 97 Step by Step, by Catapult, Inc. ISBN: 1-57231-314-5

Expert level:

Microsoft Word 97 Step by Step, Advanced Topics, by Catapult, Inc.
ISBN: 1-57231-563-6

Microsoft Excel 97 Step by Step, Advanced Topics, by Catapult, Inc.
ISBN: 1-57231-564-4

Microsoft Access 97 Step by Step, by Catapult, Inc. ISBN: 1-57231-316-1

Microsoft PowerPoint 97 Step by Step, by Perspection, Inc. ISBN: 1-57231-315-3

Microsoft Outlook 97 Step by Step, by Catapult, Inc. ISBN: 1-57231-382-X

Microsoft FrontPage 97 Step by Step, by Catapult, Inc. ISBN: 1-57231-336-6

Candidates may take exams from any participating Sylvan Test Center, participating corporations, or participating employment agencies. Exams have a suggested retail price of $50 each.

To become a candidate for certification, or for more information about the certification process, please visit the CMOU program World Wide Web site at

http://www.microsoft.com/office/train_cert/

or call 1-800-933-4493 in the United States.

New Features in PowerPoint 97

The following table lists the major new features in Microsoft PowerPoint 97 that are covered in this book. The table shows the lesson in which you can learn about each feature. You can also use the index to find specific information about a feature or a task you want to do.

To learn how to	See
Use the new and improved AutoContent Wizard to create informal, formal, and Internet presentations.	Lesson 1
Find, insert, rearrange, and catalog slides.	Lesson 2
Expand bullets to create individual slides.	Lesson 4
Spell check different languages.	Lesson 5
Look up references in Microsoft Bookshelf and other CD-ROM reference tools.	Lesson 5
Add new fill effects for backgrounds and objects.	Lessons 7 and 8
Draw new and expanded AutoShape objects.	Lesson 8
Connect objects together with connector lines.	Lesson 8
Add new shadows and 3-D effects, such as lighting direction and perspective, to objects.	Lesson 8

To learn how to	See
Insert new clip art, pictures, sounds, and videos with the Microsoft Clip Gallery.	Lessons 9 and 12
Rotate text on chart axes, add chart data tables, and add fill effects to chart elements.	Lesson 10
Create animated slides and custom slide shows.	Lesson 11
Add new sounds and custom soundtracks to slide shows.	Lesson 12
Add narration to slide shows.	Lesson 12
Creating self-navigating slide show presentations.	Lesson 12
Create an agenda slide or home page.	Lesson 13
Create hyperlinks to a slide, file, and the Internet.	Lesson 13
Save a presentation for the Internet.	Lesson 13
Access the Internet from PowerPoint.	Lesson 13
Insert comments and send out presentations for review.	Lesson 14
Run a presentation conference through the Internet or display a presentation on two screens.	Lesson 14

Corrections, Comments, and Help

Every effort has been made to ensure the accuracy of this book and the contents of the practice files disk. Microsoft Press provides corrections and additional content for its books through the World Wide Web at

> http://www.microsoft.com/mspress/support/

If you have comments, questions, or ideas regarding this book or the practice files disk/disc, please send them to us.

Send e-mail to

> mspinput@microsoft.com

Or send postal mail to

> Microsoft Press
>
> Attn: Step by Step Series Editor
>
> One Microsoft Way
>
> Redmond, WA 98052-6399

Please note that support for the PowerPoint software product itself is not offered through the above addresses. For help using PowerPoint, you can call Microsoft PowerPoint AnswerPoint at 206-635-7145 on weekdays between 6 a.m. and 6 p.m. Pacific time.

Visit Our World Wide Web Site

We invite you to visit the Microsoft Press World Wide Web site. You can visit us at the following location:

> http://www.microsoft.com/mspress/

You'll find descriptions for all of our books, information about ordering titles, notice of special features and events, additional content for Microsoft Press books, and much more.

You can also find the latest in software developments and news from Microsoft Corporation by visiting the following World Wide Web site:

> http://www.microsoft.com/

We look forward to your visit on the Web!

Perspection, Inc.

The writers, editors, and production team of *Microsoft PowerPoint 97 Step by Step* invite you to visit the Perspection World Wide Web site at:

> http://www.perspection.com

You'll find descriptions for all of our books, additional content for our books, information about Perspection, and much more.

Installing and Using the Practice Files

The disk attached to the inside back cover of this book contains practice files that you'll use as you perform the exercises in the book. For example, when you're learning how to print a presentation, you'll open one of the practice files —a partially completed presentation—and then print slides, speaker's notes, and audience handouts. By using the practice files, you won't waste time creating the samples used in the lessons—instead, you can concentrate on learning how to use PowerPoint. With the files and the step-by-step instructions in the lessons, you'll also learn by doing, which is an easy and effective way to acquire and remember new skills.

IMPORTANT Before you break the seal on the practice disk in the back of this book, be sure that this book matches your version of the software. This book is designed for use with Microsoft PowerPoint 97 for the Windows 95 and Windows NT 4.0 operating systems. To find out what software you're running, you can check the product package or you can start the software, and then on the Help menu at the top of the screen, click About Microsoft PowerPoint. If your program is not compatible with this book, a Step by Step book matching your software is probably available. Many of the Step by Step titles are listed on the second page of this book. If the book you want isn't listed, please visit our World Wide Web site at http://www.microsoft.com/mspress/ or call 1-800-MSPRESS for more information.

Install the practice files to your hard disk

Follow these steps to install the practice files to your computer's hard disk so that you can use them with the exercises in this book.

 NOTE If you are new to Windows 95 or Windows NT, you might want to work through Appendix A, "If You Are New to Windows or PowerPoint" before you copy the practice files.

In Windows 95, you will also be prompted for a username and password when starting Windows 95 if your computer is configured for user profiles.

1 If your computer isn't already on, turn it on now.

2 If you're using Windows NT, press CTRL+ALT+DEL to display a dialog box asking for your username and password. If you are using Windows 95, you will see this dialog box if your computer is connected to a network.

3 Type your username and password in the appropriate boxes, and then click OK. If you see the Welcome dialog box, click the Close button.

4 Remove the disk from the package inside the back cover of this book.

5 Insert the disk in drive A or drive B of your computer.

6 On the taskbar at the bottom of your screen, click the Start button, and then click Run.

Start

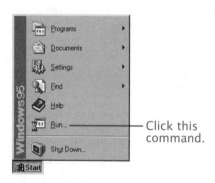

Click this command.

The Run dialog box appears.

7 In the Open box, type **a:\setup** (or **b:\setup** if the disk is in drive B). Do not add spaces anywhere in the command line.

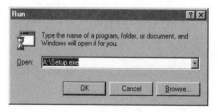

8 Click OK, and then follow the directions on the screen.

The setup program window appears with recommended options preselected for you. For best results in using the practice files with this book, accept these preselected settings.

9 When the files have been installed, remove the disk from your drive and replace it in the package inside the back cover of the book.

A folder called PowerPoint SBS Practice has been created on your hard disk, and the practice files have been put in that folder.

Microsoft
Press
Welcome

Camcorder
Files On The
Internet

NOTE In addition to installing the practice files, the Setup program created two shortcuts on your Desktop. If your computer is set up to connect to the Internet, you can double-click the Microsoft Press Welcome shortcut to visit the Microsoft Press Web site. You can also connect to this Web site directly at http://www.microsoft.com/mspress/

You can double-click the Camcorder Files On The Internet shortcut to connect to the *Microsoft PowerPoint 97 Step by Step* Camcorder files Web page. This page contains audiovisual demonstrations of how to do a number of tasks in PowerPoint, which you can copy to your computer for viewing. You can connect to this Web site directly at http://www.microsoft.com/mspress/products/353/

Using the Practice Files

Each lesson in this book explains when and how to use any practice files for that lesson. When it's time to use a practice file, the book will list instructions for how to open the file. The lessons are built around scenarios that simulate a real work environment, so you can easily apply the skills you learn to your own work. For the scenarios in this book, imagine that you're the Director of Communications at Ferguson & Bardell, a financial investment firm that is committed to using technology to be effective in the financial planning market. In the lessons you will take part as the Director of Communications who uses PowerPoint to create a progress report, an investment seminar presentation, and a standard company presentation.

List of the Practice Files

For those of you who like to know all the details, here's a list of the files included on the practice disk.

Lesson	File name	Description
Lesson 1	New presentation	Create a new presentation
Lesson 2	02 PPT Lesson	Work with a presentation
Lesson 3	03 PPT Lesson	Print a presentation
Part 1 Review & Practice	New Presentation	Practice what you learned in Part 1
Lesson 4	04 Market Outline	Insert an outline
Lesson 5	05 PPT Lesson	Add and modify text
Part 2 Review & Practice	Part 02 Review Part 02 Outline	Practice what you learned in Part 2
Lesson 6	06 PPT Lesson 06 PPT Template	Apply a template and change the title and slide masters
Lesson 7	07 PPT Lesson	Choose and create a color scheme
Lesson 8	08 PPT Lesson	Draw and modify objects
Part 3 Review & Practice	Part 03 Review Part 03 Template	Practice what you learned in Part 3
Lesson 9	09 PPT Lesson 09 Funds Rates 09 Service Picture 09 Logo Picture	Insert clip art, a table, a chart, a picture and WordArt in slides
Lesson 10	10 PPT Lesson 10 Funds Data	Create and edit a graph
Part 4 Review & Practice	Part 04 Review Part 04 Data Part 04 Rates	Practice what you learned in Part 4
Lesson 11	11 PPT Lesson	Produce a slide show
Lesson 12	12 PPT Lesson	Create a multimedia presentation
Lesson 13	13 PPT Lesson 13 Review Results	Create an Internet presentation
Lesson 14	14 PPT Lesson	Set up and run a presentation conference over a network
Part 5 Review & Practice	Part 05 Review Part 05 Pres	Practice what you learned in Part 5

Need Help with the Practice Files?

Each lesson in this book explains when and how to use any practice files for Every effort has been made to ensure the accuracy of this book and the contents of the practice files disk. If you do run into a problem, Microsoft Press provides corrections for its books through the World Wide Web at

> http://www.microsoft.com/mspress/support/

We also invite you to visit our main Web page at

> http://www.microsoft.com/mspress/

You'll find descriptions for all of our books, information about ordering titles, notices of special features and events, additional content for Microsoft Press books, and much more.

Deleting the Practice Files

Use the following steps to delete the shortcuts added to your Desktop and the practice files added to your hard drive by the Step by Step Setup program.

1   Click Start, point to Programs, and then click Windows Explorer.

If you are using Windows NT, click Windows NT Explorer.

2   In the All Folders area, scroll up and click Desktop.

The contents of your Desktop appear.

3   Click the Microsoft Press Welcome shortcut icon, hold down CTRL, and click the Camcorder Files On The Internet shortcut icon. Press DELETE.

If you are prompted to confirm the deletion, click Yes. The Desktop shortcut icons are removed from your computer.

4   In the All Folders area, click Drive C.

The contents of your hard drive appear. If you installed your practice files on another drive, view the contents of that drive.

5   Click the PowerPoint SBS Practice folder, and then press DELETE.

If you are prompted to confirm the deletion, click Yes. The practice files are removed from your computer.

6   In the Contents area, double-click the Windows folder, and then double-click the Favorites folder.

7   Click the PowerPoint SBS Practice shortcut icon, and then press DELETE.

If you are prompted to confirm the deletion, click Yes. All practice files installed on your computer are now deleted.

Conventions and Features in this Book

You can save time when you use this book by understanding, before you start the lessons, how instructions, keys to press, and so on are shown in the book. Please take a moment to read the following list, which also points out helpful features of the book that you might want to use.

 NOTE If you are unfamiliar with Windows, Windows NT or mouse terminology, see Appendix A, "If You Are New to Windows or PowerPoint."

Conventions

- Hands-on exercises that you are to follow are given in numbered lists of steps (**1**, **2**, **3**, and so on). An arrowhead bullet (➤) indicates an exercise with only one step.
- Text that you are to type appears in **bold**.
- A plus sign (+) between two key names means that you must press those keys at the same time. For example, "Press ALT+TAB" means that you hold down the ALT key while you press TAB.

- Notes or Tips that appear either in the text or in the left margin provide additional information or alternative methods for a step.

- Notes labeled "Important" alert you to essential information that you should check before continuing with the lesson.

- Notes labeled "Troubleshooting" alert you to possible error messages or computer difficulties, and provide solutions.

- Skills that are demonstrated in audiovisual files available on the World Wide Web.

Other Features of this Book

Outlook FrontPage

- You can learn how to use other Microsoft products, such as Outlook and FrontPage, with PowerPoint by reading the shaded boxes that appear throughout the lessons. You'll see identifying icons next to information about Outlook and about FrontPage.

- You can learn about options or techniques that build on what you learned in a lesson by trying the optional "One Step Further" exercise at the end of the lesson.

- You can get a quick reminder of how to perform the tasks you learned by reading the Lesson Summary at the end of a lesson.

- You can quickly determine what online Help topics are available for additional information by referring to the Help topics listed at the end of each lesson. The Help system provides a complete online reference to Microsoft PowerPoint. To learn more about online Help, see Appendix A, "If You Are New to Windows or PowerPoint."

- You can practice the major skills presented in the lessons by working through the Review & Practice sections at the end of each part. These sections offer challenges that reinforce what you have learned and demonstrate new ways you can apply your newly acquired skills.

- If you have Web browser software and access to the World Wide Web, you can view audiovisual demonstrations of how to perform some of the more complicated tasks in PowerPoint by downloading supplementary files from the Web. Double-click the Camcorder Files On The Internet shortcut that was created on your Desktop when you installed the practice files for this book, or connect directly to:

  http://www.microsoft.com/mspress/products/353/

The Web page that opens contains full instructions for copying and viewing the demonstration files.

Part 1

Learning Basic Skills

Creating a Presentation

In this lesson you will learn how to:

Estimated time
35 min.

- Start PowerPoint.
- Use the AutoContent Wizard.
- Move around in a presentation.
- Change text in Outline view.
- Understand and change presentation views.
- Move from slide to slide.
- Change and add text in Slide view.
- Preview slides in Slide Sorter view.
- Save a presentation.

With Microsoft PowerPoint you can create overhead slides, speaker's notes, audience handouts, and an outline, all in a single presentation file. PowerPoint offers powerful wizards to help you create and organize your presentation step by step.

As the Director of Communications for Ferguson & Bardell, you're responsible for managing the development of an investment seminar series. For your manager, you need to present a progress report for the seminar series.

In this lesson, you'll learn to start PowerPoint, use the AutoContent Wizard to create a presentation, and change and insert text. You'll edit title and bulleted text, move around in your presentation, look at your content in different views, and save your work.

Starting PowerPoint

After you've installed PowerPoint and the practice files, you're ready to start PowerPoint. The quickest way to start PowerPoint and all your other applications is by using the Start button on the taskbar.

Start Microsoft PowerPoint

Start

1 On the taskbar, click the Start button.

The Start menu appears.

2 On the Start menu, point to Programs.

The Programs menu appears displaying all the programs on your hard drive, including Microsoft PowerPoint. A portion of the Program menu should look like the following illustration:

If you have installed PowerPoint 97 as a separate application, your menu might look different.

3 Click the Microsoft PowerPoint icon to start PowerPoint.

The first time you run PowerPoint after installing it, PowerPoint displays the Office Assitant shown in the margin and instructions for getting help with PowerPoint. The Office Assistant answers your questions, offers tips, and provides help for a variety of Office 97 program features.

The Office Assistant appears with options to get information for new users and upgraders, to find out about the Office Assistant, and to start using PowerPoint. For more information about using the Office Assistant and getting help in PowerPoint, see Appendix A "If You Are New to Windows or PowerPoint."

4 Click the Start Using Microsoft PowerPoint option button or click the Close button for the Office Assistant to continue.

The PowerPoint Startup dialog box appears, giving you a choice of four presentation types, as shown on the next page.

NOTE You can also start PowerPoint by creating a shortcut icon on the Windows 95 desktop. To create a shortcut icon, see Appendix B "Customizing PowerPoint," or your Microsoft Windows 95 documentation.

PowerPoint Startup Dialog Box

When you first start PowerPoint, the PowerPoint Startup dialog box appears. This dialog box gives four options for beginning your PowerPoint session.

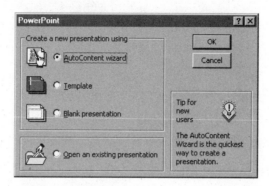

To begin your PowerPoint session, choose from one of four options to create a new presentation or open an existing one in the PowerPoint Startup dialog box. The following table describes the available options:

Select	To	Toolbar button
AutoContent Wizard	Create a new presentation using the AutoContent Wizard, which prompts you for a presentation title and information about your topic. Click a presentation style, type, and then PowerPoint provides a basic outline to help guide you in organizing your content into a professional presentation.	
Template	Create a new presentation based on a design template, which is a presentation with predefined slide colors and text styles. The New Presentation dialog box appears, where you can choose a template.	▣
Blank Presentation	Create a new blank presentation. The New Slide dialog box appears with 24 predesigned slide layouts you can choose from to help you create a new slide.	
Open An Existing Presentation	Open an existing PowerPoint presentation. The Open dialog box appears. Select a presentation file.	

5

Using the AutoContent Wizard

If you have trouble thinking of what you want to present in your presentation, let PowerPoint help you get started with the AutoContent Wizard. Creating a presentation can be much easier with the AutoContent Wizard, because it helps you organize your presentation in minutes.

Select the AutoContent Wizard

The AutoContent Wizard helps to get you started with ideas and an organization for your presentation in an easy, step-by-step process.

1   Click the AutoContent Wizard option button.
2   Click the OK button.

Read the AutoContent Wizard Introduction

The *AutoContent Wizard* displays a Start dialog box and then leads you through choosing a presentation type and entering title slide information.

➤   After reading the introduction, click the Next button.

Choose a presentation type

First, the AutoContent Wizard prompts you to select a presentation type. To help you identify presentation types quickly, the wizard organizes presentations by category.

1   Click the General button.
2   In the presentation type box, click Reporting Progress.

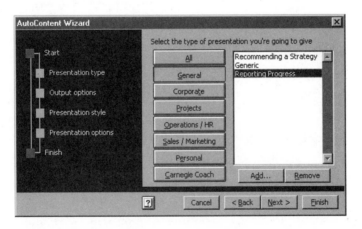

3   Click the Next button.

Choose output options

The AutoContent Wizard now prompts you to select the way you want to use the presentation.

1 Click the Presentation, Informal Meetings, Handouts option button.
2 Click the Next button.

Choose a presentation style

The AutoContent Wizard now prompts you to select the media type for your presentation.

1 In the What Type Of Output Will You Use area, click the Color Overheads option button to select a presentation type.
2 Click the Yes option to print handouts, if necessary.
3 Click the Next button.

Enter presentation title slide information

The AutoContent Wizard now prompts you to enter information for the *title slide*, the first slide in your presentation. Type in some title slide information. If you make a mistake as you type, press the BACKSPACE key to delete the mistake, and then type the correct text.

In the steps throughout this book, bold indicates text you should type exactly as it appears; italic indicates text that you supply.

1 In the Presentation Title box, type **Investment Seminar Series** and press TAB.
2 If your name appears correctly in the Your Name box, press TAB to continue. Otherwise, type *Your Name* and then press TAB.
3 In the Additional Information box, type **Ferguson & Bardell**

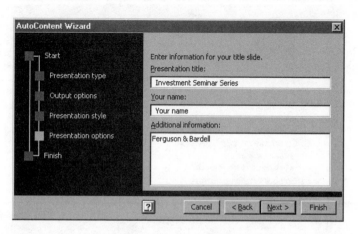

4 Click the Next button.

Finish the AutoContent Wizard

If you want to make any changes to the information before the AutoContent Wizard creates your presentation, you can click the Back button.

➤ Click the Finish button.

Upon completion, the PowerPoint presentation window appears with content provided by the AutoContent Wizard in outline form.

Moving Around in a Presentation

The *presentation window* is the canvas on which you type text, draw shapes, create graphs, add color, and insert objects. Along the top of the presentation window are the menus and buttons you'll use to do most common presentation tasks. The buttons you see are organized on *toolbars*. Toolbar buttons are shortcuts to commonly used menu commands and formatting tools. Simply click a button on the appropriate toolbar for one-step access to tasks such as formatting text and saving your presentation. At the bottom of the presentation window are view buttons that allow you to look at your presentation in different ways—in Slide, Outline, Slide Sorter, Notes Pages, and Slide Show views. At the left of the presentation window are the tools you'll use to rearrange title and paragraph text in Outline view. In Outline view, a slide icon appears to the left of each slide's title. The paragraph text underneath each title appears indented with bullets. The title, your name, and the company name you entered appear selected on the first slide along with a miniature of the presentation slide to the right, as shown in the following illustration:

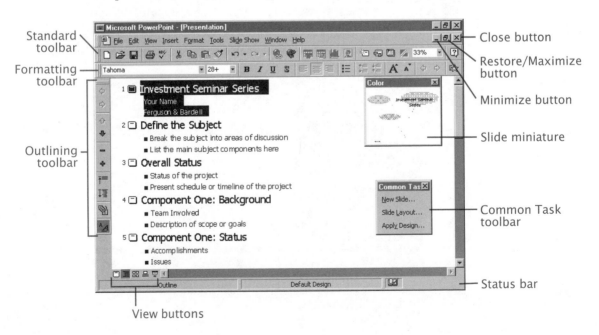

8

As with any Windows program, you can adjust the size of the PowerPoint and presentation windows with the Minimize and Restore/Maximize buttons or close Microsoft PowerPoint or the presentation window with the Close button.

 NOTE Your screen might look different than the above illustration if your presentation window is minimized or resized. In this book, all illustrations of the presentation window are shown maximized.

ScreenTips and the Status bar

ScreenTip

To find out about different items on the screen, you can display a *ScreenTip*. Click the What's This? command on the Help menu and click the item you want to show information. A yellow box appears telling you more information about the item. When you place your mouse pointer over a toolbar button a yellow box, appears telling you the name of the button, as shown in the margin. You can turn ScreenTips on and off by choosing the Toolbars command on the View menu.

Messages appear at the bottom of the window in an area called the *status bar*. These messages describe what you are seeing and doing in the PowerPoint window as you work.

Scrolling in a Window

The presentation outline you're working on contains more text than you can see on the screen at one time. To see the rest of the text, you need to scroll through the outline. You can click the scroll arrows or drag the scroll box located on the vertical and horizontal scroll bars to move through the window.

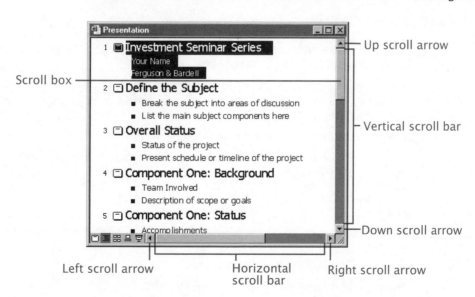

Scroll in a window

You can use one of three methods for scrolling in PowerPoint, depending on how quickly you want to move through a window. You can scroll line by line, scroll window by window, or jump immediately to the beginning, middle, or end of a window.

1   Click the down scroll arrow a few times to see the text below the current window.

Each time you click a scroll arrow, PowerPoint changes the screen to show you one more line.

2   Click below the scroll box in the scroll bar.

The bottom of the outline appears. When you click below or above the scroll box, PowerPoint scrolls window by window. You can also press the PAGE UP key or the PAGE DOWN key to scroll window by window.

3   Drag the scroll box to the top of the scroll bar—you cannot drag it off the scroll bar.

The top of the outline appears. With this method, you can quickly jump to the beginning, middle, or end of an outline, or anywhere in between.

Changing Text in Outline View

The AutoContent Wizard helps you get started with a suggested presentation outline. Now, your job is to modify and add the outline text to meet your specific needs.

Edit text in Outline view

1   Position the I-beam cursor to the right of the text "Define the Subject" in slide 2 and click to select the title text.

PowerPoint selects the text so that it is highlighted. Once you've selected text, the subsequent text you type—regardless of its length—replaces the selection.

2   Type **Investment Seminar Development**

Four-headed Arrow

3   Position the I-beam cursor (which changes to a four-headed arrow) over the bullet next to the text "Break the subject into areas of discussion" in slide 2 and click.

4   Type **Basic Investment Strategies**

5   In slide 2, click the bullet next to the text "List the main subject components here."

6   Type **Tax Free Investment Strategies**

You can add a new bullet by pressing the ENTER key.

7 Press the ENTER key.

A new bullet appears underneath the previous line of text.

8 Type **Retirement Investment Strategies**

Your presentation window should look like the following illustration:

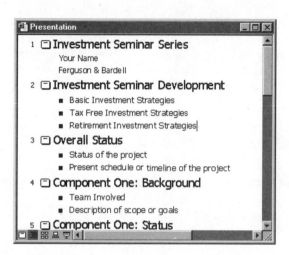

Change your mind

A handy feature in PowerPoint is the Undo command on the Standard toolbar or Edit menu, which reverses up to your last 20 actions. For example, choosing the Undo command now will remove the paragraph text you just entered. Whenever something happens that is not what you intended, click Undo to reverse previous actions. If you decide that the undo action is not exactly what you wanted, you can click the Redo button to restore the undo action.

Undo

1 On the Standard toolbar, click the Undo button to reverse your last action.

To undo a number of actions at the same time, you can use the Undo drop-down menu.

2 On the Standard toolbar, click the Arrow next to the Undo button.

The Undo drop-down menu appears.

3 Drag down to select the top two items in the list and click.

The last two entires in the outline have been reversed.

Redo

4 On the Standard toolbar, click the Redo button.

5 On the Standard toolbar, click the Redo button drop-down arrow, drag to select the top two items, and click to restore the text.

Understanding PowerPoint Views

For a demonstration of how to work in PowerPoint views, double-click the Camcorder Files On The Internet shorcut on your Desktop or connect to the Internet address listed on p. xxiii.

PowerPoint has five views to help you create, organize, and show your presentation. *Slide view* allows you to work on individual slides. *Outline view* allows you to work on the title and body text of your presentation. *Slide Sorter view* allows you to organize the order and status of the slides in your presentation. *Notes Pages view* allows you to create speaker's notes. *Slide Show view* allows you to see your slides as an electronic presentation on your computer. Slide Show view displays your slides as you would see them in Slide view using the entire screen. You can switch among views using the view buttons at the bottom of the presentation window. An illustration of Slide view, Outline view, Notes Pages view, and Slide Sorter view is shown below.

Click this button
for Slide view

Click this button
for Outline view

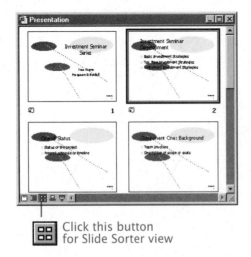

Click this button
for Slide Sorter view

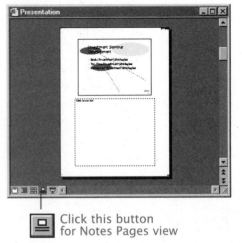

Click this button
for Notes Pages view

Changing Presentation Views

The view buttons at the bottom of the presentation window let you view or work on your presentation in different ways—in Slide view, Outline view, Slide Sorter view, and Notes Pages view. These view commands are also available on the View menu.

Change to Slide view

You can change to Slide view and look at the slide you just changed in your outline. In Slide view, you can see how the title and paragraph text appear on the slide. PowerPoint changes the view of the current slide when you click one of the view buttons.

Slide View

➤ Click the Slide View button.

 TIP Double-clicking the slide number or slide icon in Outline view also takes you to the selected slide in Slide view.

Your presentation window should look like the following illustration:

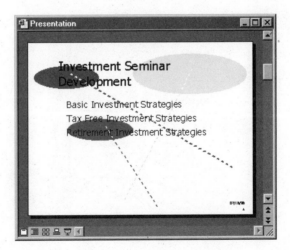

Changes to the text that you make in Outline view appear in Slide view. You change text in Slide view the same way you change text in Outline view.

Moving from Slide to Slide

To move from one slide to another in Slide view or Notes Pages view, click the Next Slide and Previous Slide buttons located in the lower-right corner of the presentation window to move one slide at a time. To move more than one slide at a time, drag the scroll box in the vertical scroll bar. As you drag the scroll box, a slide indicator box appears showing you the number of the slide you're about to display.

Move from slide to slide

Previous Slide

1 Click the Previous Slide button.

Slide 1 appears in Slide view. Use the Next Slide button to look at the slides in your presentation.

Next Slide

2 Click the Next Slide button until you reach the end of the presentation.

As you can see, each slide contains suggestions for how you might develop and organize your presentation.

3 Drag the scroll box up the vertical scroll bar to view slide 3 but don't release the mouse button.

Your presentation window should look like the following illustration:

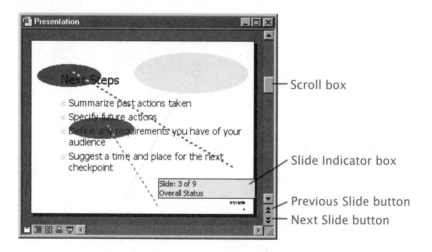

A slide indicator box appears telling you which slide is selected. The scroll box displays the slide number and title, and indicates the relative position of the slide in the presentation on the scroll bar.

4 Release the mouse button.

The status bar changes from "Slide 9 of 9" to "Slide 3 of 9."

 TIP In Slide view or Notes Pages view, you can press the PAGE UP key or click above the scroll box to view the previous slide or press the PAGE DOWN key or click below the scroll box to view the next slide.

Changing and Adding Text in Slide View

You can work with your presentation's text in Slide or Outline view. In Slide view you work with one slide at a time while in Outline view you can view and edit text for all your slides at once.

Change text in Slide view

I

I-beam Cursor

1 Position your pointer (which changes to an I-beam) over the title text in slide 3 and click to let PowerPoint know that you want to change text.

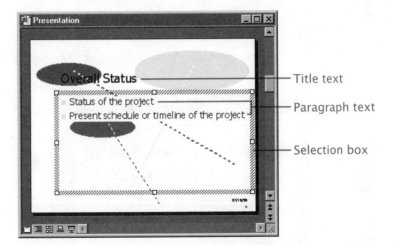

The text is surrounded by a rectangle of gray slanted lines called a *selection box* with the I-beam cursor placed in the text. The selection box lets PowerPoint know what object you want to change on the slide. An object containing slide text is called a *text object*. A typical slide contains a title, called *title text*, and the major points beneath the title, called *paragraph* or *bullet* text.

2 Drag to select the title text "Overall Status."

3 Type **Seminar Development Status**

4 Position your pointer (which changes to an I-beam) over any of the bulleted text in slide 3 and click.

15

Four-headed Arrow

5   Position the I-beam cursor (which changes to a four-headed arrow) over the bullet next to the text "Status of the project" in slide 3 and click.

PowerPoint selects the text so that it is highlighted.

6   Type **Content Development Stage**

7   Click the bullet next to the text "Present schedule or timeline of the project" in slide 3 or drag to select the text.

8   Type **Final Content Scheduled for Q2**

Add text in Slide view

To add more bulleted text to the text object, you place the insertion point at the end of a line of text and press ENTER. With the insertion point at the end of the text, add another line of text.

1   Press ENTER to create a new bullet.

A new bullet automatically appears in the outline.

2   Type **Seminar Rollout Scheduled for Q4**

3   Click outside of the selection box to deselect the text object.

Your presentation window should look like the following illustration:

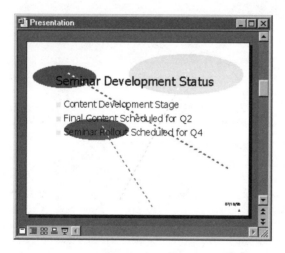

Previewing Slides in Slide Sorter View

Another way to view your presentation is to use Slide Sorter view. Slide Sorter view allows you to preview your entire presentation as if you were looking at slides on a light board. In this view—as well as in Outline view—you can easily rearrange the order of the slides in your presentation, which you'll learn in a later lesson.

Change to Slide Sorter view and preview slides

Slide Sorter View

1 Click the Slide Sorter View button.

All the slides now appear in miniature on the screen, and the slide you were viewing (the one with the insertion point) in Slide view is surrounded by a black box indicating that the slide is selected. Just as you scrolled through Outline view to see all the slides in your presentation, you can do the same in Slide Sorter view.

2 Click below the scroll box in the scroll bar to see the slides at the end of the presentation.

3 Click above the scroll box.

The top of Slide Sorter view appears.

Your presentation window should look like the following illustration:

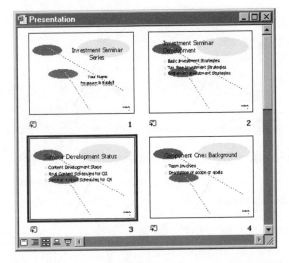

When slides are formatted in Slide Sorter view, titles might be hard to read. PowerPoint allows you to surpress the slide formatting to read the slide titles.

4 Hold down the ALT key and click an individual slide.

The formatting for the slide disappears and the title appears clearly. When you release the mouse, the display format reappears.

Change to a specific slide in Slide view

In Slide Sorter view, you can double-click a slide miniature to switch to Slide view for a specific slide. Try switching to slide 1 in Slide view.

▶ Double-click slide 1.

The presentation view changes to Slide view showing slide 1.

Saving a Presentation

The work you've done is currently stored only in the computer's memory. To save the work for further use, you must give the presentation a name and store it on your hard drive.

Save

1 On the Standard toolbar, click the Save button.

PowerPoint displays the Save As dialog box. The insertion point is positioned in the box next to the label "File name," so that you can type a presentation name.

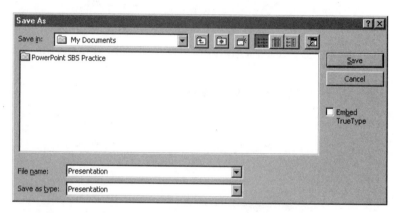

2 In the File Name box, type **F&B Report Pres 01**

The word "Pres" in the file name is an abbreviation for Presentation.

3 In the Save In box, ensure that the My Documents folder is selected (if that is where you stored your Step by Step practice files). Typically, you'll find the My Documents folder, which is on your hard drive (C:).

If you need information about using dialog boxes, see "If You Are New to Windows or PowerPoint," in Appendix A at the end of this book.

4 In the list of file and folder names, double-click the PowerPoint SBS Practice folder.

 TIP You can save a slide as an overhead picture to use in other programs. Display or select the slide that you want to save and click Save As on the File menu. In the Save As Type box, click Windows Metafile and click the Save button.

---

5 Click the Save button or press ENTER to save the presentation.

The Title bar name changes from "Presentation" to "F&B Report Pres 01."

TIP PowerPoint automatically saves presentations for recovery in case the program hangs (stops responding) or you lose power. The changes are saved in a recovery file based on the AutoRecover save Interval. For more information about the AutoRecover feature, see Appendix B "Customizing PowerPoint,"

One Step Further

In this lesson, you have learned how to start PowerPoint and use the AutoContent Wizard to enter your ideas into a PowerPoint presentation. In addition, you have learned how to enter and change text in Slide and Outline views, how to switch between views, how to move from slide to slide, and how to preview and save your presentation.

Add presentation properties

With PowerPoint's Presentation Properties dialog box, you can enter information about your presentation that will help you find the file if you forget its name or location. You can use the property information to search for your presentation by its contents, a keyword, or a date.

1   On the File menu, click Properties.

    The Presentation Properties dialog box appears displaying summary information. Generally, you should enter keywords that might help you identify the file later.

2   In the Category text box, type **Progress Report**

3   In the Keywords text box, type **Investment Seminars**

    You can click other tabs in the Presentation Properties dialog to display other information about your presentation.

4   Click the OK button.

If you want to continue to the next lesson

1   On the File menu, click Close (CTRL+W).

2   If a dialog box appears asking whether you want to save the changes to your presentation, click the Yes button.

If you want to quit PowerPoint for now

1   On the File menu, click Exit (CTRL+Q).

2   If a dialog box appears asking whether you want to save the changes to your presentation, click the Yes button.

Lesson Summary

To	Do this	Button
Create a presentation using the AutoContent Wizard	In the PowerPoint Startup dialog box, click the AutoContent Wizard option button.	
Scroll in a window	Click a scroll arrow on the vertical or horizontal scroll bars.	
Change text in Outline view or Slide view	Select the text and then make the changes you want.	
Reverse an action	On the Edit menu, click Undo or click the Undo toolbar button.	
Redo an undo action	On the Edit menu, click Redo or click the Redo toolbar button.	
Change presentation views	Click any of the view buttons: Slide, Outline, Slide Sorter, Notes Pages, or Slide Show.	
Move from slide to slide	Click the Next Slide button or click the Previous Slide button.	
Preview slide miniatures	Click the Slide Sorter View button.	
Save a new presentation	On the File menu, click Save or click the Save toolbar button.	
Enter presentation properties	On the File menu, click Properties and type text in the appropriate text box.	
End a PowerPoint session	On the File menu, click Exit.	

For online information about	Use the Office Assistant to search for
Creating a presentation	**Create a presentation**, and then click Create A New Presentation
Using Slide or Outline views	**Slide view** or **Outline view**, and then click PowerPoint Views

To use the Office Assistant, see Appendix A, in the back of this book.

Preview of the Next Lesson

In the next lesson, you'll learn how to start a new presentation, create new slides in Slide view and Outline view. You'll also learn how to rearrange slides in Slide Sorter view, create speaker's notes, and present a slide show.

Working with a Presentation

Estimated time
40 min.

In this lesson you will learn how to:

- Start a new presentation.
- Enter text in a slide.
- Create new slides.
- Enter text in an outline.
- Insert slides from other presentations.
- Rearrange slides.
- Create speaker's notes pages.
- Show your slides in Slide Show view.

To work efficiently with PowerPoint, you need to become familiar with the important features of the product. In the previous lesson, you learned how to create a presentation using the AutoContent Wizard, change title and paragraph text, change views, move from slide to slide, and preview slides.

After quickly and easily creating a progress report presentation for the investment seminar series, you decide to use PowerPoint to develop the seminar content. The next step is to start a new presentation and develop the content for the first investment seminar, "Basic Investment Strategies."

In this lesson, you'll learn how to start a new presentation with a presentation design, enter slide text, create new slides, insert slides from other presentations, rearrange slides in Slide Sorter view, enter text in Notes Pages view, and show your slides in Slide Show view.

Starting a New Presentation

In addition to starting a presentation with sample text from the AutoContent Wizard, as you did in Lesson 1, you can also start a new presentation without any text, with a pre-formatted or blank design. To start a new presentation, use the New command on the File menu.

Start a new presentation with a presentation design

If you quit PowerPoint at the end of the last lesson, restart PowerPoint now. If you are continuing from the previous lesson, click the New button on the Standard toolbar.

1 In the PowerPoint Startup dialog box, click the Template option button, and then click the OK button.

or

Click the File menu and then click New or click the New button on the Standard toolbar to display a list of presentations.

The New Presentation dialog box appears.

2 Click the Presentation Designs tab.

A list of different presentation designs appears.

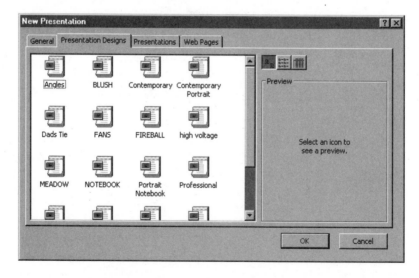

From the New Presentation dialog box, you can also start a blank presentation from the General tab, start an AutoContent Wizard from the Presentations tab, or create Internet pages from the Web Pages tab.

3 Click the scroll down arrow and click the Contemporary icon.

A sample slide appears in the Preview box.

4 Click the OK button.

The New Slide dialog box appears. You can choose a different layout for each slide to create a specific design look, such as a slide with a graph. Choose a layout by clicking it in the AutoLayout gallery list. You can scroll down to see more layouts. The layout title for the selected slide type appears to the right of the gallery list.

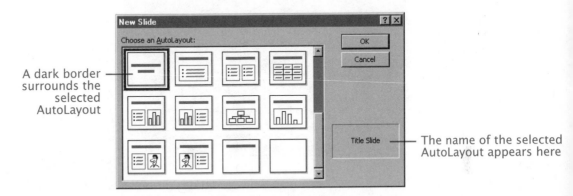

A dark border surrounds the selected AutoLayout

The name of the selected AutoLayout appears here

5 Click the OK button to use the default Title Slide.

The title slide appears in the presentation window.

Entering Text in Slide View

The new presentation window includes an empty slide with two text boxes called *text placeholders*. The box at the top is a placeholder for the slide's title text. The lower box is a placeholder for the slide's subtitle text. After you enter text into a placeholder, the placeholder becomes a *text object*.

Type title and subtitle text in Slide view

To give your slide a title, you can click the title placeholder and start typing.

1 Click the text "Click to add title."

The placeholder is surrounded by a rectangle of gray slanted lines called a *selection box* to indicate the placeholder is ready to enter or edit text. A blinking insertion point appears.

2 Type **Basic Investment Strategies**

3 Click the text "Click to add sub-title."

The title object is deselected, and the subtitle object is selected.

4 Type *Your Name* and press ENTER.

5 Type **Ferguson & Bardell**

Your presentation window should look like the following illustration:

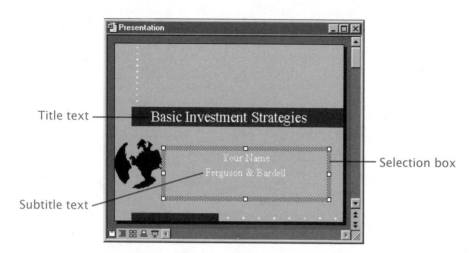

Title text — Basic Investment Strategies

Selection box

Subtitle text — Your Name Ferguson & Bardell

PowerPoint puts a wavy-red line under mispelled or nonrecognized words by the dictionary. For more information, see lesson 5, "Adding and Modifying Text."

Creating a New Slide in Slide View

You can create a new slide in your presentation using the Insert New Slide button on the Status bar, the Insert New Slide button on the Standard toolbar, or the New Slide command on the Insert menu.

Create a new slide

Insert New Slide

1   On the Standard toolbar, click the Insert New Slide button.

    The New Slide dialog box appears.

2   Click the OK button to use the default Bulleted List.

    A new empty slide is added after the current slide in Slide view. The Status bar displays "Slide 2 of 2."

 TIP   You can hold down SHIFT and click the Insert New Slide button to add a new slide that has the same layout as the current slide without having to select the layout from the New Slide dialog box.

Enter text in a new slide

If you start typing on an empty slide with nothing selected, PowerPoint enters the text into the title object.

➤ Type **Develop An Investment Plan**

PowerPoint lets you work directly in Slide view or Outline view to enter your ideas. Let's change views and complete this slide in Outline view.

Change to Outline view

Outline view shows your presentation text in outline form just as if you had typed the text in Microsoft Word. From Slide view, switch to Outline view.

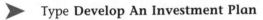

Outline View

➤ Click the Outline View button.

Slide Icon

A slide icon appears to the left of each slide's title. Body text underneath each title appears indented one level. The title from slide 2 is selected, as shown in the following illustration:

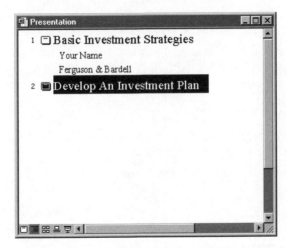

Entering Text in Outline View

To enter text in Outline view, position the insertion point where you want the text to start or click New Slide on the Status bar, and begin typing. Adding a new slide in Outline view creates a new slide icon.

Enter paragraph text

In this section, you'll change a paragraph text indent level, and type in paragraph text to complete slide 2. If you make a mistake as you type, press the BACKSPACE key to delete the mistake and then type the correct text.

1 Click to the right of the title in slide 2.

A blinking insertion point appears.

25

2   Press ENTER.

PowerPoint adds a new slide. To add paragraph text to slide 2 instead of starting a new slide, change the outline level from slide title to a bullet.

Demote

3   On the Outlining toolbar, click the Demote button or press the TAB key.

The Demote button indents your text to the right one level and moves the text from slide 3 to slide 2. The slide icon changes to a small bullet on slide 2.

4   Type **Diversity** and press ENTER.

A new bullet is added at the same indent level.

5   Type **Invest for Your Goals and Objectives** and press ENTER.

6   Type **Re-Evaluate Your Portfolio Regularly**

Create a new slide and enter text

With the insertion point after the word "Regularly," create a new slide from an indented outline level using a toolbar button and a keyboard command.

1   Press ENTER.

2   On the Outlining toolbar, click the Promote button.

Promote

A new slide is created with the insertion point to the right of the slide icon. Type title and paragraph text.

3   Type **Focus on Your Objectives** and press ENTER.

4   Press TAB.

A new indent level is created for slide 3. Now enter three bullet points under slide 3 at the same indent level to finish the slide.

5   Type **Retirement** and press ENTER.

6   Type **Education** and press ENTER.

7   Type **Tax Free** and press ENTER.

8   Hold down the CTRL key and press ENTER.

A new slide is created using a keyboard command.

9   Type **Summary**, press ENTER, and then press TAB.

A new indent level is created for slide 4.

10   Type **Develop an Investment Plan Tailored to Your Objectives** and press ENTER.

11   Type **Begin Your Investment Program as Early as Possible** and press ENTER.

12   Type **Diversify Your Investment Portfolio**

Insert new text

You can easily insert new text anywhere in Outline view and in Slide view.

1 Position the I-beam cursor just after the word "Regularly" and click.

This places the blinking insertion point where you are to begin typing, as shown in the following illustration:

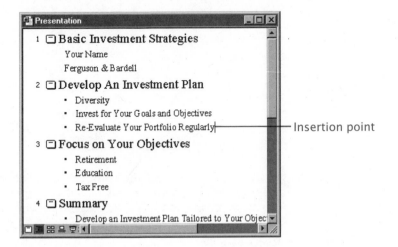

TROUBLESHOOTING If the insertion point is not where you want it, reposition the I-beam cursor and click again to place the insertion point in the desired location.

2 Press the SPACEBAR and type **and Make Adjustments as Needed**

PowerPoint makes room in the outline for the new text.

Select and replace text

You can select individual characters, sentences, paragraph text, or title text in either Outline or Slide view. Selecting text in PowerPoint works just as it does in Microsoft Word 97 for Windows.

1 Position the I-beam cursor over any part of the word "Free" in the third bullet point of slide 3.

2 Double-click to select the word.

To select one or more words or characters, you can also drag.

Your presentation window should look like the following illustration:

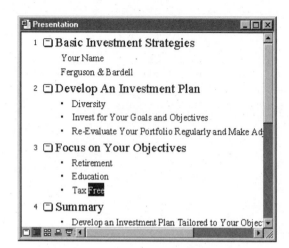

The text is now highlighted, indicating it has been selected. When you double-click a word, PowerPoint also selects the space that follows. This maintains correct spacing if you delete a word. Once you've selected text, the next text you type—regardless of its length—replaces the selection.

3 Type **Reduction**

The new word replaces the text in the outline.

Select and rearrange text

You can easily select and rearrange title and paragraph text in Outline and Slide views. In Outline view, you can select and rearrange text, a range of text, an individual slide, or a group of slides. To select paragraph text or an individual slide, click the associated bullet or slide icon to its left.

Four-headed Arrow

1 Move your pointer over the bullet entitled "Tax Reduction" in slide 3.

The pointer changes to a four-headed arrow.

2 Click the bullet to select the entire line.

3 On the Outlining toolbar, click the Move Up button.

The entire line moves up one level.

Move Up

4 Double-click slide 3 to display the slide in Slide view.

Inserting Slides from Other Presentations

You can save time creating a presentation by using work that has already been done by you or a co-worker. When you insert slides from another presentation, the new slides conform to the color and design of your presentation, so you don't have to make many changes.

Insert slides into your presentation

*For a demon-
stration of how
to insert slides,
double-click the
Camcorder Files
On The Internet
shorcut on your
Desktop or con-
nect to the In-
ternet address
listed on p. xxiii.*

1 On the Insert menu, click Slides From Files.

The Slide Finder dialog box appears.

2 Click the Browse button.

The Insert Slides From File dialog box appears.

3 In the Look In box, ensure that the My Documents folder is selected (if that is where you stored your Step by Step practice files).

Typically, you'll find the My Documents folder on your hard drive (C:). If you can't find the My Documents folder, click the Look In drop-down arrow, click your hard drive (C:), and double-click the My Documents folder to open it.

4 In the list of file and folder names, double-click the PowerPoint SBS Practice folder.

*If you do not see
PowerPoint SBS
Practice in the
list of folders,
see "Installing
and Using the
Practice Files,"
earlier in this
book.*

5 In the list of file names, click 02 PPT Lesson and then click the Open button.

The Find Slides dialog box appears.

6 Click the Display button.

7 Click slide 2, click slide 3, click the right scroll arrow, and then click slide 4 to select the slides you want to insert.

Your Slide Finder dialog box should look like the following illustration:

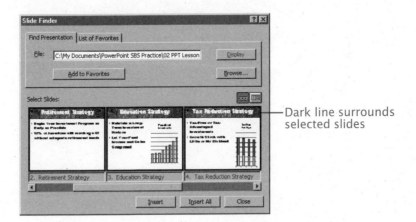

Dark line surrounds selected slides

8 Click the Insert button.

PowerPoint inserts the slides into your presentation after the current slide.

9 Click the Close button.

The last inserted slide appears in Slide view.

Rearranging Slides in Slide Sorter View

After copying slides from your other presentation into your new one, you'll want to rearrange the slides into the order that most effectively communicates your message.

Move a slide in Slide Sorter view

In Slide Sorter view, you can drag one or more slides from one location to another.

Slide Sorter View

Insert Pointer

1 Click the Slide Sorter View button.

2 Click slide 6.

3 Drag the slide between slide 4 and slide 5.

You'll notice the mouse pointer changes to an insert pointer when you begin to drag. When you release the mouse button, slide 5 and slide 6 move to their new positions and the other slides in the presentation are repositioned and renumbered.

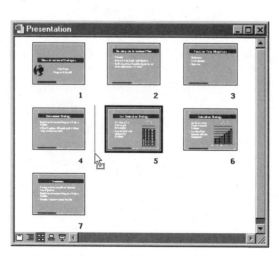

4 Click the scroll up arrow and click slide 2.

5 On the Standard toolbar, click the Zoom Control drop-down arrow and click 50%.

Zoom Control

 **TIP** In Slide Sorter view, you can also move slides between two or more open presentations. Open each presentation, switch to Slide Sorter view, and click Arrange All on the Window menu. Drag the slides from one presentation window to the other.

Entering Text in Notes Pages View

In Notes Pages view, you can create speaker's notes for your presentation. Each slide in your presentation has a corresponding notes page. At the top of each notes page is a reduced image of the slide. To enter speaker's notes, on a notes page, change to Notes Pages view, select the Notes placeholder, and begin typing. Entering and changing text in Notes Pages view works the same as it does in Slide view. You can also enter speaker notes from other views by clicking Speaker Notes on the View menu.

Notes Pages View

1   Click the Notes Pages View button.

Notes Pages view appears at 33% view for most screens to display the entire page. Your view scale might be different depending on the size of your monitor.

Your presentation window should look like the following illustration:

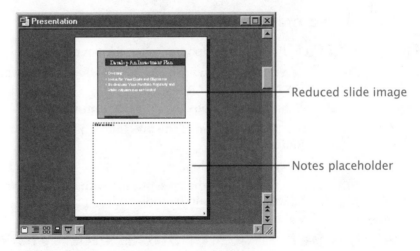

Reduced slide image

Notes placeholder

2   Click the Notes placeholder to select it.

Zoom Control

3   On the Standard toolbar, click the Zoom Control drop-down arrow and click 75%.

The view scale size increases to 75%, and displays the selected Notes placeholder for the notes page.

4   Type the paragraph below without pressing the ENTER key. If you make a mistake as you type, press the BACKSPACE key to delete the mistake, and type the correct text.

While no investment portfolio is right for everyone, there are a few elements to keep in mind as you plan your investment strategy.

Move from notes page to notes page

In Notes Pages view, you can move from notes page to notes page in the same way as in Slide view.

Next Slide

1 Click the Next Slide button.

2 Click the Notes placeholder to select it.

3 Type **Many investors believe these three investment objectives are important elements in their investment plans. As you plan, define your goals and the time you need to obtain them.**

4 On the Standard toolbar, click the Zoom Control drop-down arrow and click Fit.

Slide View

5 Click the Slide View button.

Switch to Slide view so PowerPoint saves your presentation in Slide view instead of Notes Pages view.

Save the presentation

Save

For information about saving a presentation, see Lesson 1.

1 On the Standard toolbar, click the Save button.

PowerPoint displays the File Save dialog box, in which you can type a new name for your presentation.

2 In the File Name box, type **F&B Training Pres 02**

The "02" at the end of the presentation file name matches the lesson number.

3 Click the Save button.

PowerPoint saves the presentation with the new name F&B Training Pres 02, which appears in the title bar.

Showing Your Slides in Slide Show View

For information about using slide show, see Lesson 11.

Now that you have saved your presentation, review the slides for accuracy and flow. You can review your slides easily in Slide Show view. Slide Show view displays your slides using the entire screen as an on-screen presentation on your computer.

Slide Show

1 Drag the scroll box to slide 1.

2 Click the Slide Show button.

PowerPoint displays the first slide in the presentation.

3 Click to advance to the next slide.

4 Click once for each slide to advance through the presentation.

After the last slide in the presentation, PowerPoint returns to the current view.

One Step Further

You have learned how to open a presentation, insert and rearrange text, copy and paste slides between presentations, and rearrange slides in Slide Sorter view. You can open recently used files by accessing them on the File menu. With the Options command, you can change the number of recently used files that appear on the File menu.

Change PowerPoint options

1   On the Tools menu, click Options, and then click the General tab.

The Options dialog box appears with the General tab.

2   Click the Recently Used File List up arrow twice to reach 6 entries, as shown in the following illustration:

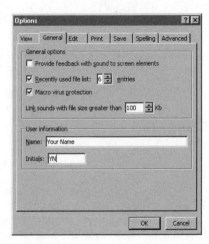

3   Click the OK button.

4   Click the File menu to see the expanded list of recently used files and then press the ESC key to cancel the menu.

If you want to continue to the next lesson

1   On the File menu, click Close (CTRL+W).

2   If a dialog box appears asking whether you want to save the changes to your presentation, click the Yes button.

If you want to quit PowerPoint for now

1   On the File menu, click Exit (CTRL+Q).

2   If a dialog box appears asking whether you want to save the changes to your presentation, click the Yes button.

Lesson Summary

To	Do this	Button
Start a new presentation using a presentation design	On the File menu, click New, and then click a tab for the presentation type. Double-click a presentation icon.	
Type title or subtitle text on a slide	Click the title object or subtitle text object and begin typing.	
Create a new slide	Click the Insert New Slide button on the Standard toolbar or click New Slide on the Insert menu.	
Insert slides from a presentation file	On the Insert menu, click Slides From Files. Click Browse to select a file. Click Display and click the slides you want to insert. Click Insert and click Close.	
Rearrange slides in Slide Sorter view	Select slides in Slide Sorter view. Drag the slides to the new location.	
Enter text in Notes Pages view	Click the Notes Pages View button. Click the placeholder and type.	
Show your slides in Slide Show	Click the Slide Show button. Click each slide.	
Change PowerPoint options	On the Tools menu, click Options.	

For online information about	Use the Office Assistant to search for
Using a presentation template	**Design template**, and then click Create A New Presentation
Making a new slide	**New slide**, and then click Make A New Slide
Creating speaker's notes pages	**Notes pages**, and then click Create Speaker Notes And Handouts

To use the Office Assistant, see Appendix A, in the back of this book.

Preview of the Next Lesson

In the next lesson, you'll preview your presentation in black and white, add a header and footer, change the page setup, choose a printer, and print presentation slides, speaker's notes, and audience handouts. In the One Step Further section, you'll also change the slide format for 35mm slides.

Printing a Presentation

In this lesson you will learn how to:

Estimated time
20 min.

- Open an existing presention.
- Preview slides in black and white.
- Add a header and footer.
- Change a presentation slide setup.
- Choose a printer.
- Print presentation slides, audience handouts, and speaker's notes.

PowerPoint gives you great flexibility for printing both the slides of the presentation and any additional supplements. For example, you can preview your presentation in black and white to see how color slides will look after printing, add headers and footers, and print your presentation slides, speaker's notes, audience handouts, and outlines. You can easily customize the printing process by selecting paper size, page orientation, print range, and printer type to meet your needs.

As the Director of Communications for Ferguson & Bardell, you want to create a series of investment seminars. In the previous lesson you created a Basic Investment Seminar presentation, and now you'd like to open and print the presentation and accompanying speaker's notes pages.

In this lesson, you'll learn how to open an existing presentation, preview slides in black and white, add a footer and header, choose a printer, print slides, speaker's notes, and audience handouts, and change a slide size.

Opening an Existing Presentation

You can open an existing presentation—one that you or a co-worker have already created—and work on it in the same way you would a new presentation. To open an existing presentation, you must first tell PowerPoint the name of the presentation and where it's located. You do this by using the Open command on the File menu.

Open a presentation

Open

1   On the Standard toolbar click the Open button, or click the File menu and then click Open to display a list of presentations.

PowerPoint displays the Open dialog box, in which you can select the name of the presentation you want. The dialog box you see might look different from the following, depending on where the practice files are located:

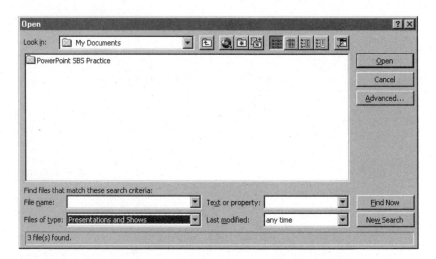

2   In the Look In box, ensure that the My Documents folder is selected (if that is where you stored your Step by Step practice files).

Typically, you'll find the My Documents folder on your hard drive (C:). If you can't find the My Documents folder, click the Look In drop-down arrow, click your hard drive (C:), and then double-click the My Documents folder.

3   In the list of file and folder names, double-click the PowerPoint SBS Practice folder to open it.

If you don't remember the name of a presentation file, but you know some of the presentation contents, you can search for the presentation.

4   Click the Text Or Property text box to place the insertion point.

5   Type **Basic Investment**

"Basic Investments" appears in the text box. The next time you would like to find presentations with Basic Investments in it, you can click the Text Or Property drop-down arrow and click Smart Investment in the list. PowerPoint remembers what you enter.

6   Click the Find Now button.

The Find Now button changes to Stop as PowerPoint searches through your presentation and then changes back to Find Now when the search is complete. The presentations that meet the search criteria in the current folder are displayed in the list of file and folder names.

7   In the list of file names, click 03 PPT Lesson, if it's not already selected.

 TIP   You can also click the Advanced button to search for files on your hard drive by property and text criteria. In the Advanced dialog box, select and type your search information, add the criteria to the match list, and then click the Find Now button.

8   Click the Open button.

PowerPoint displays the presentation 03 PPT Lesson.

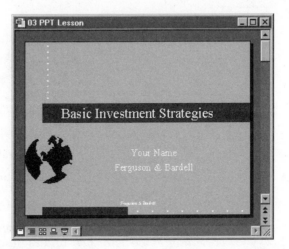

 TIP   PowerPoint makes it easy to open recently used files by adding your most recently opened presentation names to the bottom of the File menu. You can open one of these presentations by clicking the file name.

Previewing Slides in Black and White

If you are printing a color presentation on a black and white printer, you need to be sure it will be legible on paper. For example, dark red text against a shaded background shows up in color, but when seen in black and white or shades of gray, the text might be indistinguishable from the background. To prevent this, you can preview your color slides in black and white to see how they will look when printed on a black and white or grayscale printer.

Change to black and white view

Black And White View

1   On the Standard toolbar, click the Black And White View button.

Your slide switches from color to black and white and a slide miniature window appears showing the slide in color. The slide miniature window shows your slide in the opposite color view making it easier to compare how your slide looks in both color and black and white.

Next Slide

2   Click the Next Slide button.

The next slide also appears in black and white and the slide miniature in color.

Slide Sorter View

3   Click the Slide Sorter View button.

All the slides in the Slide Sorter view also appear in black and white.

4   Double-click slide 2.

5   On the Standard toolbar, click the Black And White View button.

Your slide switches back to color and the slide miniature window closes.

Black And White View

View a slide miniature in black and white

Instead of clicking the Black And White View button back and forth to see how your presentation looks in color and in black and white, you can simply click the slide miniature window.

1   On the View menu, click Slide Miniature.

The slide miniature window appears with the slide in black and white.

2   Right-click the Slide Miniature window and then click Color View.

The display changes from black and white to color.

3   Click the Slide Miniature window Close button.

Adding a Header and Footer

Before you print your work, consider adding a header or footer that can appear on every page, like your company name or product name. You can add a header and footer to your slides, speaker's notes, and audience handouts quickly and easily with the Header And Footer command on the View menu. This command also allows you to add and customize the slide number and date.

Add a header and footer to your presentation

1   On the View menu, click Header And Footer.

The Header and Footer dialog box appears.

2   Click the Footer check box and type **Ferguson & Bardell**

In the Preview box, a black rectangle highlights the placement of the footer.

Your dialog box should look like the following illustration:

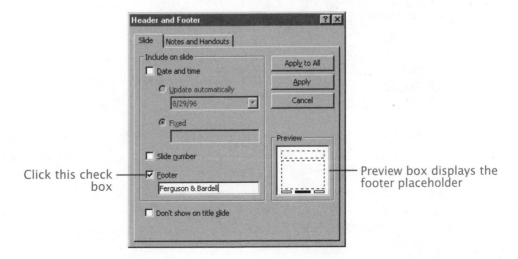

Click this check box

Preview box displays the footer placeholder

3   Click the Notes And Handouts tab.

The header and footer settings for the Notes and Handout pages appear.

4   Click the Page Number check box to select the option.

5   Click the Header check box and type **F&B Investments**

6   Click the Apply To All button.

The header and footer information is applied to your slides, notes pages, and handouts pages. Notice that the current slide appears with the footer in place.

Changing the Page Setup

The page setup determines the size and orientation of your slides, notes pages, handouts, and outline on the printed page. For a new presentation, PowerPoint opens with default slide format settings: on-screen show, landscape orientation, and slide numbers starting at one, which you can change at any time.

Change the slide size

Change the slide size setting from on-screen show to Letter Paper.

1   On the File menu, click Page Setup.

The Page Setup dialog box appears.

2   Click the Slides Sized For drop-down arrow.

Your dialog box should look like the following illustration:

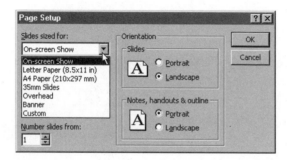

PowerPoint has seven slide size formats to choose from:

On-screen Show   Use this setting when designing an on-screen slide show. The slide size for the screen is smaller than the Letter Paper size.

Letter Paper (8.5 x 11 in)   Use this setting when printing a presentation on U.S. letter paper (8.5 x 11 in).

A4 Paper (210 x 297 mm)   Use this setting when printing on international A4 paper (210 x 297 mm or 10.83 x 7.5 in).

35mm Slides   Use this setting when designing a presentation for 35mm slides. The slide size is slightly reduced to produce the slides.

Overhead   Use this setting when printing overhead transparencies on U.S. letter size paper (8.5 x 11 in).

Banner   Use this setting when designing a banner (8 x 1 in).

Custom   Use this setting to design a presentation with a special size. Change the width and height settings to create a custom size.

3   Click Letter Paper (8.5 x 11 in).

4   Click the OK button.

Choosing a Printer

PowerPoint prints presentations on the default Windows printer unless you select a different printer. Your default printer is set up in the Windows 95 or Windows NT print settings. You can select another printer in PowerPoint's Print
dialog box.

1 Make sure your printer is turned on and connected to your computer.

2 On the File menu, click Print.

  The Print dialog box appears.

3 In the Printer area, click the Name drop-down arrow.

  A drop-down list appears with the installed printers on your computer.
  Your list of installed printers might look different than the following
  illustration:

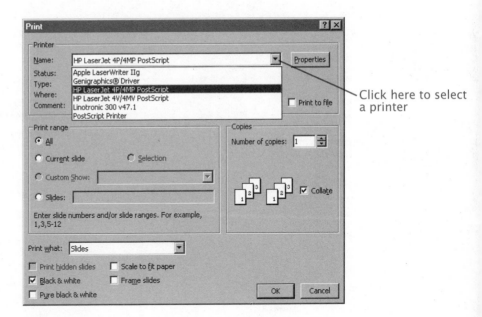

Click here to select a printer

4 Click a printer.

  After choosing a printer, you can customize your printer settings.

5 Click the Properties button.

  The Properties dialog box appears, showing current printer settings. The
  Properties dialog settings differ depending on your specific printer.

6 Click the OK button.

  The Properties dialog closes to display the Print dialog box.

Printing in PowerPoint

PowerPoint allows you to print your presentation four different ways: You can print slides, speaker's notes, audience handouts, and the outline. A sample of each printing type is shown in the following illustrations:

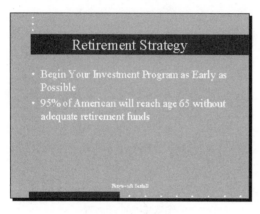

Slide (landscape)

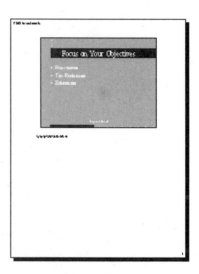

Notes Page

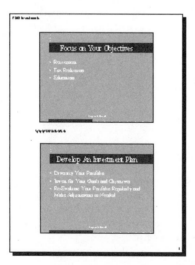

Handout Page

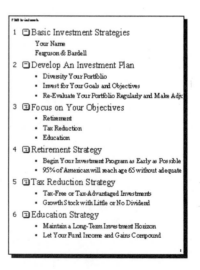

Outline

Printing Slides, Handouts, and Notes

PowerPoint makes it easy to print your slides, audience handouts, and speaker's notes with the Print command. When you use the Print command to print your slides or presentation supplements, PowerPoint automatically detects the type of printer chosen and prints the appropriate color or black and white version of the slides.

Print presentation slides

Print

PowerPoint prints your slides based on the settings in the Print dialog. If you know the current Print dialog settings, you can click the Print button on the Standard toolbar to print directly. Otherwise, choose the Print command on the File menu to print with new settings.

1   On the File menu, click Print, if the Print dialog is not already displayed.

The Print dialog box appears.

2   Click the Print What drop-down arrow.

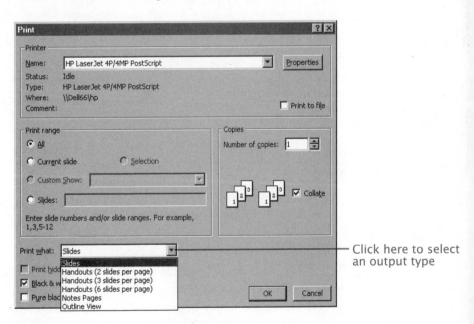

Click here to select an output type

Six print options are available.

Slides   Prints your slides as they appear on the screen, one per page.

Handouts (2 slides per page)   Prints two slides per page.

Handouts (3 slides per page)   Prints three slides per page.

Handouts (6 slides per page)   Prints six slides per page.

Notes Pages   Prints the speaker's notes pages that correspond to the slide numbers selected in the Print Range.

Outline View   Prints your outline according to the current view setting. What you see in Outline view is what you get on the printout.

3   In the Print What drop-down list, click Slides.

4   In the Print Range area, click the Current Slide option button.

5   Click the OK button.

When you click the OK button, PowerPoint prints the current slide in your presentation. A small print icon appears in the status bar, giving your printing status.

 NOTE   In PowerPoint, your presentation slides automatically size to the printer you have chosen. Using scalable fonts, such as TrueType fonts allows you to print your presentation on different printers with the same great results.

Print audience handouts

You can print audience handouts in three different formats: 2 slides per page, 3 slides per page, and 6 slides per page. When printing the audience handouts, you'll add a frame around the slides.

1   On the File menu, click Print.

The Print dialog box appears.

2   Click the Print What drop-down arrow and click Handouts (2 slides per page).

To enhance the look of your audience handouts, you click the Frame Slide check box at the bottom of the Print dialog box, which adds a black frame or border around the slides.

3   Click the Frame Slide check box.

The print options available in the Print dialog box include the following:

Print to File   Use this option to print slides to a presentation file that you can send to a Genigraphics service center. See "One Step Further" later in this lesson for more information.

Collate   Use this option to print multiple copies of your presentation. This option is usually available for laser printers only.

Print Hidden Slides   Use this option to print all hidden slides.

Scale to Fit Paper   Use this only if the paper in the printer does not correspond to the slide size and orientation settings. This option scales slides automatically to fit the paper size in the printer.

Black & White   Use this option to turn all fills to white (or black and white, if patterned). Unbordered objects that have no text appear with a thin black frame.

Pure Black & White   Use this option when printing draft copies of your presentation on a color printer. This option turns all color fills to white, turns all text and lines to black, adds outlines or borders to all filled objects, and renders pictures in grayscale.

Frame Slides   Prints a frame around the presentation slides.

4   Click the OK button.

A small print icon appears in the status bar, giving your printing status.

Print speaker's notes

You can print speaker's notes in the same way you print presentation slides. A reduced image of the presentation slide prints on each notes page. Before you print the speaker's notes, you'll want to turn off the Frame Slides option in the Print dialog box.

1   On the File menu, click Print.

The Print dialog box appears.

2   Click the Print What drop-down arrow, scroll down, and click Notes Pages.

3   In the Print Range area, click the Slides option button.

The insertion point appears in the range box.

4   Type **1-3, 5**

The numbers 1-3 appear in the slide range. PowerPoint will print notes pages 1 through 3 and 5. You can print notes pages or slides in any order by entering slide numbers and ranges separated by commas.

5   Click the Frame Slides check box to turn it off.

6   Click the OK button.

A print message box appears, giving your printing status.

Save the presentation

1   On the File menu, click Save As.

The Save As dialog box opens. Be sure the PowerPoint SBS Practice folder appears in the Save In box.

2   In the File Name box, type **F&B Training Pres 03**

3   Click the Save button.

The presentation is saved and the title bar changes to the new name.

One Step Further

In this lesson, you have learned to preview slides in black and white, add headers and footers to slides, notes pages, and handouts, set your slide format, and print your presentation in different ways. You can also send your presentation to a Genigraphics Service Center that will create 35mm color slides directly from your PowerPoint slides.

Order 35mm slides from Genigraphics

1 On the File menu, point to Send To, and then click Genigraphics.

   The Genigraphics Wizard displays an introduction dialog box. Read the instructions carefully before you continue.

2 Click the Next button.

   The Genigraphics Wizard asks you what output products and services you would like to order.

3 Click the 35mm check box to select the option, if necessary.

4 Click the Next button.

   The Genigraphics Wizard asks you what presentation file you would like to send. Your active presentation file is selected by default.

5 If you have a modem installed, click the Send Via Direct Dial Modem option button, otherwise click the Send On Disk option button.

6 Click the Next button and follow the instructions until the wizard indicates your order is ready to send on disk or to transmit by modem.

   The Genigraphics Wizard asks you to choose slide mounts and to provide information about processing your order, shipping, and billing.

7 Click the Finish button.

   The Genigraphics Wizard transmits your presentation file to a Genigraphics Service Center or saves it on disk.

   If you selected the Send File Via Modem option, the Genigraphics Wizard transmits your presentation file using GraphicsLink (Graflink). A Send Status dialog appears, showing you the progress of your transmission. After your transmission is final, a transmission summary appears, telling you the results of your transmission.

   GraphicsLink is an application that allows you to send your presentation file to a Genigraphics Service Center and to keep track of all presentation files, their job descriptions, and their billing information. You can also use the GraphicsLink application independently of the wizard by starting the Windows Explorer, and then double-clicking the GraphicsLink icon located in the PowerPoint folder.

Graflink

If you want to continue to the next lesson

1 On the File menu, click Close (CTRL+W).

2 If a dialog box appears asking whether you want to save the changes to your presentation, click the No button.

If you want to quit PowerPoint for now

1 On the File menu, click Exit (CTRL+Q).

2 If a dialog box appears asking whether you want to save the changes to your presentation, click the No button.

Lesson Summary

To	Do this	Button
Open a presentation	Click the File menu, and then click Open. Click the file you want to open and click the Open button.	
Preview a slide in black and white	On the Standard toolbar, click the Black and White View button.	
Add a header and footer	On the View menu, click Header And Footer. Click the appropriate check boxes and type your text.	
Change the slide format	On the File menu, click Page Setup and then select a slide format.	
Choose a printer	On the File menu, click Print. Click the Name drop-down arrow and click a printer.	
Print slides	On the File menu, click Print. Click the Print What drop-down arrow and click Slides.	
Print with the current Print dialog box settings	On the Standard toolbar, click the Print button (no dialog box appears).	
Print audience handouts	On the File menu, click Print. Click the Print What drop-down arrow and click Handouts (2, 3, or 6 slides).	
Print notes pages	On the File menu, click Print. Click the Print What drop-down arrow and click Notes Pages.	
Create 35mm slides	On the File menu, point to Send To, and then click Genigraphics.	

For online information about	Use the Office Assistant to search for
Viewing in black and white	**Black and white view**, and then click Change View To Black And White
Adding headers and footers	**Header or footer**, and then click Add Or change The Date, Time, Slide Number, Or Footer
Printing a presentation	**Print slides**, and then click Print Slides, Notes, Handouts, And Outlines

To use the Office Assistant, see Appendix A, in the back of this book.

Preview of the Next Lesson

In the next lesson, you'll import an existing outline, select and rearrange outline text and slides, and save an outline. You'll also learn how to view your outline with only titles and unformatted text.

Review & Practice

In the lessons in Part 1, you learned skills to start a new presentation, create a new slide, enter and edit text, create speaker's notes, and print and save your presentation. If you want to practice these skills and test your understanding before you proceed with the lessons in Part 2, you can work through the Review & Practice section following this lesson.

Review & Practice

You will review and practice how to:

Estimated time
20 min.

- Create a new presentation.
- Create a new slide.
- Enter and modify your ideas.
- Create speaker's notes pages.
- Add a header and footer.
- Print a presentation.
- Save a presentation.

Practice the skills you learned in the Part 1 lessons by working through this Review & Practice section. You'll practice creating a new presentation.

Scenario

You are an account manager at Ferguson & Bardell and have many years of experience working directly with personal investment portfolios. To develop a solid customer base and market for the company, you need to create an investment presentation that portrays stability and confidence, yet that can be customized for specific customer needs.

After recently learning PowerPoint techniques, you realize creating a presentation with PowerPoint is easy and effective. In this section, you'll create a new presentation, create a new slide, enter and modify an outline, create speaker's notes pages, print the presentation, and save the final product.

Step 1: **_Create a New Presentation_**

Since you are a financial expert and not an artist, use PowerPoint's Presentation Designs to help you customize the look of your presentation.

1 Start PowerPoint, use the Template option, and then view the Presentation Designs tab.

   or   _File New_

   Use the New Presentation button on the Standard toolbar.

2 Use the Professional presentation design.   _Pick_

3 Add the title slide.

For more information on	See
Starting a new presentation	Lesson 2

Step 2: **_Create a New Slide_**

Enter presentation title information and create a new slide.

1 Type **Investment Presentation** as the presentation title.

2 Type **Prepared for** <client name> as the sub-title.

3 Insert a New Slide with the Bulleted List layout.

4 Enter the following information on the new slide:

Ferguson & Bardell	(as a title)
Independently owned and managed	(as a bullet point)
Over 20 years of investment experience	(as a bullet point)
Relationship-driven client service	(as a bullet point)
Quantitative investment process	(as a bullet point)

For more information on	See
Creating a new slide and entering text	Lesson 2

Step 3: **_Enter and Modify Your Ideas_**

Modify the presentation content to meet your specific needs.

1 Switch to Outline view.

2 Create a new slide in Outline view.

3 Enter the following information in Outline view:

3 ☐Overview
- Investment Review
- Investment Strategy

You can use the Demote toolbar button or TAB key to change indent levels.

4 Switch to slide 3 in Slide view.

For more information on	See
Entering text in Outline view	Lesson 2

Step 4: ### *Create Speaker's Notes Pages*

Enter speaker's notes for important slides in your presentation.

1 Switch to Notes Pages view for Slide 2 and type the following paragraph.

Ferguson & Bardell, independently owned and managed, has been servicing the investment community for over 20 years. Since each investor comes with different needs, we strive to meet their individual investment needs through a personal commitment and a quantitative investment process.

2 Switch to Notes Pages view for Slide 3 and type the following paragraph.

As an overview, we will start with an investment review and conclude with an investment strategy. The investment review determines your current investment status, and looks at different alternatives and implications. The investment strategy reviews objectives and markets, and then selects programs.

For more information on	See
Creating speaker's notes pages	Lesson 2

Step 5: ### *Add a Header and Footer*

Add a header to your speaker's notes and audience handouts and a footer to your slides.

1 Add the header **Investment Presentation** to the notes pages and handouts.

2 Add a slide number and a page number to the presentation slides and the notes pages and handouts.

3 Add the footer **Ferguson & Bardell** to the presentation slides and the notes pages and handouts.

For more information on	See
Adding headers and footers	Lesson 3

Step 6: *Print a Presentation*

Print the slide and notes pages to review your presentation.

1 Check your presentation slides in Black and White view.
2 Print your presentation slides in black and white and then, if your printer is capable, print the presentation in color.
3 Print speaker's notes pages.
4 Print audience handouts with 2 slides per page.

For more information on	See
Printing a presentation	Lesson 3

Step 7: *Save a Presentation*

Save your presentation, so you can work on it later.

1 Save your presentation with the name **R&P Investment Pres 01** in the PowerPoint SBS Practice folder.
2 Add summary information to your presentation properties.

For more information on	See
Saving a presentation	Lesson 1
Entering presentation properties	Lesson 1

If you want to continue to the next lesson

1 On the File menu, click Close (CTRL+W).
2 If a dialog box appears asking whether you want to save the changes to your presentation, click the Yes button.

If you want to quit PowerPoint for now

1 On the File menu, click Exit (CTRL+Q).
2 If a dialog box appears asking whether you want to save the changes to your presentation, click the Yes button.

Organizing Your Ideas

Outlining Your Ideas

In this lesson you will learn how to:

Estimated time
40 min.

- View and enter text in Outline view.
- Insert an outline from Microsoft Word into PowerPoint.
- Change the view of an outline.
- Edit and rearrange outline text.
- Format text and change fonts.
- Send an outline or notes to Microsoft Word.

In PowerPoint, as you have seen, you can enter and organize your thoughts and ideas in Outline view to see the slide title text and paragraph text for each slide in your presentation. You can edit and rearrange both title and paragraph text in Outline view. You can also import outlines created in other applications into your PowerPoint outline and export the result when you are done.

In the previous lessons, you created an investment seminar presentation for Ferguson & Bardell. Later, Ferguson, one of the partners, asks you to develop a company presentation for next month's stockholders meeting.

In this lesson, you'll enter text into a PowerPoint outline, insert a Microsoft Word outline into your presentation, change the way you view your outline, rearrange and format your text, and export the outline into Microsoft Word for later use.

Start the lesson with a blank presentation

If you quit PowerPoint at the end of the last lesson, restart PowerPoint now. If you are continuing from the previous lesson, click the New button on the Standard toolbar.

New

1 In the PowerPoint Startup dialog box, click the Blank Presentation option button, and then click the OK button.

or

On the Standard toolbar, click the New button, click the Presentations tab, double-click the Blank Presentation icon, and then click the OK button to open a new blank presentation.

2 On the File menu, click Save As.

The Save As dialog box opens. Be sure the PowerPoint SBS Practice folder appears in the Save In box.

3 In the File Name box, type **F&B Company Pres 04**

4 Click the Save button.

The presentation is saved and the title bar changes to the new name.

Viewing and Entering Text in Outline View

In Outline view, each title appears on the left side of the window with a slide icon and slide number. Paragraph text is indented under its title on the outline. If there are graphic objects on a slide, the slide icon appears with shapes inside.

Enter text in Outline view

In this section, you'll type in paragraph text, and change a paragraph text indent level, to complete the title slide.

Outline View

1 Click the Outline View button.

The slide icon for slide 1 appears, as shown in the following illustration:

2 Type **Ferguson & Bardell** and press ENTER.

After you enter title text and press the ENTER key, the insertion point shifts down to start a new slide.

Demote

3 On the Outlining toolbar, click the Demote button or press TAB.

The insertion point shifts to the right to start a new paragraph.

4 Type **Your Personal Investment Managers**

The insertion point appears at the end of the phrase, as shown in the following illustration:

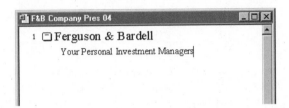

In the next section, you'll insert an outline from Microsoft Word into your presentation. When you insert an outline, PowerPoint creates a new slide and then inserts the outline text to create more slides.

Inserting an Outline from Another Application

PowerPoint can insert outlines created in other applications, such as Microsoft Word, into a presentation outline. When you insert a Microsoft Word document that is set up with outline heading styles, PowerPoint creates slide titles and paragraphs based on the heading and paragraph text indent levels. In this section, you'll insert an outline you developed for a previous project that describes the company.

1 On the Insert menu, click Slides From Outline.

The Insert Outline dialog box appears.

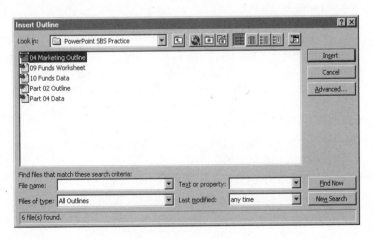

2 In the Look In box, ensure that the PowerPoint SBS Practice folder is open. If it is not, select the hard drive and folder where the Step by Step practice files are stored. Typically, you'll find the PowerPoint SBS Practice folder in the My Documents folder.

3 In the list of file and folder names, click 04 Marketing Outline.

4 Click the Insert button.

The Microsoft Word outline is inserted into the PowerPoint outline.

 TIP You can start a new presentation from an outline using the Open command. On the Standard toolbar, click the Open button, click the Files Of Type drop-down arrow, click All Outlines, and click the outline file you want to use.

The outline you're working on contains more text than you can see on the screen at one time.

Changing the View of an Outline

There are different ways of viewing your presentation in Outline view. You can change the view scale, collapse or expand your outline, or use plain or formatted text. To make it easier to view the entire outline you imported, reduce the view scale of the presentation window.

Change the view scale

You can change the scale of your view by using the Zoom Control on the Standard toolbar or the View menu. The standard view scales available in Outline view are 25%, 33%, 50%, 66%, 75%, and 100%. In other views, 150%, 200%, 300%, 400%, and Fit are also available for working on detailed items—such as graphics or objects.

Zoom Control

1 On the Standard toolbar, click the Zoom Control drop-down arrow and click 25%.

The view scale decreases from 33% to 25%. The Zoom Control command allows you to increase the view size to see small text that is hard to read or decrease the view size to see more of the presentation outline.

2 Scroll to the top of the outline.

3 On the Standard toolbar, click the Zoom Control box to select the percentage size.

Zoom Control

4 Type **33** and press ENTER.

The view scale changes to 33%. You can type in any view size.

Your presentation window should look like the following illustration:

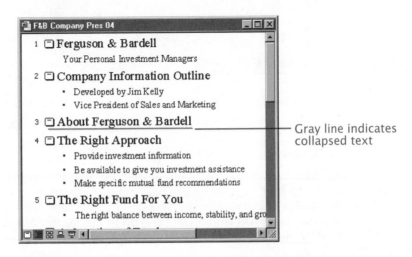

Collapse and expand the outline

To make it easier to work on certain parts of your outline, PowerPoint lets you view only slide titles for the entire presentation or for individual slides.

1 Click to the right of the slide 3 title to place the insertion point in the line.

Collapse

2 On the Outlining toolbar, click the Collapse button.

Slide 3 collapses down to show the title only. The rest of the outline remains fully expanded.

Your presentation window should look like the following illustration:

To make it easier to work on the main points of your outline, view only slide titles for the presentation.

Collapse All

3 On the Outlining toolbar, click the Collapse All button.

The view switches from titles and paragraphs to titles only. The Collapse All button allows you to work with the main points of your outline.

4 Click to the right of the slide 7 title to place the insertion point in the line.

Expand

5 On the Outlining toolbar, click the Expand button.

Slide 7 expands back to include the paragraph text.

Expand a slide

The Expand Slide feature in PowerPoint allows you to create individual slides quickly from the paragraphs found on a single slide.

1 On the Tools menu, click Expand Slide.

The bulleted paragraphs on the slide expand to titles on new slides, as shown in the following illustration:

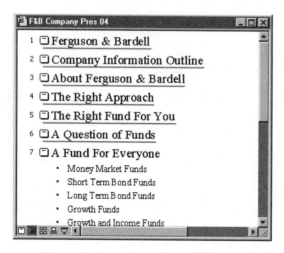

Expand All

2 On the Outlining toolbar, click the Expand All button.

Outline view expands to include title and paragraph text.

Show outline formatting

The Show Formatting feature in PowerPoint allows you to work on your content without formatting, so you can see your content more easily. The formatting information is not deleted or cleared; it's just turned off. When you print an outline, it will print with formatting on or off, depending on how you set the Show Formatting command.

*Show
Formatting*

1 On the Outlining toolbar, click the Show Formatting button.

The view switches from formatted text to plain text, as shown in the following illustration:

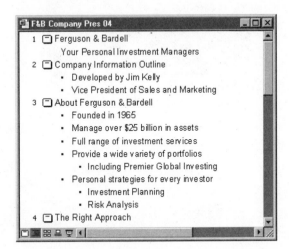

2 On the Outlining toolbar, click the Show Formatting button again.

The text in Outline view changes from plain to formatted text.

Editing and Rearranging in Outline View

In Outline view, you can select, edit, and then rearrange slides, paragraphs, and text by using the Outlining toolbar buttons or by dragging the slides, paragraphs, or text. In this section you need to delete a slide and rearrange a few points in your presentation.

Selecting and Editing Slide and Paragraph Text

To edit or rearrange slides and paragraphs, you'll need to select the text first. To select a slide or paragraph, click the corresponding slide icon or paragraph bullet. To select a word, double-click the word, and to select text, drag the insertion point across the text.

Select an entire slide

*Four-headed
Arrow*

➤ Scroll to the top of the outline and position the I-beam cursor (which changes to a four-headed arrow) over the icon for slide 2 and click to select the slide.

The entire slide, including all text and graphic objects (even those that are not visible in Outline view), is selected. You can also select a slide by clicking its slide number.

Your presentation window should look like to the following illustration:

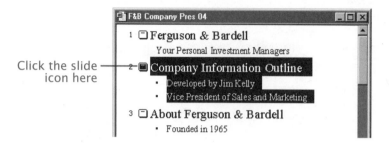

Click the slide icon here

Delete a slide

After selecting a slide or any other text in Outline view, you can delete the entire slide at any time. Delete slide 2 which contains unnecessary text.

➤ Press the DELETE key.

PowerPoint deletes slide 2 and renumbers the other slides.

 TIP You can also delete the currently selected or displayed slide in any view by clicking Delete Slide on the File menu. You can also drag through multiple paragraphs to select them.

Select and delete a paragraph

Selecting paragraphs works the same way as selecting slides.

1 Position the I-beam cursor (which changes to a four-headed arrow) over the bullet next to the paragraph titled "Full range of investment services" in slide 2 and click.

PowerPoint selects the paragraph, including all related indented paragraphs. After selecting a paragraph or any text in Outline view, you can delete it at any time. Slide 2 contains to much text, delete a paragraph.

2 Press the DELETE key.

PowerPoint deletes the paragraph.

Select multiple paragraphs

1 Click the bullet next to the paragraph titled "Provide a wide variety of portfolios" in slide 2.

2 Hold down the SHIFT key and click the bullet for the paragraph titled "Risk Analysis." Notice that the bullet points in between are also selected.

Your presentation window should look like the following illustration:

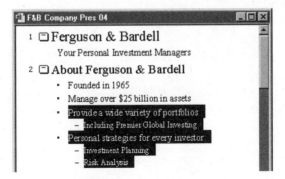

 TIP You can also select multiple paragraphs with the mouse button. Click the I-beam cursor where you want the selection to begin, then drag to where you want the selection to end. PowerPoint selects everything between the first click and the drag.

Select text

Selecting text in Outline view is the same as selecting text in Slide view. To select any part of a title or paragraph, you can drag the I-beam cursor to highlight the text. In Outline view, you can also click the blank area at the end of a title or paragraph to select the entire line of text. This technique works well especially when selecting slide titles.

1   Position the I-beam cursor in the middle of the word "Manage" in the paragraph text of slide 2.

2   Drag through the title "Manage over $25 billion in assets" to select the text.

   With the Automatic Word Selection feature turned on, even though you started the selection in the middle of the word "Manage," PowerPoint automatically selects the entire word.

 NOTE You can turn off the Automatic Word Selection command by choosing Options on the Tools menu, clicking the Edit tab, and removing the check mark in the Automatic Word Selection check box.

3 Position the I-beam cursor to the right of the word "Bardell" in slide 2.

4 Double-click to select the entire title.

Only the slide title is selected.

Rearranging Slides, Paragraphs, and Text

You can rearrange slides and paragraphs in Outline view by using the Move Up button and the Move Down button on the Outlining toolbar or by dragging selected slides and paragraphs to where you want them to appear.

Rearrange a slide

In Lessons 1 and 2, you learned how to move text in Outline view by using the Demote, Promote, Move Up, and Move Down buttons on the Outlining toolbar. In this part of the lesson, you'll learn how to rearrange slides and text by dragging to improve the flow of your company presentation.

1 In slide 4, position the four-headed arrow over the bullet of the text line titled "The Right Fund For You."

2 Drag the slide icon down between the last bullet point in slide 5 and the title text in slide 6, as shown in the following illustration:

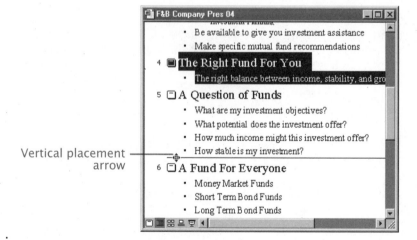

Vertical placement arrow

Notice that the four-headed arrow changes into a four-headed placement arrow that indicates which direction you are moving the text. A placement line appears showing you where you can place the text. After you release the mouse, the slides are reordered and renumbered.

3 Click in a blank area of the outline to deselect the text.

Rearrange paragraphs

You can rearrange paragraphs by dragging them just like you do entire slides. Instead of moving a paragraph up or down, this time try moving a paragraph so it becomes a part of another paragraph.

1 In slide 5, position the four-headed arrow over the bullet of the text line titled "The right balance between income, stability, and growth."

2 Drag the text line horizontally to the left one level as shown in the following illustration.

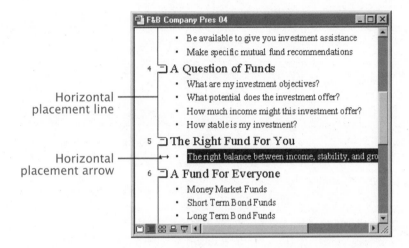

Horizontal placement line

Horizontal placement arrow

The text line moves one indent level to the left.

3 Click the I-beam cursor to the right of the text to deselect the paragraph.

Rearrange words

You can move selected words by simply dragging the selection to a new position.

1 Position the I-beam cursor over the word "stability," in slide 5.

2 Drag to select the entire word, the comma, and the space that follows it.

3 Position the I-beam cursor (which changes to the pointer) over the selection.

4 Drag the selection to the left of the word "income" on the same line.

After you press the mouse down, the cursor changes to the Insert pointer. When you release the mouse, the word "stability" moves to its new position.

Insert Pointer

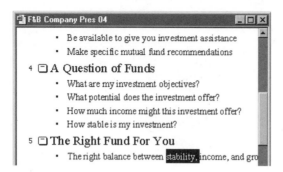

Formatting Text

In Outline view, you can modify the style of text by changing fonts, sizes, and styles, just as you can in Slide view.

Format paragraph text

1 Drag the scroll box to the top of the vertical scroll bar.

2 Position the I-beam cursor to the right of the word "Managers" in slide 1.

3 Double-click to select the entire line.

The paragraph text is selected.

Italic

4 On the Formatting toolbar, click the Italic button.

5 On the Formatting toolbar, click the Font Size drop-down arrow button and click 28.

The selected text is formatted, as shown in the following illustration:

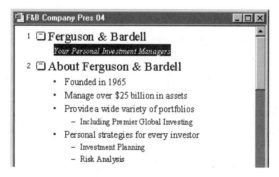

6 Position the I-beam cursor to the right of the word "Bardell" in slide 1.

7 Double-click to select the entire line.

8 On the Formatting toolbar, click the Bold button.

The selected text appears bold.

Bold

Increase Font Size

9 On the Formatting toolbar, click the Increase Font Size button.

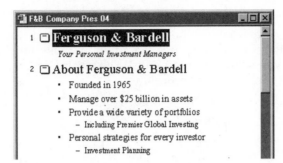

The slide title font changes from 44 points to 48 points.

Change the font

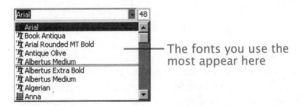

Font

1 On the Standard toolbar, click the Font drop-down arrow, scroll to the top of the list, and then click Arial.

The selected text changes from Times New Roman to Arial.

2 On the Standard toolbar, click the Font drop-down arrow again.

Notice the Arial font is at the top of the list. PowerPoint places the fonts you use the most at the top of the list, separated by a double line, so you don't have to scroll down the list of fonts.

The fonts you use the most appear here

3 Click a blank space to the right of the Font drop-down list.

The slide 1 title text is deselected.

Sending an Outline or Notes to Microsoft Word

In PowerPoint, you can turn your presentation information into a report. With the Send to Microsoft Word feature, you can export your presentation outline or speakers' notes directly into Microsoft Word. PowerPoint launches Microsoft Word and sends or copies the outline or note pages in your presentation to a blank Word document. You'll need to have Microsoft Word installed on your computer to perform this task.

Send the outline to Microsoft Word

1 On the File menu, point to Send To and then click Microsoft Word.

The Write-Up dialog box appears with five page layout options and two pasting options. The page layout options determine the type of information you want to send to Word. The pasting options determine how you want to send the information.

2 Click the Outline Only option.

3 Click the OK button.

PowerPoint launches Microsoft Word and inserts your presentation slides with the title text and main text format into a blank Word document.

4 Click the Close button to close the Office Assistant, if necessary.

5 On the Microsoft Word File menu, click Save As.

6 In the Save In box, ensure that the PowerPoint SBS Practice folder is open. If it is not, select the hard drive and folder where the Step by Step practice files are stored. Typically, you'll find the PowerPoint SBS Practice folder in the My Documents folder.

7 In the File Name box, type **F&B Company Doc**

8 Click the Save As Type drop-down arrow and click Word Document.

9 Click the Save button.

Word saves your presentation slide text in a document called F&B Company Doc in your Step by Step practice folder.

10 On the Microsoft Word File menu, click Exit.

Word closes and returns you to PowerPoint.

 NOTE If you don't have Microsoft Word, then you can save your presentation in outline format. For more information and step-by-step instructions, see "One Step Further," at the end of this lesson.

Save the presentation in Outline view

PowerPoint saves your presentation in the current view and view scale. Choosing the Save command in Outline view saves your presentation in Outline view with the current view scale setting.

Save

➤ On the Standard toolbar, click the Save button.

When you open this presentation the next time, PowerPoint will open it in Outline view at the view scale it was last saved.

One Step Further

In this lesson, you learned how to insert a Microsoft Word outline into PowerPoint, add text to the outline, change the view of outline, select and rearrange slides and paragraphs, export a PowerPoint outline to Microsoft Word, and save a PowerPoint outline in Microsoft Word as a document.

You can also save your PowerPoint outline in Microsoft Word using a special format called *Rich Text Format* (RTF). One nice feature of using the RTF format to save your outline is that it saves any formatting you may have done to the text of your outline. Also, there are many other applications that can import outlines saved in the RTF format.

Save the presentation outline

1   On the File menu, click Save As.

2   In the Save In box, ensure that the PowerPoint SBS Practice folder is open. If it is not, select the hard drive and folder where the Step by Step practice files are stored. Typically, you'll find the PowerPoint SBS Practice folder in the My Documents folder.

3   In the File Name box, type **F&B Company Pres RTF**

4   Click the Save As Type drop-down arrow and click Outline/RTF.

5   Click the Save button.

PowerPoint saves your presentation slide text in a document called F&B Outline RTF in your Step by Step practice folder.

If you want to continue to the next lesson

1   On the File menu, click Close (CTRL+W).

2   If a dialog box appears asking whether you want to save the changes to your presentation, click the Yes button.

If you want to quit PowerPoint for now

1   On the File menu, click Exit (CTRL+Q).

2   If a dialog box appears asking whether you want to save the changes to your presentation, click the Yes button.

Lesson Summary

To	Do this	Button
Start with a blank presentation	On the Standard toolbar, click the New button, and then double-click the Blank icon.	
Insert an outline into a presentation	On the Insert menu, click Slides From Outline.	
View an outline with titles only	On the Outlining toolbar, click the Collapse All button.	
Expand a slide	Select a slide in Outline or Slide Sorter view. On the Tools menu, click Expand Slide.	
View an outline with unformatted text	On the Outlining toolbar, click the Show Formatting button.	
Increase or decrease the Outline view size	On the Standard toolbar, click the Zoom Control drop-down arrow and click a view size.	33%
Select a slide or paragraph	Position the four-headed arrow to the left of the text and click.	
Move a slide or paragraph	Select the slide or paragraph. On the Outlining toolbar, click one of the outlining buttons or drag the selection.	
Move text	Select the text. Drag it to a new position.	
Send an outline to Microsoft Word	On the File menu, point to Send To, then click Microsoft Word. Click the Outline Only option button.	

For online information about	Use the Office Assistant to search for
Inserting an outline	**Insert outline**, and then click Create A Presentation From An Outline
Editing and arranging text	**Edit outline view**, and then click Ways To Organize My Content In Outline View

To use the Office Assistant, see Appendix A, in the back of this book.

Preview of the Next Lesson

In the next lesson, you'll correct text while you type, add text to slides, select and deselect text objects, format text, check spelling, and check presentation styles.

Adding and Modifying Text

In this lesson you will learn how to:

Estimated time
35 min.

- Select and deselect objects.
- Correct text as you type.
- Add text to slides.
- Adjust and format text.
- Find and replace text and fonts.
- Check spelling.
- Check presentation styles.
- Look up information in Microsoft Bookshelf.

In PowerPoint, adding and modifying text is simple. PowerPoint offers several alternatives for placing text on your slides; you can use text placeholders for entering your slide titles and subtitles, text labels for short notes and phrases, text boxes for longer supporting text, and finally, you can place text inside shaped objects.

As Director of Communications at Ferguson & Bardell, you have been working on a company presentation. After working with your presentation outline in the previous lesson, you're ready to fine-tune your message.

In this lesson, you'll learn how to let PowerPoint automatically correct text while you type, create several kinds of text objects, edit text, change the appearance of text, find and replace text, replace fonts, check spelling, check presentation style, and look up information in Microsoft Bookshelf.

Start the lesson

Follow the steps below to open the practice file called 05 PPT Lesson, and then save it with the new name F&B Company Pres 05. If you haven't already started PowerPoint, do so now.

Open

For information about opening a presentation, see Lesson 3.

1 On the Standard toolbar, click the Open button or click the Open An Existing Presentation option button on the Start-up dialog box and click OK.

2 In the Look In box, ensure that the PowerPoint SBS Practice folder is open. If it is not, select the hard drive and folder where the Step by Step practice files are stored.

3 In the file list box, double-click the file named 05 PPT Lesson to open it.

4 On the File menu, click Save As.

The Save As dialog box opens. Be sure the PowerPoint SBS Practice folder appears in the Save In box.

5 In the File Name box, type **F&B Company Pres 05**

6 Click the Save button.

The presentation is saved and the title bar changes to the new name.

Selecting and Deselecting Objects

To make formatting changes to all of the text in a text object, you need to select the object. To select an object, click a part of the object using the Select Objects tool or "pointer." To deselect an object, move your pointer off the object into a blank area of the slide and click.

Select and deselect a text object

Selection Cursor

1 Position the pointer near the edge of the bulleted text box until it changes to the selection cursor shown in the margin, as shown in the following illustration:

2 Click the mouse button to select the text box.

The text object is surrounded by a fuzzy outline called a *dotted selection box* indicating it's selected and ready to be edited as an object. The white squares at each corner of the object are resize handles, which are used to adjust and resize objects.

3 Click outside the selection box to deselect the text box.

The text box is deselected.

AutoCorrecting Text While Typing

With AutoCorrect, PowerPoint automatically replaces common misspellings as you type with the correct spelling. For example, if you always type "tehm" instead of "them," you can create an AutoCorrect entry named "tehm." Whenever you type **tehm** followed by a space or punctuation mark, PowerPoint replaces it with "them." Before beginning your work on the company presentation, you decide to use AutoCorrect to prevent errors in spelling the company name.

Add an AutoCorrect entry

1 On the Tools menu, click AutoCorrect.

The AutoCorrect dialog box appears.

2 In the Replace box, type **Fergusen**

Ferguson is commonly misspelled as Fergusen.

3 Press TAB.

4 In the With box, type **Ferguson**

Your AutoCorrect dialog box should look like the following illustration:

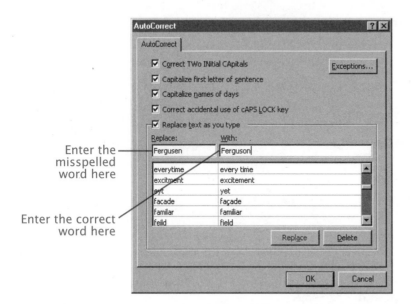

Enter the misspelled word here

Enter the correct word here

Now, whenever you type Fergusen, PowerPoint will automatically replace it with Ferguson. In the next section, you'll see this in practice.

5 Click the OK button.

Change to another slide

➤ Drag the scroll box to advance to slide 3.

Adding Text to Your Slide

Usually, slides contain a title placeholder and a main text placeholder in which to enter your main ideas, as you saw in Lesson 1. With PowerPoint, you can also place other text objects on your slide with the Text Box tool.

There are two primary types of text objects: a *text label*, which refers to text that does not word-wrap within a defined box, and a *word processing box*, which refers to text that word-wraps inside the boundaries of an object. You usually use a text label to enter short notes or phrases, while for longer sentences, you use a word processing box.

Add text in a text object

You can add text in any PowerPoint text object by placing the insertion point where you want and typing your new text.

I-Beam Cursor

1 Click the I-beam cursor just to the right of the word "Provide" in the bulleted list to place the insertion point.

A blinking insertion point appears where you clicked the I-beam cursor.

2 Press the SPACEBAR and type **comprehensive**

The paragraph automatically wraps in the text object.

Your presentation window should look like the following illustration:

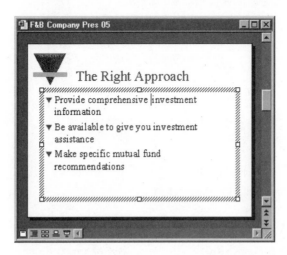

3 Click outside the slanted-line selection box to deselect the text object.

Create a text label

To create a text label on your slide, use the Text Box tool to select a place on the slide for your text, and start typing. Text created on a slide with the Text Box tool doesn't appear in Outline view. Only text entered in a title place-holder and a main text placeholder appears in Outline view.

Text Box

1 On the Drawing toolbar, click the Text Box button.

2 Position your pointer at the bottom of the slide directly below the last bullet.

3 Click to create a text label.

An empty text box with a dotted selection appears. When a text box is empty, you can enter text by simply typing.

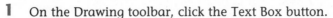

Empty Text Box

4 Type **Mutual funds are not insured by the FDIC**

As you enter text in an empty text box, the selection box changes to a slanted-line selection box. The slanted-line selection box lets you know you're ready to enter or edit the text within a text object.

75

Your presentation window should look like the following illustration:

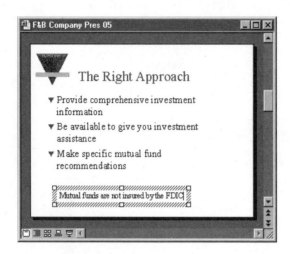

5 Click outside the slanted-line selection box to deselect the text label.

The text label is deselected.

Change to the next slide

Next Slide

➤ Click the Next Slide button to advance to slide 4.

Create a word processing box

To create a word processing box, use the Text Box tool just as you did for the text label, but instead of clicking, drag the box to the width you want it, and start typing.

Text Box

Cross Hairs Cursor

1 On the Drawing toolbar, click the Text Box button.

2 Position your pointer below the last bullet.

3 Drag to create a box approximately 5 inches long.

As you drag, the pointer changes to the cross hairs cursor shown to the left. When you release the mouse button, a slanted-line selection box appears. PowerPoint is ready for you to enter your text.

4 Type **Fergusen & Bardell is committed to helping you achieve your financial goals**

As you enter your text, the misspelled word, "Fergusen," is automatically corrected with the AutoCorrect feature. The width of the box stays the same, the words wrap, and the box height increases to accommodate the complete entry.

Your presentation window should look like the following illustration:

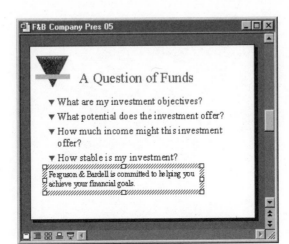

> **TIP** You can convert a word processing box to a text label by selecting the word processing box, clicking Text Box on the Format menu, and then clicking the Text Box tab and turning off the Word-wrap Text in Object check box. To covert a text label to a word processing box, turn on the Word-wrap Text in Object check box.

Adjusting Text

You have complete control over the placement and position of your text in PowerPoint. You can adjust the arrangement, alignment, and line spacing of text in an object to achieve the best look.

Adjust text in an object

You can adjust text in an object by setting the word-wrap option and the fit text option in the Format AutoShape dialog box. Turning on the word-wrap setting changes a text attribute from a text label to a word processing box. Turning on the fit text setting adjusts a text object to the size of the text.

*Selection
Cursor*

1 Position the pointer near the edge of the bulleted text (which changes to the selection cursor) and click to select it.

Notice that the dotted selection box is larger than it needs to be.

2 On the Format menu, click AutoShape.

The Format AutoShape dialog box appears.

3 Click the Text Box tab.

4   Click the Resize Autoshape To Fit Text check box.

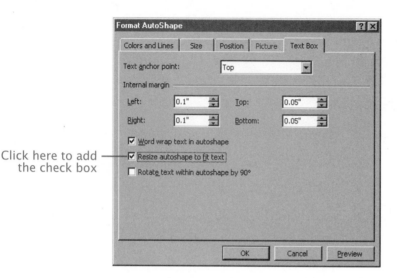

Click here to add — the check box

5   Click the OK button.

The object adjusts to fit the size of the text.

Change spacing between lines of text

Using PowerPoint's Line Spacing command, you can easily adjust the vertical space between selected lines and paragraphs to achieve a certain look.

Decrease Paragraph Spacing

1   On the Formatting toolbar, click the Decrease Paragraph Spacing button.

The paragraph spacing in the text box decreases by 0.1 from 1.0 to 0.9. To make other line spacing changes, use the Line Spacing command.

2   On the Format menu, click Line Spacing.

The Line Spacing dialog box appears.

3   Click the Before Paragraph down arrow until 0.1 appears.

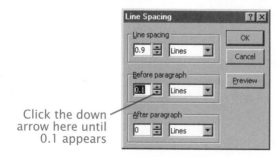

Click the down arrow here until 0.1 appears

The paragraph spacing before each paragraph decreases by 0.1.

4   Click the OK button.

Your presentation window should look like the following illustration:

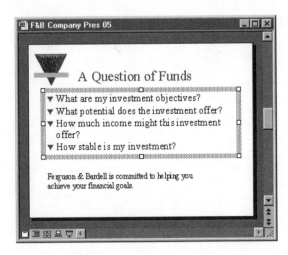

Formatting Text

After you have finished adjusting your text, you can change text formatting, such as bullets, font size, italic, bold, underline, or shadow, by selecting the text object and clicking one or more formatting buttons on the PowerPoint Formatting toolbar.

Remove text bullets and decrease font size

Bullets

1   Ensure that the bulleted text box is still selected.

2   On the Formatting toolbar, click the Bullets button.

The bullets for the four bulleted lines disappear.

3   On the Formatting toolbar, click the Decrease Font Size button to reduce the font size a setting down to 28.

Format text in a text object

*Selection
Cursor*

Italic

1   Position the pointer near the edge of the text "Ferguson & Bardell . . ." (which changes to the selection cursor) and click to select it.

A dotted line selection box appears around the text object indicating it's selected.

2   On the Formatting toolbar, click the Italic button.

The text in the object changes to italic.

Font Color

3 On the Drawing toolbar, click the Font Color drop-down arrow button.

A text color menu of the current color scheme appears.

4 Click the purple color as indicated in the following illustration:

Click the purple color here

The font color changes to purple. The line on the Font Color button also changes to purple indicating the currently selected font color.

Change text alignment

To align text in an object, first select the object and then click Alignment on the Format menu. A submenu opens, giving you four options: Left, Center, Right, and Justify.

Center Alignment

➤ On the Formatting toolbar, click the Center Alignment button.

The text in the text object aligns to the center.

Move a text object

You can move a text object to any place on a slide to give your presentation the best look. To move a text object, drag the edge of the text object's selection box.

➤ Drag the edge of the selection box to center the text object between the bottom of the slide and the bulleted text box.

Your presentation window should look like the following illustration:

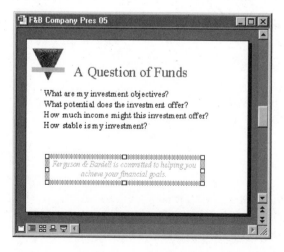

Finding and Replacing Text and Fonts

The Find and Replace commands allow you to locate and change specific text in your presentation. Find helps you locate a specific word, while Replace locates all occurrences of a word and replaces them with a different one.

Replace text

Use the Replace command to find the word "Exchange" and replace it with the word "Transfer" for the company presentation.

1 On the Edit menu, click Replace (CTRL+H).

The Replace dialog box appears.

2 In the Find What box, type **Exchange**

3 Press TAB or click the I-beam cursor in the Replace With box.

4 Type **Transfer**

Type Exchange here →

Type Transfer here →

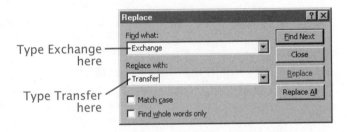

5 Click the Find Next button.

PowerPoint finds the word "Exchange" on slide 7. If you can't see the selected text, drag the Replace dialog box title bar up so you can see the text.

6 Click the Replace button.

A dialog box appears telling you PowerPoint is finished searching the presentation.

7 Click the OK button.

8 Click the Close button in the Replace dialog box.

The Replace dialog box closes.

Replace fonts

With the Replace Fonts command, you can replace a current font style you have been using with another style throughout your entire presentation. Try changing Arial to Times New Roman.

1 On the Format menu, click Replace Fonts.

The Replace Font dialog box appears with Arial in the Replace box.

2 Click the With drop-down arrow.

3 Scroll down and click Book Antiqua.

4 Click the Replace button.

Throughout your presentation, the text formatted with the Times New Roman font changes to the Book Antiqua font.

5 Click the Close button.

Checking Spelling

The spelling checker checks the spelling of the entire presentation, including all slides, outlines, notes pages, and handout pages. To help you identify misspelled words, PowerPoint underlines them with a wavy red line. To turn off this feature, you can click Options on the Tools menu. PowerPoint uses different built-in dictionaries to check your presentation in more than one language. You can also create custom dictionaries in PowerPoint to check spelling for unique words or use custom dictionaries from other Microsoft applications.

Select another language to check in your presentation

1 Double-click the Spanish word "Espanol" in the bulleted text box.

The word "Espanol" appears with a red underline indicating it is misspelled or not recognized by the dictionary.

2 On the Tools menu, click Language.

The Language dialog box appears.

3 Scroll down and click Spanish (Mexican).

PowerPoint marks the selected word as a Mexican Spanish word for the spell checker.

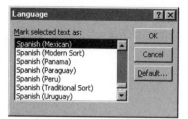

4 Click the OK button.

You'll notice the red line under the word doesn't appear indicating the word is recognized by the dictionary. You can also correct the spelling of a word by right-clicking the misspelled word and clicking the correct spelling of the word from the list in the shortcut menu.

Correct the spelling of a word

> Right-click the word "Guidence," and then click Guidance.

The misspelled word is replaced with the correct spelling.

Check the spelling in your presentation

Spelling

1   On the Standard toolbar, click the Spelling button.

PowerPoint begins checking the spelling on the current slide. The spelling checker stops and highlights the proper name "Ferguson."

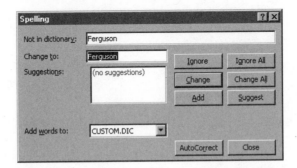

"Ferguson" doesn't appear in your dictionary. The custom dictionary allows you to add words that your dictionary doesn't recognize. Since Ferguson is a proper name, add the word to your custom dictionary.

2   Click the Add button.

The custom dictionary adds the word "Ferguson" and continues to check your presentation. The spelling checker stops when it fails to recognize the word "Bardell."

3   Click the Ignore All button.

All appearances of the word "Bardell" are ignored by the spelling checker. The spelling checker stops and highlights the misspelled word "portfolioes." A list appears, showing possible correct spellings of the misspelled word. The correct word spelling, "portfolios," appears selected.

   TIP   You can click the AutoCorrect button to add the misspelled and correct spelling of the word to the AutoCorrect table of entries to avoid the misspelling in the first place.

---

4   Click the Change button to correct the spelling.

The spelling checker continues to check your presentation for misspelled words or words not found in the dictionary. A dialog box appears, indicating PowerPoint finished checking the entire presentation.

5   Click the OK button.

Checking Presentation Styles

Use PowerPoint's Style Checker to help you correct common presentation style design mistakes so your audience focuses on you and not your mistakes. The Style Checker reviews your presentation for typical mistakes like font size, number of fonts, number of words, punctuation, and other readability problems and then suggests ways to improve your presentation.

Check the style of your presentation

1 On the Tools menu, click Style Checker.

The Style Checker dialog box appears.

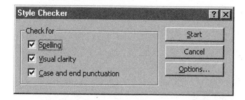

Since you already checked the spelling of the presentation, turn off the spelling option.

2 Click the Spelling check box to uncheck the option.

3 Click the Options button.

The Style Checker Options dialog box appears, displaying tabs for Case And End Punctuation and Visual Clarity.

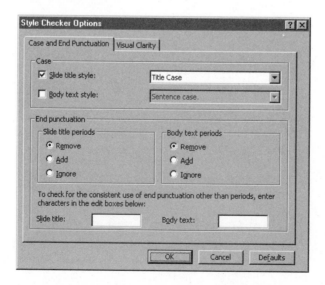

4 In the Case area, click the Body Text Style check box.

The Style Checker disregards the case of body text style in the presentation. You'll see another way to change text case in the "One Step Further" at the end of this lesson.

5 Click the OK button.

The Style Checker dialog box appears.

6 Click the Start button.

The Style Checker dialog box reappears to warn you of an inconsistency. Paragraph 1 of placeholder 2 of slide 5 has end punctuation.

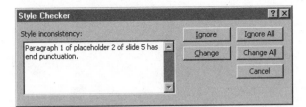

7 Click the Change button.

The Style Checker Summary dialog box appears.

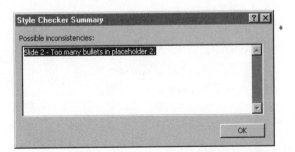

The Style Checker found other possible style inconsistencies. Based on the current Style Checker settings, slide 2 contains too many bullets in placeholder 2.

8 Click the OK button.

Looking Up Information in Microsoft Bookshelf

When Microsoft Bookshelf 97 or Microsoft Bookshelf Basics, a multimedia reference collection with online books, is installed with Microsoft Office 97, a special command, Look Up Reference, is added to PowerPoint so you can look up information in Bookshelf without leaving your presentation. In addition, you can also right-click a word in your presentation and then click Define on the shortcut menu to quickly find a definition from information provided on the Bookshelf 97 or Bookshelf Basics CD-ROMs.

Look up information in Microsoft Bookshelf

1 Insert the Bookshelf CD into your CD-ROM drive.

2 On the Tools menu, click Look Up Reference.

The Look Up Reference dialog box appears.

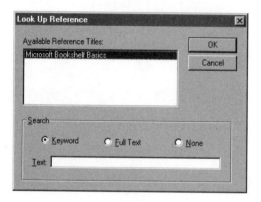

3 In the Available Reference Titles area, click Microsoft Bookshelf Basics.

4 Click OK.

Bookshelf Basics opens.

For information about using Bookshelf Basics, see Office 97 on-line help.

5 Select information from the Bookshelf Basics CD-ROM.

6 On the Bookshelf Basics Edit menu, click Copy To PowerPoint.

7 Choose the locaton where you want the information and click Copy.

The information from Bookshelf Basics appears on your slide.

Save the presentation

Save

➤ On the Standard toolbar, click the Save button.

No dialog box appears because the presentation already has a name. The current information in your presentation is saved with the same name.

One Step Further

You have learned to create and edit a text object, format text using the toolbar, adjust text alignment and line spacing, find and replace text, check spelling, and check presentation style. As part of the style checking process, PowerPoint checks case, but you can independently change text case for sentences with a command from the Format menu.

Change the case of text

1 Drag the scroll box to slide 7, if necessary.

2 Position the pointer near the bulleted text box (which changes to the selection cursor) and click to select it.

3 On the Format menu, click Change Case.

   The Change Case dialog box appears with the Sentence Case option button set as the default.

4 Click the OK button.

   The paragraph text changes to sentence case.

If you want to continue to the next lesson

1 On the File menu, click Close (CTRL+W).

2 If a dialog box appears asking whether you want to save the changes to your presentation, click the Yes button.

If you want to quit PowerPoint for now

1 On the File menu, click Exit (CTRL+Q).

2 If a dialog box appears asking whether you want to save the changes to your presentation, click the Yes button.

Lesson Summary

To	Do this	Button
Select text	Click a text box with the selection cursor.	
Deselect text	Click a blank area on the slide.	
Add AutoCorrect text	On the Tools menu, click AutoCorrect and type in an entry.	
Create a text label	On the Drawing toolbar, click the Text Box button. Click the slide and type your text.	
Create a word processing box	On the Drawing toolbar, click the Text Box button. Drag to create a text box, and then type your text.	
Change line spacing	Select a text object. On the Format menu, click Line Spacing or click one of the paragraph spacing buttons on the Formatting toolbar.	

To	Do this	Button
Adjust text	Select a text object. On the Format menu, click Drawing Object.	
Remove a bullet	Select the bulleted text. On the Formatting toolbar, click the Bullets button.	
Change text alignment	Select the text. On the Formatting toolbar, click the alignment buttons.	
Replace fonts	On the Format menu, click Replace Fonts.	
Find or replace text	On the Edit menu, click Find or Replace.	
Check spelling	On the Standard toolbar, click the Spelling button.	
Check style	On the Tools menu, click Style Checker.	
Look up information in Bookshelf	On the Tools menu, click Look Up Reference and select a reference.	

For online information about	Use the Office Assistant to search for
Working with text	**Add text**, and then click Add Text
Selecting and editing text	**Select text**, and then click Select Text
Formatting text	**Format text**, and then click Change The Way Text Looks
Finding and replacing text	**Find text**, and then click Find Text Or Replace Text

To use the Office Assistant, see Appendix A, in the back of this book.

Preview of the Next Lesson

In the next lesson, you'll apply a design template, change the Slide Master, change bullets, work with the ruler and tabs, and save a design template.

Review & Practice

In the lessons in Part 2, you learned skills to open a presentation and insert an outline, edit and rearrange slides and text, create text objects, format text, check your presentation's spelling and style, and report your presentation outline text to Microsoft Word. If you want to practice these skills and test your understanding before you proceed with the lessons in Part 3, you can work through the Review & Practice section following this lesson.

Review & Practice

Estimated time
25 min.

You will review and practice how to:

■ Insert an outline.

■ Edit and rearrange slides and text.

■ Create text objects and add text to a slide.

■ Format text.

■ Check spelling and presentation style.

■ Save an outline.

Practice the skills you learned in the Part 2 lessons by working through this Review & Practice section. You'll use PowerPoint to edit and modify text in a presentation.

Scenario

As the account manager at Ferguson & Bardell, continue to work on the investment presentation you started in the first Review & Practice.

In this section, you'll open a presentation and insert an outline from Microsoft Word, edit and rearrange the outline, create a text label or word processing box, format text, check the spelling and style of the presentation, and then report your results in Microsoft Word for use by co-workers.

Step 1: **_Open a Presentation and Insert an Outline_**

1 From the PowerPoint SBS Practice folder, open the presentation called Part 02 Review.

2 Save the presentation with the name **R&P Investment Pres 02** in the PowerPoint SBS Practice folder.

3 Switch to Outline view.

4 Insert the Microsoft Word outline called Part 02 Outline after the last slide in the outline.

5 Scroll to the top of the outline and select slide 4.

For more information on	See
Inserting an outline	Lesson 4
Selecting a slide	Lesson 4

Step 2: **_Edit and Rearrange Slides and Text_**

1 Add the entry "investmnet" and "investment" to the AutoCorrect table.

2 Edit the text in slide 3 of the current outline to reflect the following text:

As you enter the word "investment," type the word as indicated to demonstrate the AutoCorrect feature.

3 ⊞ Overview
  ■ Investment Process
  ■ Investment Review
    – Evaluate Financial Status
    – Formulate Guidelines
  ■ Investment Strategy
    – Select Investments
    – Review & Report Status

3 Move the slide entitled "Investment Review" after the slide entitled "Investment Characteristics" and then move the slide entitled "Investment Strategy" after the slide entitled "Investment Trends."

4 Delete slide 4.

5 Switch to slide 2 in Slide view.

For more information on	See
Editing and rearranging text in Outline view	Lesson 4
AutoCorrecting text while typing	Lesson 5

Step 3: *Create Text Objects for Your Slides*

work with slide 2

1 Select the bulleted text object and adjust the text object to fit the text using the Drawing Object command.

2 Create a text label or a word processing box with the following text:
Your Personal Investment Manager

For more information on	See
Adjusting text	Lesson 5
Adding text to your slide	Lesson 5

Step 4: *Format Text*

1 Select the text object with "Your Personal Investment Manager."

2 Increase the font size to 28 points.

3 Change the font to Arial Rounded MT Bold and italic.

4 Change the text color to match the title.

5 Move the text object to be centered on the slide between the bulleted text and the footer.

Your presentation window should look like the following illustration:

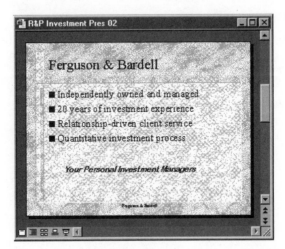

For more information on	See
Formatting text	Lesson 5
Adjusting text	Lesson 5

Step 5:   *Check the Presentation's Spelling and Style*

1   Add a foriegn language word to your presentation and mark the word.

2   Click the Spelling toolbar button.

3   Correct any words that are clearly misspelled. Add all proper names to the dictionary.

4   Check presentation style and correct any text case problems and remove periods.

5   After you have finished proofing the presentation, save it.

For more information on	See
Checking spelling	Lesson 5
Checking presentation style	Lesson 5

Step 6:   *Send the outline to Microsoft Word*

If you don't have Microsoft Word installed on your computer, then save your outline from PowerPoint as described in the "One Step Further" for Lesson 4.

1   Report your presentation outline to Microsoft Word.

2   Save your outline in Microsoft Word with the name **R&P Investment Doc** in the PowerPoint SBS Practice folder.

3   Exit Microsoft Word and return to PowerPoint.

For more information on	See
Sending an Outline to Microsoft Word	Lesson 4

If you want to continue to the next lesson

1   On the File menu, click Close (CTRL+W).

2   If a dialog box appears asking whether you want to save changes to the presentation, click the Yes button.

If you want to quit PowerPoint for now

1   On the File menu, click Exit (CTRL+Q).

2   If a dialog box appears asking whether you want to save changes to the presentation, click the Yes button.

Making Your Ideas Communicate

Part 3

Applying and Modifying Templates

In this lesson you will learn how to:

Estimated time
25 min.

- Understand and apply a template.
- Understand and view a master.
- Change the display using master objects.
- Modify and format master text.
- Adjust master text indents.
- Reapply a layout from the master.
- Save a presentation as a template.

A *template* is a presentation file that has a predefined set of color and text characteristics. You can create a presentation from a template or you can apply a template to an existing presentation. When you apply a template to a presentation the slides in the presentation take on the characteristics of the template, so you can maintain a uniform design. To make maintaining a uniform design even easier, PowerPoint uses *masters* that control the look of the individual parts of the presentation, including formatting, color, graphics, and text placement. Every presentation has a set of masters, one for each view.

As Director of Communications at Ferguson & Bardell, you have been working on a company presentation. After adding and modifying your text in the previous lesson, you're ready to apply a presentation design template.

In this lesson, you'll learn how to apply a PowerPoint template, change the display for master objects, modify and format the master text, reapply a layout from the master, and save a presentation as a template.

Start the lesson

Follow the steps below to open the practice file called 06 PPT Lesson, and then save it with the new name **F&B Company Pres 06**. If you haven't already started PowerPoint, do so now.

Open

1 On the Standard toolbar, click the Open button or click the Open An Existing Presentation option button on the Start-up dialog box and click OK.

2 In the Look In box, ensure that the PowerPoint SBS Practice folder is open. If it is not, select the hard drive and folder where the Step by Step practice files are stored.

For information about opening a presentation, see Lesson 3.

3 In the file list box, double-click the file named 06 PPT Lesson to open it.

4 On the File menu, click Save As.

The Save As dialog box opens. Be sure the PowerPoint SBS Practice folder appears in the Save In box.

5 In the File Name box, type **F&B Company Pres 06**

6 Click the Save button.

The presentation is saved and the title bar changes to the new name.

Understanding and Applying Templates

PowerPoint comes with a wide variety of templates that are professionally designed to help you achieve the look you want. When you apply a template to your presentation, PowerPoint copies the information from each master in the template to the corresponding masters in your presentation. All slides in your presentation then acquire the look of the template. You can use the templates that come with PowerPoint, or you can create your own from existing presentations. Moreover, you can apply any number of templates to your presentation at any point during the development process until you find the look you like best.

Apply a template

To apply a template to an existing presentation, you can open the presentation and then use the Apply Design dialog box to locate and select the template you want. For the Ferguson & Bardell presentation, you'll apply a company template one of your employees in the Communications department created.

Apply Design

1 On the Standard toolbar, click the Apply Design button.

The Apply Design dialog box appears.

2 In the Look In box, ensure that the PowerPoint SBS Practice folder is open. If it is not, select the hard drive and folder where the Step by Step practice files are stored.

3 In the list of file and folder names, click 06 PPT Template.

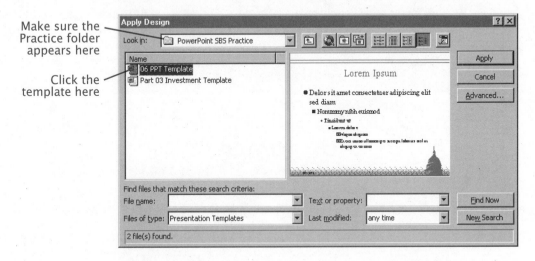

Make sure the Practice folder appears here

Click the template here

4 Click the Apply button.

The information from the template file, 06 PPT Template, is applied, or copied, to the masters in your presentation. The text style and format, slide colors, and background objects change to match the template. Your content remains the same.

Your presentation window should look like the following illustration:

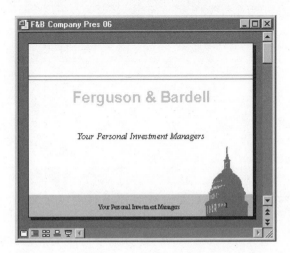

Understanding PowerPoint Masters

PowerPoint comes with a special slide called the *Slide Masters.* The Slide Master controls the properties of every slide in the presentation. All the characteristics (background color, text color, font, and font size) of the slide master appear on every slide in the presentation. When you make a change on the slide master, the change affects every slide. For example, if you want your company's logo or the date to appear on every slide, you can place it on the Slide Master. Note that the Slide Master controls all slides except for the title slide, which has its own master, the Title Master.

View the Slide Master

Your company presentation has a new look now that you've applied a different template, but you'd like to make some changes to the Slide Master.

➤ On the View menu, point to Master, and then click Slide Master.

The Slide Master contains master placeholders for title text, paragraph text, the date and time, footer information, and slide number. The master title and text placeholders control the text format for your slide presentation. For example, when you change the master title text format to italic, the title on each slide changes to italic to follow the master. If for some reason you don't want to follow the Slide Master on a particular slide, you can easily override it using commands on the Format menu. To omit background graphics from a slide, you can easily turn it off the option using the Background command.

Your presentation master should look like the following illustration:

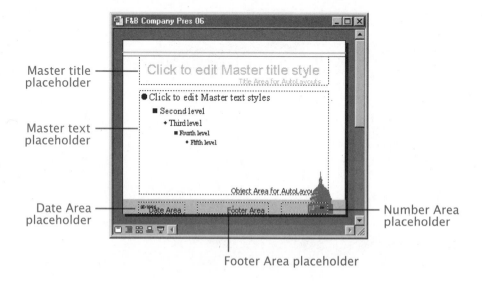

View the Title Master

The Title Master contains placeholders similar to the Slide Master. The main difference between the two Slide view masters is the Title Master's use of a master subtitle style instead of the master text style.

➤ On the View menu, point to Master and then click Title Master.

The Title Master slide appears, as shown in the following illustration:

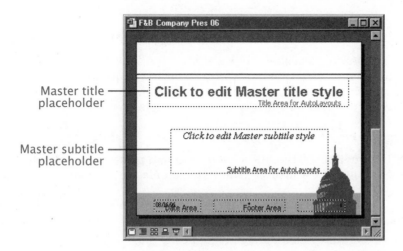

TROUBLESHOOTING   If you don't have a Title Master, you can create one by switching to the Slide Master and clicking the New Title Master button on the status bar at the bottom of the PowerPoint screen.

Switch between the Title Master and the Slide Master

➤ In Title Master view, drag the scroll box on the scroll bar up.

The Slide Master appears.

Switch to Handout Master and Notes Master

PowerPoint also comes with a handout master and a notes pages master, where you can add items you want to appear on each page.

1   On the View menu, point to Master, and click Handout Master.

The Handout Master view and Handout Master toolbar appear. With the Handout Master toolbar you can show the positioning of 2, 3, or 6 per page hanouts and outline view.

3   On the Master Handout toolbar, click the Show Positioning Of 3-Per-Page Handouts button.

4   On the View menu, point to Master, click Notes Master.

The Notes Master view appears, showing the slide and speaker note text positioning for the notes pages.

5   On the Master toolbar, click the Close button.

PowerPoint returns you to the first slide in your presentation.

Changing the Display Using the Master

Each master contains placeholders where you can add background objects, such as text and graphics, that can appear on every page. Some examples are your company name, logo, or product name. With PowerPoint you can determine what appears on your slides.

Remove footer display from the Title Slide

The footer information on the title slide for the F&B presentation already appears in the subtitle of the slide, so remove the duplicate information from the title slide.

1   On the View menu, click Header And Footer.

The Header And Footer dialog box appears.

2   Click the Don't Show On Title Slide check box.

Click this check box ———

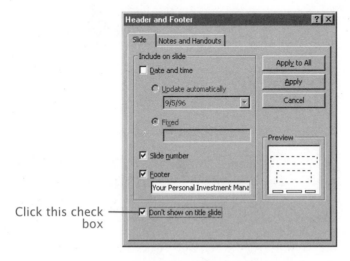

3   Click the Apply To All button.

The slide footer information disappears from the title slide.

Next Slide

4 Click the Next Slide button to view slide 2.

The slide footer information remains on the rest of the slides in the presentation.

Modifying Master Placeholders

You can modify and arrange placeholders for the date and time, footers, and slide numbers on all of the master views.

Edit master placeholders

The footer, date and time, and slide number appear on the Slide Master in the default position. For the F&B company presentation, customize the position of the placeholders.

Slide View

1 Hold down the SHIFT key and click the Slide View button.

The Slide Master view appears. Holding down the SHIFT key and clicking a view button switches you to the corresponding master view. With the title slide displayed, the Slide View button becomes the Title Master button. With any of the other slides displayed, the Slide View button becomes the Slide Master button.

2 Select the Date Area placeholder (bottom left corner).

Be sure you click the placeholder border so the resize handles appear.

3 Press the DELETE key.

 TIP If you delete a placeholder by mistake, you can click Master Layout on the Format menu, click the appropriate placeholder check box, and click the OK button to reapply the placeholder.

---

4 Click the dotted edge of the Footer Area placeholder to select it.

Be sure the resize handles appear around the placeholder.

5 Hold down the SHIFT key and drag the Footer Area placeholder to the left until the edge of the placeholder matches the edge of the master text placeholder.

Holding down the SHIFT key while you drag a PowerPoint object constrains the movement of the object horizontally or vertically. For more information on moving objects, see Lesson 8.

6 Click a blank area of the slide to deselect the placeholder.

Formatting Master Text

Formatting the placeholders in Slide Master view provides consistency to your presentation. The master placeholders for the title, bulleted text, date and time, slide number, and footer determine the style and placement of those objects.

Format master text attributes

To format master text, you select the text placeholder and change the format until it looks the way you want it. Format the text in the Footer and Number Area placeholders for the F&B company presentation.

1 Hold down the SHIFT key, click the Footer Area placeholder, and click the Number Area placeholder to select both objects.

2 On the Formatting toolbar, click the Font Size drop-down arrow, and click 20.

Font Size

3 Hold down the SHIFT key and click the Footer Area placeholder.

The Footer Area placeholder is deselected.

4 On the Formatting toolbar, click the Italic button.

The Number Area placeholder becomes italic.

Italic

5 Click the Slide View button.

Your presentation window should look like the following illustration:

Slide View

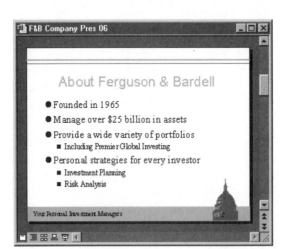

Format master title and bulleted text

To format bulleted text, you have to place the insertion point in the line of the bulleted text you want to change.

Slide View

Italic

1 Hold down the SHIFT key and click the Slide View button.

2 In the master text placeholder, position the I-beam cursor to the right of the text "Second level."

3 On the Formatting toolbar, click the Italic button.

4 Click outside the master text placeholder in a blank area to deselect it.

Your Slide Master should look like the following illustration:

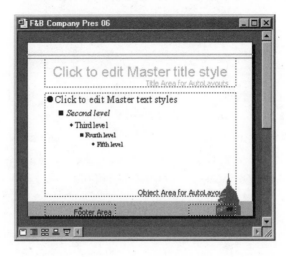

Format master bullets

PowerPoint allows you to customize the bullets in your presentation for individual paragraphs or entire objects.

1 Click the first line of text titled "Click to edit Master text styles" in the master text placeholder.

The insertion point is placed in the text.

2 On the Format menu, click Bullet.

The Bullet dialog box appears, with the current bullet symbol selected. You can change the symbol font in the Bullets From drop-down list, click a different bullet color in the Special Color drop-down list, or adjust the font size percentage in the Size box.

3 In the dialog box, click the diamond bullet, as shown in the following illustration:

Click the diamond
bullet here

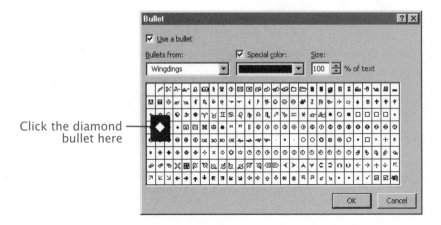

4 Click the Special Color drop-down arrow and click the blue color.

5 Click the Size down arrow until 85% appears.

The new bullet size is reduced by 15% on the slide.

6 Click the OK button.

The bullet appears in the first line of text.

7 Click the Slide View button.

PowerPoint returns to slide 2 and shows the font and bullet changes as shown in the following illustration:

New diamond
bullet

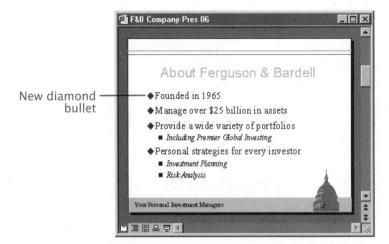

Adjusting Master Text Indents

PowerPoint uses indent markers to control the distance between bullets and text levels. To work with indented text and bullets, select a text object and show its ruler to make adjustments. Adjusting indents in PowerPoint works the same way it does in Microsoft Word for Windows.

Display the ruler

To change the distance between a bullet and its corresponding text, you first display the ruler, which shows the current bullet and text placement.

Slide View

1 Hold down the SHIFT key and click the Slide View button.

   The Slide Master appears.

2 Click the first line of text titled "Click to edit Master title style" in the master text placeholder.

3 On the View menu, click Ruler.

   Your presentation window should look like the following illustration:

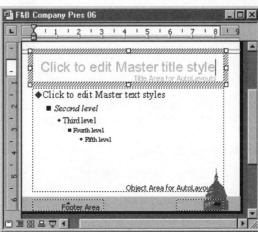

Setting Indent Markers

Margin Markers

Indent Marker

The indent markers on the ruler control the indent levels of the master text object. Each indent level consists of two triangles, called *indent markers*, and a small box, called a *margin marker*. The upper indent marker controls the first line of the paragraph; the lower indent marker controls the left edge of the paragraph. Each indent level is set so that the first line extends to the left of the paragraph, with the rest of the paragraph "hanging" below it. This indent setting is called a *hanging indent*.

Adjust indent markers

To adjust an indent marker, you move the triangle on the ruler to a new position. In the F&B company presentation, the diamond bullet in the first indent level appears too close to the text. Adjust the indent markers of the first indent level to put more space between the bullet and the text to create a hanging indent.

1 Click the line of text titled "Click to edit Master text styles" in the master text placeholder.

The ruler adds indent markers for each level of text represented in the bulleted list. Five indent markers appear.

2 Drag the lower indent marker of the first indent level to the left margin of the ruler, as shown in the following illustration:

Move the lower indent marker to here

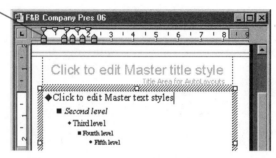

When you release the mouse button, the text for the first indent level moves next to the bullet on the left margin.

Adjust the margin level

You can move the entire level, including bullet and text, using the margin marker.

1 Slowly drag the margin marker of the first indent level to the 0.5 inch mark on the ruler.

NOTE If you drag an indent level or margin marker into another indent level, the first indent level (or marker) pushes the second indent level until you release the mouse button. To move an indent marker back to its original position, drag the indent level's margin marker or click the Undo button.

Your presentation window should look like the following illustration:

Move the margin marker to here

Moving the first indent marker repositions the left margin of the master text object to the 0.5 inch mark. (Notice the first text level in the master text object.)

 TROUBLESHOOTING If the ruler on your screen looks different from the one in the previous illustration, you might not have moved the indent margin marker. If the indent markers are not aligned over one another, drag one of the markers back to the other.

2 Drag the upper indent marker of the first indent level to the left edge of the ruler.

The first indent level of your ruler is formatted again as a hanging indent.

Your presentation window should look like the following illustration:

Move the upper indent marker to here

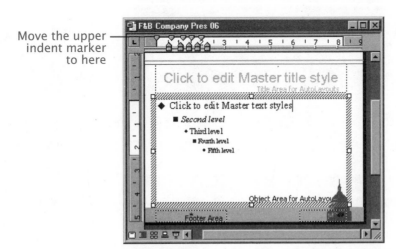

3 In a blank area of the Slide Master, click the right mouse button and then click Ruler.

The ruler closes.

4 On the View menu, click Slide.

PowerPoint returns you to slide 2.

Reapplying a Slide Layout

If you make changes to items on a slide and then decide you want the original slide layout back, you can reapply the slide layout to that slide using the Slide Layout command. You can also change the current layout of a slide by selecting a new layout from the Slide Layout dialog box.

Apply a slide layout

1 Drag the title object to the right edge of the slide.

Your presentation window should look like the following illustration:

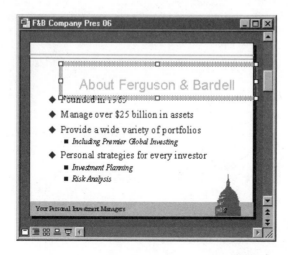

Slide Layout

2 On the Standard toolbar, click the Slide Layout button.

The Slide Layout dialog box appears with the current slide layout style selected.

3 Click the Reapply button.

PowerPoint uses the slide layout to reposition the title object to its original position on the slide.

Save the presentation

Save

➤ On the Standard toolbar, click the Save button.

No dialog box appears because the presentation already has a name. The current information in your presentation is saved with the same name.

Saving a Presentation as a Template

After changing the masters in your presentation the way you want, you can save the presentation as a template, which you can apply to other presentations in the future. You can create specialized templates for different types of presentations.

1 On the File menu, click Save As.

The File Save dialog box appears. F&B Company Pres 06 appears in the File Name box.

2 In the File Name box, type **F&B Company Template**

3 Click the Save As Type drop-down arrow and click Presentation Templates.

PowerPoint displays the Template folder. To include your new template with the others that come with PowerPoint, you need to save the template in one of the corresponding folders. A new template icon will appear in the New Presentation dialog box. For the purposes of this lesson, save this template with the rest of your practice files.

4 In the Save In box, ensure that the PowerPoint SBS Practice folder is open. If it is not, select the hard drive and folder where the Step by Step practice files are stored. Typically, you'll find the PowerPoint SBS Practice folder in the My Documents folder.

5 Click the Save button.

The template is saved in the Practice folder.

One Step Further

You have learned how to apply a template, view and switch to a master, change the master title and master text of your presentation, change bullets, adjust margin indents, reapply a slide layout, and save a presentation as a template.

For individual slides, you might want to hide background objects, such as date and time, header and footer, and slide number placeholders, graphics, shapes, and lines, so they do not appear on the screen. Try hiding the master objects from slide 2.

Hide objects from the Master

Next Slide

1 Click the Next Slide button.

2 In a blank area of the slide, click the right mouse button, and click Background.

3 Click the Omit Background Graphics From Master check box.

The Omit Background Graphics From Master option is turned on.

4 Click the Apply button.

The background objects are omitted from the slide.

If you want to continue to the next lesson

1 On the File menu, click Close (CTRL+W).

2 If a dialog box appears asking whether you want to save the changes to your presentation, click the No button.

If you want to quit PowerPoint for now

1 On the File menu, click Exit (CTRL+Q).

2 If a dialog box appears asking whether you want to save the changes to your presentation, click the No button.

Lesson Summary

To	Do this	Button
Apply a template	On the Standard toolbar, click the Apply Design button. Select the folder that contains the template you want to use, and select the template file. Click the Apply button.	
Switch to master views	On the View menu, point to Master, and then click the view you want from the menu or hold down the SHIFT key and click the View button you want.	
Format the master text	Select the master text or text object and click the formatting effects you want on the Formatting toolbar.	
Change the bullet format	Click a line of text and on the Format menu, click Bullet. Click a bullet.	
Display the text object ruler	On the View menu, click Ruler or click the right mouse button and click Ruler on the Shortcut menu.	
Set the indent marker for the first line of text	On the View menu, click Ruler. Drag the upper triangle.	
Set the indent marker for a paragraph other than the first line of text	On the View menu, click Ruler. Drag the lower indent marker.	
Adjust a paragraph margin	On the View menu, click Ruler. Drag the indent margin marker.	
Create a hanging indent	On the View menu, click Ruler. Move the upper triangle to the left of the lower indent marker.	
Reapply a slide layout	Move to the slide. Click the Slide Layout button on the Standard toolbar, select a layout, and click the Reapply button.	
Save as a template	On the File menu, click Save As. Click the Save As Type drop-down arrow, click Presentation Templates and click the Save button.	

To use the Office Assistant, see Appendix A, in the back of this book.

For online information about	Use the Office Assistant to search for
Applying a template	**Apply template**, and then click Apply A Different Design To A Presentation
Working with the slide or title master	**Master**, and then click Go To Where I Can Work On The Slide Master
Changing master text	**Indents**, and then click Display Tab And Indent Settings, or Set Paragraph Indentations
Formatting master bullets	**Bullet**, and then click Add, Change, Or Remove A Bullet
Reapplying a layout	**Slide layout**, and then click Change The Layout Of A Slide

Preview of the Next Lesson

In the next lesson, you'll change a color scheme, change colors, and add colors to menus.

Using a Color Scheme

Estimated time
20 min.

In this lesson you will learn how to:

- View and choose a color scheme.
- Change colors in a color scheme.
- Create a color scheme.
- Add other colors to color menus.
- Add a background.
- Copy a color scheme.

In the previous lesson you learned how to work with the overall look of your presentation using templates and masters. In this lesson, you'll work with a very important part of your presentation known as the color scheme. A *color scheme* is a set of eight colors designed to be used as the primary colors in your slide presentation. The color scheme determines the colors for the background, text, lines, shadows, fills, and accents of your slides. You can experiment with different colors and schemes until you've found the combination of colors you like, using PowerPoint's color scheme capabilities to ensure an aesthetically pleasing design.

As Director of Communications at Ferguson & Bardell, you have been working on a company presentation. After modifying the master in the previous lesson, you're ready to change your presentation colors to match the company colors.

In this lesson, you'll learn how to view and choose a color scheme, change colors in a color scheme, create a color scheme, add other colors, add a background to a slide, and copy a color scheme to a slide.

113

Start the lesson

Follow the steps below to open the practice file called 07 PPT Lesson, and then save it with the new name F&B Company Pres 07. If you haven't already started PowerPoint, do so now.

Open

1   On the Standard toolbar, click the Open button or click the Open An Existing Presentation option button on the Start-up dialog box and click OK.

2   In the Look In box, ensure that the PowerPoint SBS Practice folder is open. If it is not, select the hard drive and folder where the Step by Step practice files are stored.

For information about opening a presentation, see Lesson 3.

3   In the file list box, double-click the file named 07 PPT Lesson to open it.

4   On the File menu, click Save As.

The Save As dialog box opens. Be sure the PowerPoint SBS Practice folder appears in the Save In box.

5   In the File Name box, type **F&B Company Pres 07**

6   Click the Save button.

The presentation is saved and the title bar changes to the new name.

Viewing and Choosing a Color Scheme

Every presentation, even a blank one, has a color scheme. The color scheme can be a set of custom colors that you've chosen or the default color scheme. Understanding color schemes helps you create professional-looking presentations that use an appropriate balance of color for your company and subject matter.

Choose a color scheme

To view your presentation's color scheme, open the Color Scheme dialog box. This dialog box allows you to change the colors in your color scheme, choose a different color scheme, or create your own color scheme. Once you've found the look you want, you can apply the color scheme to one or all the slides in your presentation. Look at the current color scheme applied to the Ferguson and Bardell presentation, then choose another color scheme.

1   Drag the scroll bar to slide 4.

2   On the Format menu, click Slide Color Scheme.

The Color Scheme dialog box appears.

3   Click the Standard tab, if necessary.

The Standard tab appears, showing a preview of the current color scheme with a selection rectangle and other available presentation color schemes.

4   Click the first color scheme in the first row as shown in the following illustration:

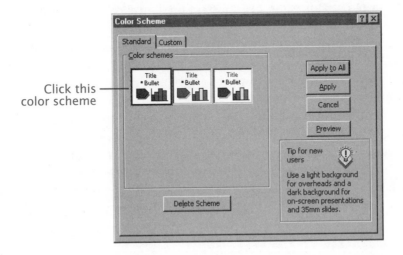

Click this
color scheme

To choose another color scheme, click a color scheme from the available choices.

5   Click the Custom tab.

The Custom tab displays a grid of eight colored boxes that correspond to the selected color scheme on the Standard tab. These eight colors make up your presentation's current color scheme.

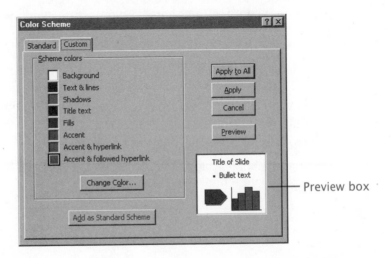

Preview box

The eight colors on the grid correspond to the following elements in your presentation:

Background   This color is the canvas color of the slide.

Text and lines   This color contrasts with the Background color. It is used for writing text and drawing lines.

Shadow   This color is generally a darker shade of the background.

Title text   This color, like the Text and Lines color, contrasts with the background.

Fills   This color contrasts with both the Background color and the Text and Lines color.

Accent   This color is designed to work as a complementary color for objects in the presentation.

Accent and hyperlink   This color is designed to work as a complementary color for objects and hyperlinks.

Accent and followed hyperlink   This color is designed to work as a complementary color for objects and visited hyperlinks.

6   Click the Apply To All button to return to slide 4. Notice how the colors on slide 4 correspond to the colors on the grid.

Changing Colors in a Color Scheme

You can modify any or all the colors within a color scheme to create your own color combinations. You can apply changes you make to a color scheme to the current slide or the entire presentation. For example, you might want to create a customized color scheme that matches your company's logo.

Change colors in a color scheme

You can change a color in the color scheme by opening the Color Scheme dialog box and then using the Change Color feature available on the Custom tab.

1   Click the right mouse button in a blank area of the slide.

A Shortcut menu appears.

2   On the Shortcut menu, click Slide Color Scheme.

The Color Scheme dialog box appears, showing the Standard tab.

3   Click the Custom tab.

The Custom tab appears.

4   In the Scheme Colors area, click the Accent & Followed Hyperlink box with the light blue color.

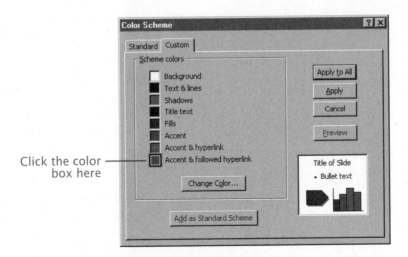

Click the color box here

With a Scheme Color selected, any color change you make is applied to that accent color.

5 Click the Change Color button.

The Accent And Followed Hyperlink Color dialog box appears, showing the Standard tab. The Standard tab displays a color palette of standard colors to choose from.

TIP You can also double-click a color scheme color box to go directly to the color dialog box.

6 In the color palette, click the maroon color, as shown in the following illustration:

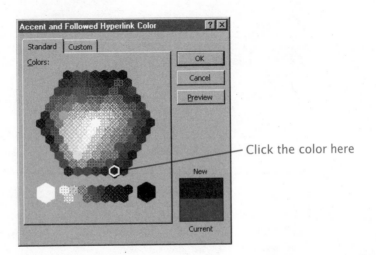

Click the color here

117

7 Click the OK button.

The accent color changes to maroon in the color scheme.

Creating a Color Scheme

You can create a new color scheme by changing the colors of an existing color scheme and then adding it to the standard set of color schemes available on the Standard tab.

Add a standard color scheme

In the last section you changed one of the accent colors in your company presentation's color scheme. Add this new color scheme to the presentation's set of color schemes.

1 Click the Add As Standard Scheme button.

The Add As Standard Scheme button turns gray, indicating that the color scheme has been added to the standard list.

2 Click the Standard tab.

The new color scheme appears, as shown in the following illustration.

The new color scheme is selected

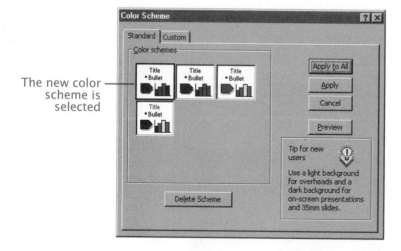

 NOTE You can delete a color scheme from the list of Standard schemes by selecting the color scheme and clicking the Delete Scheme button.

3 Click the Apply button.

The accent color changes the text object to maroon on slide 4. The color is applied only to the current slide.

Adding Other Colors to Color Menus

Along with the eight basic color scheme colors are what PowerPoint calls "Other Colors." Other colors are additional colors you can add to each of the toolbar button color menus—the Font Color button menu, for example. Other colors are very useful when you want an object or picture to always have the same color or when you want to change the color of an object to a specific color and the presentation color scheme does not have that color. Colors you add to a specific color menu appear in all color menus and remain in the menu even if the color scheme changes.

Add a color to the menus

Font Color

1 On the Drawing toolbar, click the Font Color button drop-down arrow.

   A drop-down menu appears that looks like the following illustration:

2 On the drop-down menu, click More Font Colors.

3 In the color palette, click the light blue color, as shown in the following illustration:

Click the color here ———

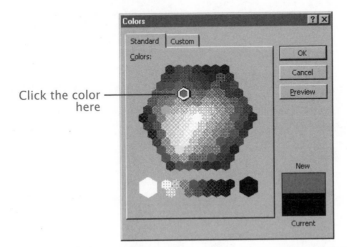

4 Click the OK button.

   The colored line on the Font Color button appears with the currently se-lected color. In this case, the light blue color appears.

119

Font Color

5 On the Drawing toolbar, click the Font Color button drop-down arrow.

The new color is now available to use throughout your presentation.

Added colors appear here
in all drop down menus

6 Click somewhere on the slide to close the drop-down menu.

Adding a Background

In PowerPoint, you can create a special background by adding a shade, a texture, a pattern, and even a picture, to your slides.

Shade a slide background

A shaded background is a visual effect in which a solid color gradually changes from light to dark or dark to light. PowerPoint offers one and two color shaded backgrounds with six styles: vertical, horizontal, diagonal right, diagonal left, from corner, and from title. For a one color shaded background, the shading color can be adjusted lighter or darker depending on your needs.

1 On the Format menu, click Background.

The Background dialog box appears.

2 Click the Background Fill drop-down arrow, as shown in the following illustration:

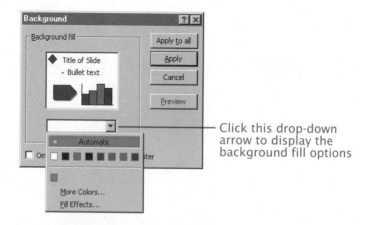

Click this drop-down
arrow to display the
background fill options

3 On the Background Fill drop-down list, click Fill Effects.

The Fill Effects dialog box appears, showing four tabs: Gradient, Texture, Pattern, and Picture.

120

The Gradient tab appears, showing six shade styles and four different shaded variants for the selected colors.

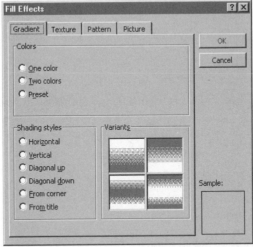

4   In the Colors area, click the Preset option button.

A Preset Color drop-down arrow appears, giving you access to a set of professionally designed backgrounds.

5   Click the Preset Color drop-down arrow, scroll down, and click Daybreak.

The shading style appears with the horizontal option selected and the variant appears with the upper left shade selected, as shown in the following illustration:

Click the Preset option button here...

...then click the Preset Colors drop-down arrow and click Daybreak here

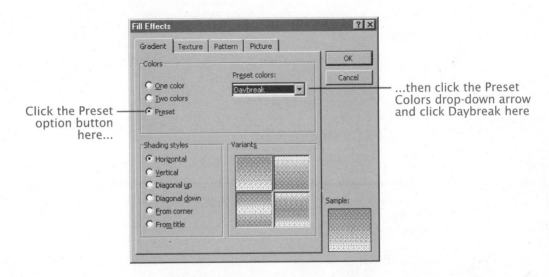

6   Click the OK button.

The Custom Background dialog box appears, showing a preview of the shaded background.

7   Click the Apply To All button.

The shaded background is applied to all the slides in the presentation.

Copying a Color Scheme

You can reuse color schemes without having to re-create them. Simply copy or pick up the color scheme from one slide and paste or apply the color scheme to another slide. You can copy a color scheme from from one presentation and apply it to another.

Pick up and apply a color scheme

With the Format Painter feature, you can copy a color scheme from one slide and apply it to other selected slides.

Slide Sorter View

1   Click the Slide Sorter View button.

Slide 4 appears selected.

2   On the Standard toolbar, click the Format Painter button.

The color scheme for slide 4 is picked up and is now ready to be applied to other slides in your presentation or any other open presentation.

Format Painter

NOTE   When you copy a color scheme from one presentation to another, colors you have defined as "other colors" on the color scheme menu are not copied.

3   On the Edit menu, click Select All (CTRL+A).

4   Click any of the selected slides.

The color scheme is applied to all the slides in your presentation.

5   Double-click slide 1.

PowerPoint returns to Slide view.

Save the presentation

➤   On the Standard toolbar, click the Save button.

No dialog box appears because the presentation already has a name. The current information in your presentation is saved with the same name.

Save

One Step Further

You have learned to view a color scheme, change a color, create a color scheme, add other colors to color menus, add a background, and copy a color scheme.

Besides a shaded background, you can also have a background with a texture, a pattern, or a picture. Try changing the shaded background to a textured background.

Texture a slide background

1   On the Format menu, click Background.

    The Background dialog box appears.

2   Click the Background Fill drop-down arrow and click Fill Effects.

    The Fill Effects dialog box appears.

3   Click the Texture tab.

4   Click the Newsprint textured fill in the upper left corner.

    The Newsprint name appears at the bottom of the dialog box.

5   Click the OK button.

    The Background dialog box appears.

6   Click the Apply To All button.

    The textured background is applied to all the slides in the presentation.

Slide Show

7   Click the Slide Show button.

    PowerPoint displays the first slide in the presentation.

8   Click once for each slide to advance through the rest of the presentation.

    After the last slide in the presentation, PowerPoint returns to the current view.

If you want to continue to the next lesson

1   On the File menu, click Close (CTRL+W).

2   If a dialog box appears asking whether you want to save the changes to your presentation, click the No button.

If you want to quit PowerPoint for now

1   On the File menu, click Exit (CTRL+Q).

2   If a dialog box appears asking whether you want to save the changes to your presentation, click the No button.

Lesson Summary

To	Do this	Button
View current slide color scheme	On the Format menu, click Slide Color Scheme.	
Choose a slide color scheme	In the Color Scheme dialog box, click the Standard tab and click a color scheme.	
Change a color in a color scheme	In the Color Scheme dialog box, click the Custom tab, and then click a color. Click the Change Color button. Click a new color.	
Add other colors to the menu	On the Drawing toolbar, click the Font Color drop-down arrow, and click More Font Colors. Click a color.	
Add a shaded background	On the Format menu, click Background. Click the Background Fill drop-down arrow and click Fill Effects. Click a Color type option. Click a Shade Style and Variant.	
Copy a color scheme	From the Slide Sorter view, select a slide with the color scheme you want. On the Standard toolbar, click the Format Painter button. Select the slide or slides to apply the color scheme to in a presentation. On the Standard toolbar, click the Format Painter button.	

To use the Office Assistant, see Appendix A, in the back of this book.

For online information about	Use the Office Assistant to search for
Changing a color scheme	**Color scheme**, and then click Change A Color Scheme
Changing a background	**Background**, and then click Change The Slide Background

Preview of the Next Lesson

In the next lesson, you'll draw shapes, edit and modify objects, and group and align objects.

Drawing and Modifying Objects

In this lesson you will learn how to:

Estimated time
50 min.

- Draw and select objects.
- Edit objects.
- Modify object attributes.
- Align objects.
- Connect objects together.
- Change objects to 3-D.
- Draw and edit an arc object.
- Rotate and flip objects.
- Group and ungroup objects.

An effective presentation includes not only meaningful text, but also shapes and pictures that complement and enhance the text on your slides. You've already seen how to create text objects, and now you'll have a chance to create drawing objects and then modify their attributes, which include size, line style, color, and shading.

As Director of Communications at Ferguson & Bardell, you have been working on a company presentation. After applying a template and changing masters in the previous lesson, you're ready to draw and modify shapes to enhance your text.

In this lesson, you'll draw and edit objects, change object attributes, align objects, connect objects together, change objects to 3-D, draw and edit arcs, rotate and flip objects, and group and ungroup objects.

Start the lesson

Follow the steps below to open the practice file called 08 PPT Lesson, and then save it with the new name F&B Company Pres 08. If you haven't already started PowerPoint, do so now.

Open

1 On the Standard toolbar, click the Open button or click the Open An Existing Presentation option button on the Start-up dialog box and click OK.

2 In the Look In box, ensure that the PowerPoint SBS Practice folder is open. If it is not, select the hard drive and folder where the Step by Step practice files are stored.

For information about opening a presentation, see Lesson 3.

3 In the file list box, double-click the file named 08 PPT Lesson to open it.

4 On the File menu, click Save As.

The Save As dialog box opens. Be sure the PowerPoint SBS Practice folder appears in the Save In box.

5 In the File Name box, type **F&B Company Pres 08**

6 Click the Save button.

The presentation is saved and the title bar changes to the new name.

Drawing an Object

The shapes you draw, the pictures you import from other applications, the text you type—these are all examples of *objects*. You create all drawing objects in PowerPoint, except freeform objects, using the same technique. Select a drawing tool from the Drawing or AutoShapes toolbar and then drag with your mouse to create the object. For your company presentation, draw an arrow that shows the right fund can produce growth.

1 Drag the scroll box to advance to slide 5.

Slide 5 appears in Slide view.

2 On the Drawing toolbar, click the AutoShapes menu button.

3 Point to Block Arrows, and point to Curved Up Arrow in the second row, as shown in the following illustration:

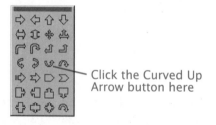

Click the Curved Up Arrow button here

Curved Up Arrow

4 Click the Curved Up Arrow button.

In the presentation window, the pointer changes to a cross hairs cursor.

NOTE You can draw a proportional object by holding down the SHIFT or CTRL keys while you draw. Holding down the SHIFT key while you draw constrains the object horizontally and vertically from the edge of the object. To draw an object from its center outward, hold the CTRL key down while you draw.

Cross Hairs Cursor

5 Position the cross hairs cursor below the bulleted text, press the SHIFT key (which constrains the proportions of the object), and then drag to draw a curved arrow shape, as shown in the following illustration:

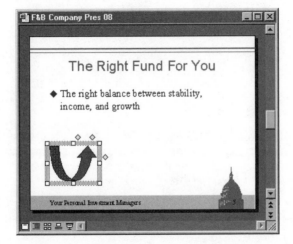

The curved arrow shape appears with white squares on each corner and side of the object, indicating the object is selected. The white squares, called *resize handles* or *sizing handles*, are used to resize the object.

NOTE When you draw an object, PowerPoint uses the default settings for the object, such as line style or fill color. For more information about changing default settings, see "Customizing PowerPoint" in Appendix B.

127

Select and deselect an object

When you draw an object, it is automatically selected. When you want to edit an object, you need to select it first. To deselect an object, move your pointer off the object into a blank area of the slide and click. To select an object, click a visible part of the object. You can apply attributes only to objects you've selected. For information on selecting multiple objects, see page 137, later in this lesson.

1 Click outside the curved arrow object in a blank area of the slide.

The curved arrow object is deselected.

2 Click a visible part of the curved arrow object.

The curved arrow object is selected.

Editing an Object

Resizing, copying, pasting, moving, cutting, and deleting are editing commands you can use on any object. To edit a PowerPoint object, select the object, and then click a command from a menu or the toolbar.

Resize an object

Often you'll draw an object or import a picture that won't be the right size for your slide. You can change the size of an object by dragging its resize handles.

1 Ensure the curved arrow object is selected.

Resize handles appear around the edges of the object.

2 Drag the arrow's top middle resize handle to match the following illustration:

Drag the top middle resize handle up to here

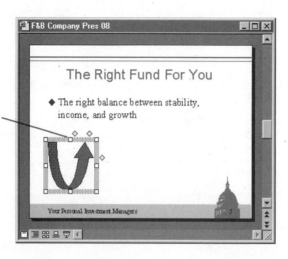

Two-headed Arrow

When you position the pointer over a resize handle, the cursor changes to a small two-headed arrow, indicating the possible directions you can resize the object.

As the object resizes, a dotted outline of the object appears, indicating what the object will look like when you release the mouse button.

Adjust an object

Some PowerPoint objects, such as triangles, parallelograms, rounded rectangles, and arrows, are adjustable. *Adjustable objects* have an adjustable resize handle (which looks like a small yellow diamond) positioned on one side of the object next to a resize handle. This handle lets you adjust the dimensions of the object without changing its size. The banner in the margin illustrates an object with an adjustable resize handle.

Adjustment Cursor

1 Position your pointer (which changes to the adjustment cursor) on the arrow object's adjustable resize handle.

2 Drag the adjustable resize handle up to match the following illustration:

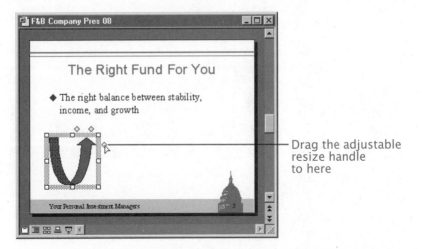

Drag the adjustable resize handle to here

As the object adjusts, a dotted outline of the object appears, indicating what the object will look like when you release the mouse button.

NOTE When you draw or edit an object, PowerPoint allows you to work with objects off of the slide area in the gray portion of the presentation window. This can be helpful if you want to include special instructions in your presentation. Any objects in the gray area will not print or display during a slide show.

129

Copy an object

You can copy the currently selected object or multiple objects to the Windows Clipboard and then paste the objects in other parts of your presentation. For the company presentation, make a copy of the arrow object.

Copy

1   On the Standard toolbar, click the Copy button.

    The curved arrow is copied to the Windows Clipboard.

Paste

2   On the Standard toolbar, click the Paste button.

    A copy of the curved arrow is pasted to the slide from the Windows Clipboard. The pasted curved arrow is selected and overlaps the original curved arrow.

    Your presentation window should look like the following illustration:

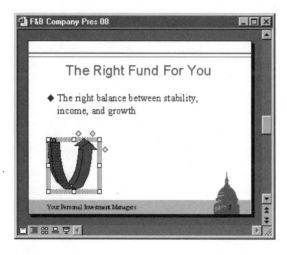

Move an object

Once you have copied and pasted the curved arrow object, move it to a new location.

▶   Hold down the SHIFT key and drag the new curved arrow about half an inch to the right of the original curved arrow.

    As the object moves, a dotted outline of the curved arrow appears, indicating where the new location will be when you release the mouse button. Holding down the SHIFT key constrains the object's movement horizontally or vertically.

Copy and move an object in one step

You can copy an object to a different location in a single movement by using the CTRL key. Simply hold down the CTRL key and drag the object that you want to be copied.

 Hold down the CTRL key and drag the new curved arrow to the right of the second curved arrow.

 TIP You can easily create another copy of the object with the same drag distance as the first by clicking Duplicate Again on the Edit menu.

A copy of the object appears to the right of the other two as shown in the following illustration:

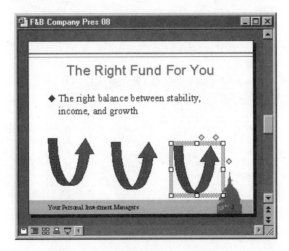

Change the shape of an object

PowerPoint allows you to change an existing shape to another shape with one easy command. For the company presentation, change the left curved arrow to a multidocument.

1 Click the left curved arrow object.

2 On the Drawing toolbar, click the Draw menu button, point to Change AutoShape, and point to Flowchart.

The AutoShape Flowchart submenu appears.

3 On the submenu, click the Multidocument shape in the second row.

131

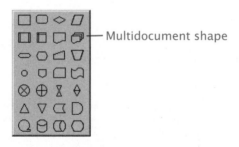

Multidocument shape

The selected curved arrow shape changes to the multidocument shape. The new multidocument shape fits in the same area and keeps the same attributes as the original curved arrow shape.

4   Click the middle curved arrow object, hold down the SHIFT key, and click the right curved arrow object to select both objects.

5   On the Drawing toolbar, click the Draw menu button, point to Change AutoShape, point to Flowchart, and then click the Multidocument shape in the second row.

Your presentation window should look like the following illustration:

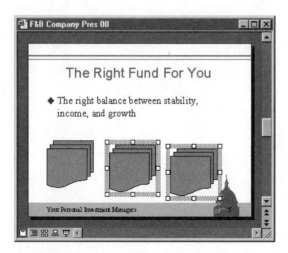

Add text to an object

When you add text to a selected object, PowerPoint automatically centers the text as you type. When you want to start a new line, you can press ENTER. You can only add text to one object at a time. For the company presentation, add text to each object to emphasize your bullet text.

1   Click the left object, then type **Stability**

As you type, a slanted-line selection box appears around the object, indicating that the object is ready for you to enter or edit text.

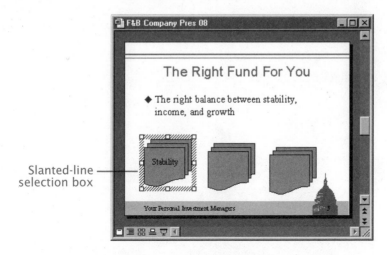

Slanted-line
selection box

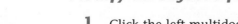

2   Click the middle object and type **Income**

3   Click the right object and type **Growth**

4   Click outside the object in a blank area to deselect the object.

Modifying Object Attributes

Objects have attributes that define how they appear on the slide. An object has graphic attributes such as fill, line, shape, and shadow, and text attributes such as style, font, color, embossment, and shadow. Objects that you draw usually have a fill and a border or frame. Before you can modify these attributes, you have to select the objects you want to change.

Modify an object's fill

Fill Color

1   Click the left multidocument object to select it.

2   On the Drawing toolbar, click the Fill Color button drop-down arrow.

A drop-down menu appears with a number of fill options.

3   On the Fill Color submenu, click Fill Effects.

The Fill Effects dialog box appears.

4   Click the Texture tab.

5 Click the Recycled Paper textured fill in the first row, as shown in the following illustration:

Click the
textured
fill here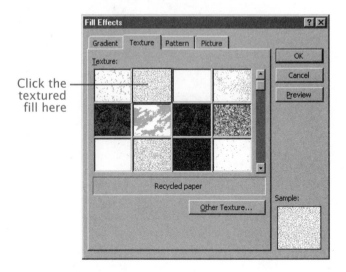

> **TIP** You can click the Other Texture button to add new textures to the list of current textured fills.

6 Click the OK button.

Modify an object's frame

Change the line style of the frame of your object to match the textured fill for the company presentation.

Line Color

1 On the Drawing toolbar, click the Line Color button drop-down arrow.

A drop-down menu appears with a selection of line styles.

2 On the Line Color menu, click the dark gray accent color box.

The new line color is applied to the object.

Add and modify an object's shadow

You can give an object a shadow to help create a three-dimensional appearance. You can choose the color of the shadow and its *offset*, the direction it falls from the object.

Shadow

1 On the Drawing toolbar, click the Shadow button.

The Shadow drop-down menu appears with a selection of shadow styles.

2 On the Shadow menu, click Shadow Style 19 on the bottom row, as shown in the following illustration:

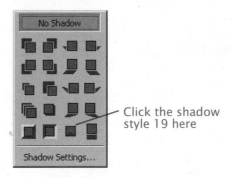

Click the shadow style 19 here

The shadow is applied to the object.

3 On the Drawing toolbar, click the Shadow button, and then click Shadow Settings.

Shadow

The Shadow Settings toolbar appears.

4 On the Shadow Settings toolbar, click the Nudge Shadow Down button four times.

Nudge Shadow Down

The shadow nudges down to display more of the shadow.

5 On the Shadow Settings toolbar, click the Shadow Color button drop-down arrow, and then click Semitransparent.

Shadow Color Arrow

The shadow color changes to semitransparent.

TIP You can click the Shadow On/Off button on the Shadow Settings toolbar or click No Shadow on the Shadow drop-down menu to turn off a shadow.

For information about working with toolbars, see Appendix B.

6 Right-click the Shadow Settings toolbar, and then click Shadow Settings or click the Close button to close the toolbar.

The Shadow Settings toolbar closes.

Change text color and style

You can also format the text in the shape by selecting the object and then using the formatting buttons to achieve the look you want.

1 On the Drawing toolbar, click the Font Color button drop-down arrow, and then click the maroon color box.

Font Color

2 On the Formatting toolbar, click the Bold button.

The text inside the object turns bold.

Bold

3 On the Formatting toolbar, click the Font drop-down arrow, scroll to the top of the font list, and then click Arial.

Your presentation should look like the following illustration:

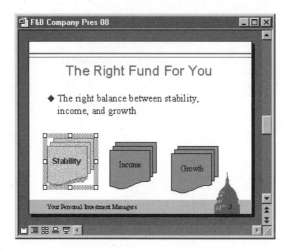

 TIP You can click the Shadow button on the Drawing toolbar to add a shadow to any selected text in PowerPoint.

Format text with the Format Painter command

Using the Format Painter command, you can copy a set of styles from selected text and objects and apply them to other selected text and objects. For the company presentation, use the Format Painter command to copy the attributes of the left multidocument object to the others.

1 Ensure the left multidocument object is selected.

2 On the Standard toolbar, click the Format Painter button.

Format Painter

PowerPoint copies and stores the specific text and object styles of the selected text object. The Format Painter button on the Standard toolbar remains depressed when styles have been copied. The pointer changes to a painter cursor, as shown in the left margin.

Painter Cursor

3 Click the middle multidocument object to copy the format to the object.

PowerPoint applies all the formats from the left multidocument object to the middle object.

4 On the Standard toolbar, click the Format Painter button.

Format Painter

5 Click the right multidocument object to copy the format to the object.

136

Your presentation window should look like the following illustration:

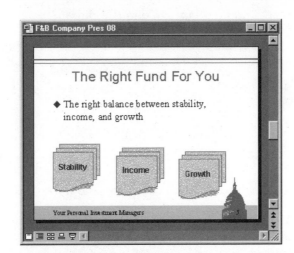

Select and deselect multiple objects

You can work with several objects at a time if you select all of them. You can select and deselect more than one object in different ways. One method uses the SHIFT key and the mouse. Another method uses a selection box.

1 Click the right multidocument object, hold down the SHIFT key, and then click the middle multidocument object.

The initially selected object remains selected, and the middle multidocument object is added to the selection. As long as you hold down the SHIFT key while clicking deselected objects, you continually add objects to the selection. Try deselecting an object that is part of a multiple selection.

2 Hold down the SHIFT key, and then click the middle multidocument object again.

The object is removed from the selection. Try dragging a selection box, also called a *marquee*, to select all three objects.

Marquee

3 Position the pointer in the lower left corner of the slide.

4 Drag a selection box until all three objects are enclosed within the marquee to select the objects.

Aligning Objects

There are two fundamentally different ways of aligning a group of objects in PowerPoint. You can either align them to each other or you can align them to a guide. For example, you can align two objects so that their tops are in a straight line or you can move your objects to a straightedge guide.

137

Align an object

The Align Or Distribute command aligns two or more objects relative to each other vertically to the left, to the center, or to the right. You can also align objects horizontally to the top, to the middle, or to the bottom. To align several objects to each other, select them and then choose an alignment option.

1 On the Drawing toolbar, click the Draw menu button, point to Align Or Distribute, and then click Align Top.

The objects align horizontally to each other at the top.

2 On the Drawing toolbar, click the Draw menu button, point to Align Or Distribute, and then click Distribute Horizontally.

The objects align horizontally across the slide at an equal distance.

Align objects with guides

The PowerPoint guides align an individual object or a group of objects to a vertical or horizontal straightedge. To align several objects to a guide, first turn the guide on. Then adjust the guide and drag the objects you want to align to the guide.

1 On the View menu, click Guides.

Vertical and horizontal dotted lines appear in the middle of the slide, indicating that the guides are turned on.

2 Position your pointer on the horizontal guide and then drag the guide to the bottom of the bulleted text.

As you drag the pointer (which changes to a Guide indicator), a number indicating inches appears. When the Guides feature is turned on, the guides appear in the middle of the slide at 0.00 inches. As you move a guide left, right, up, or down, the inches number indicates how far you are from the slide center.

3 Hold down the SHIFT key and drag the guide down until the Guide indicator reaches .50.

As you drag the pointer, the Guide indicator indicates how far you are from the starting point of the guide.

 NOTE If your Guide indicator skips numbers as you drag the guides across the slide, turn off Snap To Grid on the Draw menu. When the Snap to Grid feature is turned on, objects snap to an invisible grid of evenly spaced lines that helps you align objects.

---

4 Drag the objects toward the horizontal guide until the tops of the objects touch or snaps to the guide.

Your presentation window should look like the following illustration:

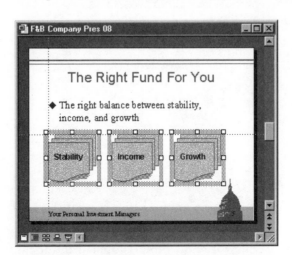

To turn off the guides, you can use a shortcut menu.

5 Click the right mouse button in a blank area of the slide.

A Shortcut menu appears.

6 On the Shortcut menu, click Guides.

Connecting Objects Together

With PowerPoint, you can connect two objects together with a connecting line. Once two objects are connected, the connecting line moves when either of the objects is moved. You can drag a connection end point to another connection point to change the connection line or drag the adjustment cursor to change the shape of the connection line.

Connect two objects together

*Curved
Double-Arrow
Connector*

*Connection
Cursor*

1 On the Drawing toolbar, click the AutoShapes menu button, point to Connectors, and then click the Curved Double-Arrow Connector button in the bottom right corner.

2 Position the cursor over the left object.

Small blue handles, known as *connection sites*, appear and the cursor changes to a small rectangle, as shown in the left margin.

3 Position the center of the cursor over the top blue handle.

4 Click and drag to the left side of the middle object over the blue handle.

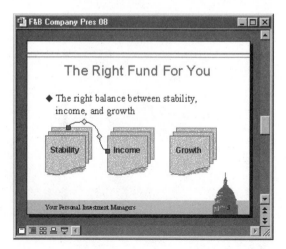

Red square handles appear at each end indicating the objects are connected. Yellow triangle handles appear in the middle of the connectore lines to resize the curve of the line. If green square handles appear at the ends, the objects are not connected.

Straight
Double-Arrow
Connector

6 On the Drawing toolbar, click the AutoShapes menu button, point to Connectors, and then click the Straight Double-Arrow Connector button in the top row.

7 Position the cursor over the right blue handle on the middle object and drag to the left blue handle of the right object

Change a connector line

Now that you have connected two objects together, change the connector line.

➤ Drag the left red handle on the selected connector line to the top of the middle object.

The line reconnects to a different point on the object.

Format a connector line

Once you have connected two objects, format the line with a dashed line.

1 Hold down the SHIFT key and click the left connector line.

The two connector lines are selected.

Dash Style

2 On the Drawing toolbar, click the Dash Style button, and then click the line second from the top.

3 On the Drawing toolbar, click the Line Style button, and then click the 3 pt. line style.

The connector lines appear dashed and 3 pt. in size.

Adding 3-D Effects to Objects

Once you draw an object, you can change the object to look 3-Dimensional. With PowerPoint's 3-D options, you can change the depth of the object and its color, rotation, angle, direction of lighting, and surface texture. For the company presentation, let's add 3-D effects to an object for emphasis.

Change an object to look 3-D

3-D

1 Click the Next Slide button to advance to slide 6.

2 Click the object labeled, "Objectives" to select it.

3 On the Drawing toolbar, click the 3-D button, and then click 3-D Style 15, as shown in the following illustration:

Click the 3-D
style here

Your presentation window should look like the following illustration:

For a demonstration of how to create 3-D objects, double-click the Camcorder Files On The Internet shorcut on your Desktop or connect to the Internet address listed on p. xxiii.

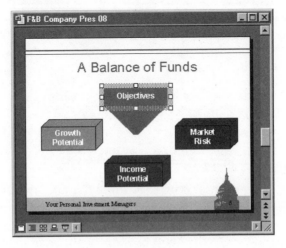

141

Change an object's 3-D settings

3-D

Lighting

1 On the Drawing toolbar, click the 3-D button, and then click 3-D Settings.

The 3-D Settings toolbar appears.

2 On the 3-D Settings toolbar, click the Lighting button, and then click the Lighting Direction button, as shown in the following illustration:

Click the Lighting Direction button here

Depth

3 On the 3-D Settings toolbar, click the Depth button, and then click 288 pt.

4 Right-click the 3-D Settings toolbar button, and then click 3D Settings or click the Close button to close the toolbar.

Drawing and Editing an Arc Object

With PowerPoint, you can draw and edit arcs of all sizes and shapes. You can change the shape of any arc by resizing it or moving its control handles. The direction in which you drag the arc determines whether the arc opens up or down, and the distance you drag the arc determines its size. To draw an arc, you use the Arc tool just like any other drawing tool.

Draw an arc

Arc

1 On the Drawing toolbar, click the AutoShapes menu button, point to Basic Shapes, and click the Arc button.

In the presentation window, the pointer changes to a cross hairs cursor.

2 Position the cross hairs cursor on the right middle edge of the object labeled, "Objectives."

3 Drag the cross hairs cursor down to the top center of the cube labeled, "Market Risk."

If the arc snaps to the top or bottom of the object labeled, "Objective," you can turn off the Snap to Shape feature. To turn off the feature, click the Draw menu button on the Drawing toolbar, point to Snap, and click To Shape.

Two adjustment handles appear at each end of the arc, as shown in the following illustration:

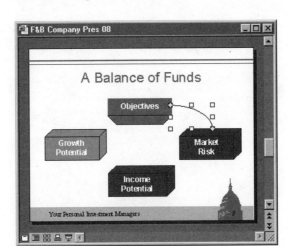

Edit the angle of an arc

Once you have drawn an arc, you can change the angle of the arc by dragging one of its adjustment handles.

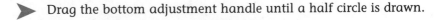 Drag the bottom adjustment handle until a half circle is drawn.

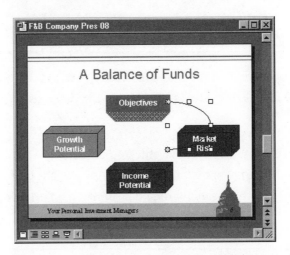

As the arc changes, a dotted outline of the arc appears, indicating what the arc will look like when you release the mouse button.

Edit the roundness of an arc

You can also change the roundness or size of the arc by resizing the object.

 Hold down the SHIFT key and drag the lower middle resize handle down to the middle of the cube labeled, "Income Potential."

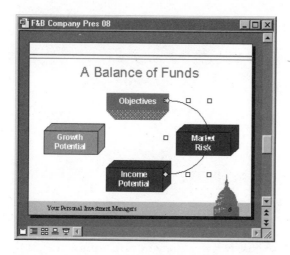

As the arc changes, a dotted outline of the arc appears, indicating what the arc will look like when you release the mouse button.

Format an arc

Once you have edited the size and shape of the arc, you can format it by changing the line thickness, adding an arrowhead, or filling the object.

Line Style

1   On the Drawing toolbar, click the Line Style button.

The Line Style menu appears, showing a variety of line widths and styles.

2   On the menu, click the 3 pt. line.

The arc line changes to a thicker point size.

Arrowheads

3   On the Drawing toolbar, click the Arrowheads button.

The Arrowheads menu appears, showing a variety of arrowhead styles.

4   On the menu, click Arrow Style 5.

 NOTE   Lines, arcs, and freeforms can't be changed using the Change AutoShape command.

Rotating and Flipping Objects

Once you have created an object you can change its orientation on the slide by rotating or flipping it. Rotating turns an object 90 degrees to the right or left and flipping turns an object 180 degrees horizontally or vertically.

1 Hold down the CTRL key and the SHIFT key, and drag the arc object to the left side of the screen.

   A new copy of the arc appears as you drag. Holding down the SHIFT key during the drag constrains the arc to the same horizontal position as the original.

2 On the Drawing toolbar, click the Draw menu button, point to Rotate Or Flip, and click Flip Horizontal.

   The object flips horizontally.

3 On the Drawing toolbar, click the Draw menu button, point to Rotate Or Flip, and click Flip Vertical.

4 Hold down the SHIFT key and drag the arc to the right until it reaches the left edge of the objects labeled, "Objectives," and "Income Potential."

   Your presentation window should look like the following illustration:

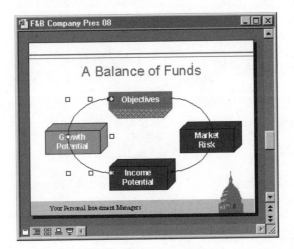

NOTE Patterns, shadows, and bitmaps don't rotate or flip. However, you can edit rotated text. PowerPoint automatically rotates the text so you can edit it and then rotates the text back when you are finished.

Grouping and Ungrouping Objects

Objects can be grouped together, ungrouped, and regrouped in PowerPoint to make editing and moving information easier. Rather than move an arrangement of objects one object at a time, you can group the objects and move them all together. Grouped objects appear as one object, but each object in the group maintains its individual attributes. You can change an individual object within a group by ungrouping the objects, making the change, and then grouping the objects together again using the Regroup command.

Group objects

For the company presentation, group the objects in the diagram together.

Marquee

1   Drag a selection marquee around the cubes, arcs, and rectangle.

    Each object has its own selection box, as shown in the following illustration:

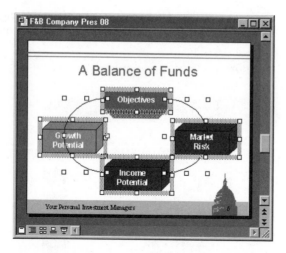

2   On the Drawing toolbar, click the Draw menu button, and click Group.

    The objects group together as one object.

Ungroup objects

To make changes to a group of objects, except editing text which you can modify directly, you need to ungroup the group of objects first.

1   On the Drawing toolbar, click the Draw menu button, and click Ungroup Objects.

2   Click a blank area of the slide to deselect the objects.

TIP You can directly edit objects with text within a group without ungrouping the objects first. Simply click the text in the object to place the insertion point, edit the text, and then deselect the object.

Object stacking order

Stacking is the placement of objects one on top of another. The drawing order determines the object stacking order. The first object you draw is on the bottom, and the last object you draw is on the top. You can change the placement of the objects by using the Bring to Front, Send to Back, Bring Forward, and Send Backward commands on the Draw menu.

1 Click the left arc object.

2 Hold down the SHIFT key and click the right arc object.

Both arcs are selected.

3 On the Drawing toolbar, click the Draw menu button, point to Order, and click Send to Back.

The arcs move to the back of the cube objects.

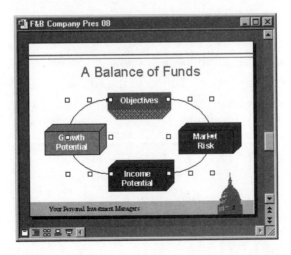

Regroup objects

Objects previously grouped can be regrouped in one easy step. After you ungroup a set of objects, PowerPoint remembers each object in the group and automatically regroups the objects with the Regroup command. When you regroup a set of objects, make sure that at least one of the grouped objects is selected before you regroup them.

147

➤ On the Draw menu, click Regroup.

All the objects are regrouped.

Save the presentation

Save

➤ On the Standard toolbar, click the Save button.

No dialog box appears because the presentation already has a name. The current information in your presentation is saved with the same name.

One Step Further

You have learned to select and deselect objects; draw and modify objects; and align, group, ungroup, rotate, and flip objects. Earlier in the lesson you learned how to rotate and flip an object in 90 degree or 180 degree intervals. With PowerPoint, you can also free rotate an object at any interval. Take another step and try the Free Rotate tool.

Free rotate an object

Previous Slide

1   Click the Previous Slide button.

Slide 5 appears in Slide view.

2   Click the left multidocument object to select it.

3   On the Drawing toolbar, click the Free Rotate button.

Free Rotate

The cursor changes to the rotate cursor. The resize handles on the selected object change to green circles handles.

4   Move the tip of the rotate cursor (which changes to small circular arrows) over one of the green circle handles.

Rotate Cursor

5   Drag with a circular motion to rotate the object.

The object rotates freely to any angle.

6   Click a blank area of the slide to turn off the Free Rotate tool.

If you want to continue to the next lesson

1   On the File menu, click Close (CTRL+W).

2   If a dialog box appears asking whether you want to save the changes to your presentation, click the No button.

If you want to quit PowerPoint for now

1   On the File menu, click Exit (CTRL+Q).

2   If a dialog box appears asking whether you want to save the changes to your presentation, click the No button.

Lesson Summary

To	Do this	Button
Draw an object	On the Drawing toolbar or the AutoShapes menu, click a drawing tool and drag to create an object.	
Select an object	Click the Select Objects button, and then click the object.	
Deselect an object	Click a blank area of the slide.	
Resize an object	Select the object. Drag a resize handle.	
Change an object's shape	Select the object. On the Draw menu, point to Change AutoShape and click a shape.	
Copy an object	Select the object. Click the Copy button and then click the Paste button or hold down the CTRL key and drag the object.	
Format text in a shape	Select the shape and click any formatting buttons on the Formatting toolbar or the Format menu.	
Format text with Format Painter	Select the object with the format you want to use. On the Standard toolbar, click Format Painter. Click the object you want to format.	
Align objects	Select the objects. On the Draw menu, click Align Or Distribute, and then click an alignment, or click the Guides command and drag the objects to a guide.	
Connect objects	On the AutoShapes menu, point to Connectors, and click a connector. Drag a line between objects.	
Change an object to 3-D	On the Drawing toolbar, click the 3-D button, and click a 3-D style.	
Draw an arc	On the Draw menu, point to Basic Shapes, and click the arc button and drag.	
Edit an arc	Select the arc. To edit the size of the arc, drag a resize handle. To edit the shape of the arc, drag one of the adjustment handles.	

To	Do this	Button
Change a line style	On the Drawing toolbar, click the Line Style button. Click a line style.	
Rotate and flip an object	Select the object. On the Draw menu, click a Rotate Or Flip command.	
Group or ungroup objects	Select the objects. On the Draw menu, click the Group or Ungroup command.	

For online information about	Use the Office Assistant to search for
Drawing objects	**Draw**, and then click Add Or Change An AutoShape
Selecting and deselecting objects	**Select objects**, and then click Select Objects Or Cancel A Selection
Changing objects	**AutoShapes**, and then click Add Or Change An AutoShape
Copying object formatting	**Copy formatting**, and then click Copy The Attributes Of An Object Or Text
Connecting objects together	**Connect object**, and then click Add, Move, Or Reroute A Connector Line
Rotating objects	**Rotate**, and then click Rotate Or Flip An Object
Grouping and ungrouping	**Group**, and then click Group, Ungroup, And Regroup Objects

To use the Office Assistant, see Appendix A, in the back of this book.

Preview of the Next Lesson

In the next lesson, you'll learn how to insert clip art, a Microsoft Word table, a Microsoft Excel chart, a picture, WordArt, and an organization chart, and then you'll learn how to scale, crop, and recolor them.

Review & Practice

In the lessons in Part 3, you learned skills to apply and modify a template, change presentation colors, add a background, and draw, modify, and adjust shapes. If you want to practice these skills and test your understanding before you proceed with the lessons in Part 4, you can work through the Review & Practice section following this lesson.

Review & Practice

Estimated time
35 min.

You will review and practice how to:

- Apply a template.
- Modify the title and slide masters.
- Choose a color scheme and change a color.
- Draw objects.
- Modify and format objects.
- Rotate, align, and group objects.

Practice the skills you learned in the Part 3 lessons by working through this Review & Practice section. You'll use PowerPoint to draw and modify objects in a presentation.

Scenario

As the account manager at Ferguson & Bardell, you continue to work on the investment presentation you worked on in the previous Review & Practice. Now you're applying and modifying a template, changing a color scheme, adding a background, and adding and modifying drawings.

In this section, you'll open a presentation, apply a template and change a title and slide master, change individual colors in a color scheme, add different backgrounds, draw, adjust, change, and format shapes, and align and group objects.

Step 1: Apply a template

After finalizing your text, apply a customized F&B company template.

1 From the PowerPoint SBS Practice folder, open the presentation called Part 03 Review.

2 Save the presentation with the name **R&P Investment Pres 03** in the PowerPoint SBS Practice folder.

3 From the PowerPoint SBS Practice folder, apply a template called Part 03 Template. *Your Choice*

For more information on	See
Applying a template	Lesson 6

Step 2: Modify the title and slide masters

The masters applied by the template need a few modifications.

1 Switch to the Slide Master.

2 Change the first bullet level to the square with a check mark as shown in the left margin and change the bullet color to dark blue. *Your Choice*

3 Adjust the indent level between the new bullet and the text.

4 Change the title font to Arial Narrow. *Your Choice*

5 Switch to the Title Master.

6 Change the title font to Arial Narrow and the format to Bold.

7 Switch to Slide view.

8 Remove the Slide Footer display from the title slide.

For more information on	See
Modifying and formatting master text	Lesson 6

Step 3: Choose a color scheme and change a color

Each template comes with several color schemes. Choose a different color scheme and then change one of the colors in the scheme.

1 Choose the top middle color scheme (light blue background) in the Color Scheme dialog box.

2 Change the title color to a dark blue to match the blue bar. *Change Fill Not Title*

3 Add the color scheme to the Standard Scheme.

4 Apply the color scheme change to all the slides.

For more information on	See
Choosing and changing a color scheme	Lesson 7

Step 4: *Draw shapes and lines*

Use the AutoShape Flowchart tools, and the Connector tools on the Drawing toolbar to draw a diagram illustrating the investment process.

1 Switch to slide 4 in Slide view.

2 Reapply a slide layout to make room for drawing shapes and lines on the slide.

3 Choose the Title Only layout.

4 Draw and modify the slide to match the following illustration:

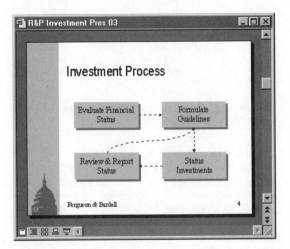

For more information on	See
Reapplying a slide layout	Lesson 6
Drawing and editing objects	Lesson 8

Step 5: *Modify, format, and rearrange shapes*

Use the partially completed slide to create a diagram by copying, changing, formatting, moving, rotating, and aligning the objects in the slide.

1 Switch to slide 5 in Slide view.

2 Change the diamond object to the 8-point star object.

3 Change the fill of the star object to the Parchment texture.

4 Copy and paste the left pentagon, labeled "Sector," two times and then change the label text to "Maturity" and "Quality."

5 Change the fill of the pentagon objects to teal.

6 Add Shadow Style 6 to the pentagon and star objects and nudge the shadow down and left for the star object.

7 Move, rotate, and align the objects to match the following illustration:

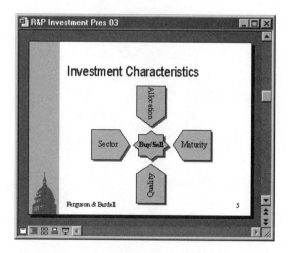

8 Group the four pentagons and the star.

For more information on	See
Modifying and formatting objects	Lesson 8
Aligning objects	Lesson 8
Rotating and flipping objects	Lesson 8
Grouping and ungrouping objects	Lesson 8

If you want to continue to the next lesson

1 On the File menu, click Close (CTRL+W).

2 If a dialog box appears asking whether you want to save the changes to your presentation, click the Yes button.

If you want to quit PowerPoint for now

1 On the File menu, click Exit (CTRL+Q).

2 If a dialog box appears asking whether you want to save the changes to your presentation, click the Yes button.

Adding Clip Art, Charts, and Graphs

Inserting Information into PowerPoint

Estimated time
45 min.

In this lesson you will learn how to:

- Insert clip art in a slide.
- Scale and recolor an object.
- Insert a Microsoft Word table.
- Insert a Microsoft Excel chart.
- Insert an organization chart.
- Insert and crop a picture.
- Insert WordArt.

You can insert information into PowerPoint several different ways. The most direct way is to copy and paste the information. You can copy and paste text, objects, and slides within a presentation, among presentations, and into other Windows-based applications. Another way to insert information into PowerPoint is to use commands on the Insert menu and the Standard toolbar, which allow you to insert clip art, tables, charts, pictures, or objects.

As Director of Communications at Ferguson & Bardell, you have been working on a company presentation. After adding shapes in the previous lesson, you're ready to add clip art, pictures, tables, and charts to enhance your text.

In this lesson, you'll learn how to insert clip art, a table, an Excel chart, an organization chart, a photograph, and a WordArt picture into your slides; scale an object; and crop and recolor a picture.

Start the lesson

Follow the steps below to open the practice file called 09 PPT Lesson, and then save it with the new name F&B Company Pres 09. If you haven't already started PowerPoint, do so now.

Open

1   On the Standard toolbar, click the Open button or click the Open An Existing Presentation option button on the Start-up dialog box and click OK.

2   In the Look In box, ensure that the PowerPoint SBS Practice folder is open. If it is not, select the hard drive and folder where the Step by Step practice files are stored.

For information about opening a presentation, see Lesson 3.

3   In the file list box, double-click the file named 09 PPT Lesson to open it.

4   On the File menu, click Save As.

The Save As dialog box opens. Be sure the PowerPoint SBS Practice folder appears in the Save In box.

5   In the File Name box, type **F&B Company Pres 09**

6   Click the Save button.

The presentation is saved and the title bar changes to the new name.

Inserting Clip Art Images

Insert Clip Art

PowerPoint comes with more than 1100 professionally designed pieces of clip art to use in your presentations. With the AutoClipArt command, PowerPoint helps you find the right clip art image for your slides. AutoClipArt searches your presentation for keywords and suggests appropriate clip art images from the Microsoft Clip Gallery for you to use. If you know what clip art image you want to use, you can add it by clicking the Insert Clip Art button on the Standard toolbar or double-clicking a clip art placeholder.

Use AutoClipArt to insert an image

1   On the Tools menu, click AutoClipArt.

A scanning message box appears, while PowerPoint checks your presentation for concepts, and then the AutoClipArt dialog box appears.

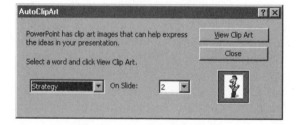

AutoClipArt checked your presentation text for keywords. The keywords appear in the drop-down list.

2 Click the drop-down arrow and click Decision.

"Decision" appears in the drop-down list and Slide 7 appears in Slide view behind the AutoClipArt dialog box.

3 Drag the AutoClipArt dialog box title to the upper right corner of the screen to see the text on the slide.

4 Click the View Clip Art button.

For information about inserting sounds and movies, see Lesson 12.

The Microsoft Clip Gallery dialog box appears with a visual preview list of the clip art images that relate to the word "Decision." The Microsoft Clip Gallery makes it easy to find clip art images, pictures, sounds, and videos by categories. After viewing the clip art images, you decide to choose another clip art image.

NOTE The first time you open the Microsoft Clip Gallery, PowerPoint asks if you want to view additional clip art available on the Office CD-ROM. Follow the instructions and click OK.

5 In the Categories list box, click the down scroll arrow, and then click Shapes.

A visual preview of images appears for the Shapes category.

6 In the Pictures list box, click the clip art shown in the following illustration:

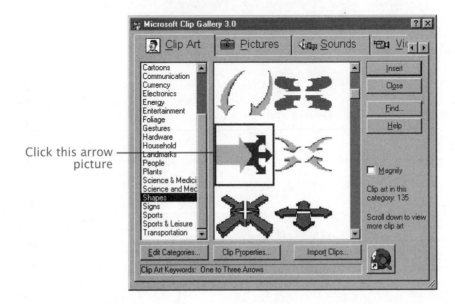

Click this arrow picture

7 Click the Insert button.

The clip art is inserted into the slide and the Picture toolbar appears. The AutoClipArt dialog box stays open in case you want to insert another clip art picture.

8 Click the Close button to exit the AutoClipArt dialog box.

The clip art image appears selected on the slide and the Picture toolbar opens. When a picture is selected, PowerPoint automatically opens the Picture toolbar.

9 Drag the arrow object to the location shown in the following illustration:

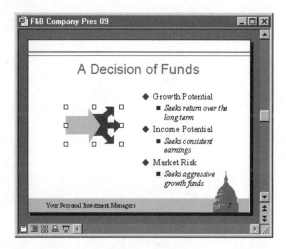

Scaling an Object

Scaling means resizing an entire object by a certain percentage. With the Scale command you can resize an object numerically instead of dragging its resize handle. An object can be scaled relative to the original picture size if the appropriate check box in the Scale dialog box is turned on.

Scale an object

Try making the arrow object 120% of its original size.

1 Ensure the arrow object is selected.

Format Picture

2 On the Picture toolbar, click the Format Picture button, or click Picture on the Format menu.

The Format Picture dialog box appears.

3 Click the Size tab.

4 In the Scale area, select the percentage in the Height box.

5 Type **120**

Since the Lock Aspect Ratio check box is turned on, the Width option setting changes to 120%. If you're not sure about the new scale size, you can click the Preview button to view the object before leaving the dialog box.

6 Click the OK button.

 TIP PowerPoint remembers the original size of a picture or text object. If you accidently change an object to the wrong size, set the scale back to 100% relative to its original size.

7 Click a blank area of the slide to deselect the object.

Your presentation window should look like the following illustration:

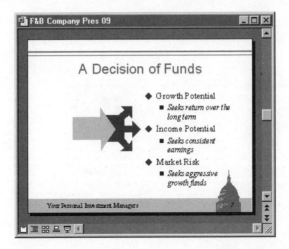

8 If necessary, click the arrow object and then use the ARROW keys to position the arrow object as shown in the above illustration.

Recoloring a Clip Art Image

You can recolor clip art images or pictures to create a better look or to follow the current color scheme. The Recolor Picture command displays a dialog box with a preview of the picture and a list of all the colors in the picture. You can change any color in the list to a color in your presentation's color scheme or to any color you want.

Recolor an image

Recolor

1 Click the arrow object to select it.

2 On the Picture toolbar, click the Recolor button.

The Recolor Picture dialog box appears.

3 Under New, click the drop-down arrow next to the purple color.

A color menu appears.

4 Click the maroon color box.

The color swatch changes to maroon. A check mark appears in the check box to the left, indicating you changed a color. Notice that PowerPoint automatically previews the color change in the Preview box.

5 Under New, click the drop-down arrow next to the green color and click the dark blue color box in the second row.

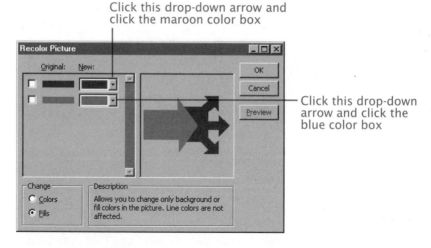

6 Click the OK button.

PowerPoint recolors the arrow object.

Inserting a Microsoft Word Table

For information on Microsoft Word, see your Microsoft Word documentation.

With the Insert Microsoft Word Table feature, you can use the power of Microsoft Word 97 for Windows or later to create a table in PowerPoint. When you insert a table, and return to your presentation slide, the table becomes an embedded object in the slide. An *embedded object* maintains a "link" with its original application for easy editing. When you embed an object, the object becomes a part of your presentation. You are the only user of the information. After returning to PowerPoint, you can edit the embedded object easily by double-clicking it.

IMPORTANT To insert a table in this lesson, you'll need Microsoft Word 97 for Windows. If you don't have this application, you can use similar techniques with other Windows-based applications that support embedding.

Insert a Microsoft Word table

Since you have a slide with a text placeholder, use the AutoLayout feature to change the current layout to one with a table. Now, you can add a table comparing mutual funds.

Slide Layout

Table

1 Click the Next Slide button to advance to slide 8.

2 On the Standard toolbar, click the Slide Layout button.

The Slide Layout dialog box appears.

3 Click the Table layout.

4 Click the Apply button.

The blank slide appears with a table placeholder.

5 Double-click the table placeholder.

The Insert Word Table dialog box appears.

 TIP You can also insert a Word table into PowerPoint by clicking the Insert Microsoft Word Table button on the Standard toolbar and dragging to create a table size.

6 Click the Number Of Rows Up Arrow button until the number reaches 7.

7 Click the OK button.

PowerPoint inserts a blank table for you to fill in with your text. The blank Word table appears in the middle of the slide and the Word toolbar appears above the presentation window.

8 Type the following text in the Word table, using TAB to move from cell to cell.

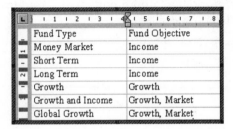

Fund Type	Fund Objective
Money Market	Income
Short Term	Income
Long Term	Income
Growth	Growth
Growth and Income	Growth, Market
Global Growth	Growth, Market

Format a Microsoft Word table

Now that you've typed the text, format the table to give it a professional look.

Tables And Borders

Table AutoFormat

1   On the Standard toolbar, click the Tables And Borders button.

The Tables And Borders toolbar appears.

2   On the Tables And Borders toolbar, click the Table AutoFormat button.

The Table AutoFormat dialog box appears.

3   In the Formats list box, scroll down and then click Classic 4.

4   In the Formats To Apply area, click the AutoFit check box to select the option.

AutoFit turns off and the table preview expands. Your dialog box should look like the following illustration:

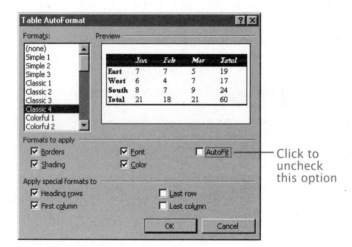

Click to uncheck this option

5   Click the OK button.

The Classic 4 AutoFormat is applied to the table.

6   Click a blank area of the slide to exit Microsoft Word.

The PowerPoint toolbars and menus return and the embedded Word table is updated on the slide.

7   Click a blank area of the slide to deselect the table.

Your presentation window should look like the following illustration:

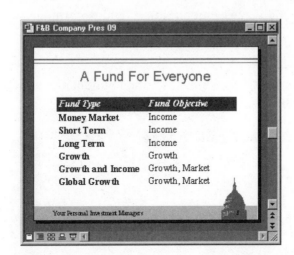

Inserting a Microsoft Excel Chart

For information on Microsoft Excel, see your Microsoft Excel documentation.

As it does for a Microsoft Word table, PowerPoint simplifies the process of inserting a Microsoft Excel chart into your presentation by embedding the chart. Besides inserting an embedded object, you can also insert a linked object. A *linked object* creates a "link" with the document that contains the object, known as the *source document*. When you link an object, the object is stored in its source document, where it was created. Your presentation becomes one of several users of the information and can be automatically updated when others update the source document. Your presentation stores only a representation of the original document. You can insert a new chart or one that you have already created in Microsoft Excel. To insert a chart, you click Object on the Insert menu.

Insert a new slide for the Microsoft Excel chart

Insert New Slide

1 On the Standard toolbar, click the Insert New Slide button.

The New Slide dialog box appears.

2 Click the Title Only layout.

3 Click the OK button.

A blank new slide appears.

Title Only

4 Click the title placeholder and type **Funds That Get Results**

The new title appears in the title text object. In the blank area below the title, you'll insert a Microsoft Excel chart that you already created.

5 Click a blank area of the slide to deselect the title text object.

Insert a Microsoft Excel chart object in a slide

For the company presentation, insert fund performance figures into your slide.

1 On the Insert menu, click Object.

The Insert Object dialog box appears.

2 Click the Create From File option button, as shown in the following illustration:

Click this option — button

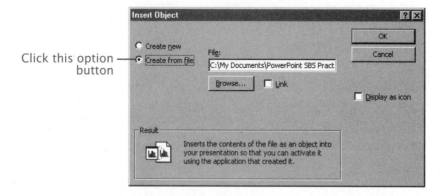

When the Link check box is turned off, PowerPoint embeds the object. To link an object, you click the Link check box to turn on the feature.

3 Click the Browse button.

The Browse dialog box appears.

4 In the Look In box, ensure that the PowerPoint SBS Practice folder is open. If it is not, select the hard drive and folder where the Step by Step practice files are stored. Typically, you'll find the PowerPoint SBS Practice folder in the My Documents folder.

5 In the list of file and folder names, click 09 Fund Rates.

6 Click the OK button to close the Browse dialog box.

7 Click the OK button.

PowerPoint embeds the chart into the new slide. To move the chart, you can drag the chart or you can use PowerPoint's Nudge feature. The Nudge feature allows you to move an object in small increments up, down, left, or right.

8 On the Drawing menu, click the Draw menu button, point to Nudge, and then click Down.

You can also nudge an object with the ARROW keys.

9 Click the DOWN ARROW key twice.

Your presentation window should look like the following illustration:

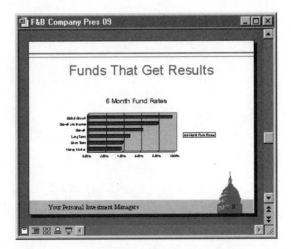

For a demonstration of how to embed an Excel chart, double-click the Camcorder Files On The Internet shorcut on your Desktop or connect to the Internet address listed on p. xxiii.

Edit an embedded Microsoft Excel object

You can edit an embedded object by double-clicking the object or by selecting the object and then clicking Object on the Edit menu. PowerPoint opens the embedded application so you can edit the object. Simply deselect the object to close the embedded application and return to PowerPoint.

1 Double-click the embedded Microsoft Excel chart.

Excel opens and displays Chart1.

2 Click the Chart2 tab button.

Your embedded object should look like the following illustration:

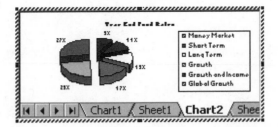

3 Click a blank area of the slide to exit Microsoft Excel.

4 Click a blank area of the slide to deselect the embedded Excel object.

The PowerPoint toolbars and menus return and the embedded Excel object is updated on the slide.

Your presentation window should look like the following illustration:

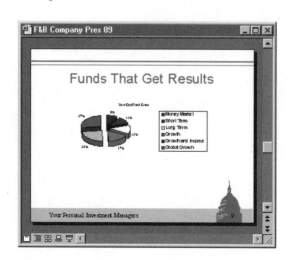

Inserting an Organization Chart

Microsoft Organization Chart is an application that PowerPoint uses to embed organization chart objects in your presentation slides. When you start and then exit the Organization Chart application, PowerPoint creates an embedded object you can edit at any time.

Insert a new slide for an organization chart

For the company presentation, insert a new slide to insert an organization chart.

Insert New Slide

Organization Chart

1 On the Standard toolbar, click the Insert New Slide button.

The New Slide dialog box appears.

2 Click the Organization Chart layout.

3 Click the OK button.

A blank new slide appears.

4 Click the title placeholder and type **An Organization on the Move**

The new title appears in the title text object. Use the org chart place-holder below the title to insert a chart.

Start Organization Chart

You can start Organization Chart by double-clicking the org chart placeholder, or by choosing the Object command on the Insert menu and clicking Microsoft Organization Chart 2.0.

1   Double-click the org chart placeholder.

PowerPoint launches Organization Chart.

The default chart displayed in the organization chart window represents the chart that will be embedded in your PowerPoint presentation. To create your own organization chart, fill in the sample chart boxes and then add new chart boxes.

2   Click the organization chart window's Maximize button.

The entire chart appears in full view.

Enter text into the top chart box

To enter text into a chart box, you need to click the chart box, select the placeholder text, and then type your own text. The top chart box text is open and ready for you to enter text.

1   Type **David Ferguson**

2   Press TAB and type **John Bardell**

3   Press TAB and type **Chief Executive Officers**

As you type, the chart box expands to fit the text.

4   Click a blank area of the chart window to deselect the chart box.

5   Click the lower left chart box to select the box.

6   Drag to select the first line of chart box text.

7   Enter chart box text to match to following illustration:

Add a chart box

You can add chart boxes to your organization chart by clicking a chart box type on the Org Chart Standard toolbar and then selecting the chart box you want to attach it to. If you add a chart box to the wrong place, you can delete it by selecting the chart box and pressing the Delete key.

Subordinate

Chart Box Cursor

1   On the Org Chart Standard toolbar, click the Subordinate button.

2   Position the cursor (which changes to chart box cursor) over the chart box with "Jim Kelly" and click to add a chart box below it.

A new chart box is added and selected. To add more employees under the chart box with "Jim Kelly," you'll need to change the chart style.

Change the chart style

The current chart type appears in the traditional style, one manager at the top with subordinates below. Use the Styles menu to change the chart style of the new chart box.

1. Ensure the new subordinate chart box is selected.

2. Type *your name* in the chart box.

   You can enter text directly in a selected chart box.

Chart Style

3. On the Styles menu, click the Styles button shown in the margin.

   The chart box style changes to match the new group style.

Subordinate

4. On the Org Chart Standard toolbar, click the Subordinate button and then click the chart box with "Jim Kelly."

   A new chart box is added below the chart box with "your name."

Chart Box Cursor

5. Type **Terry Angelle**

6. Click a blank area of the chart window to deselect the chart box.

7. Add chart boxes and enter text to match to the following illustration:

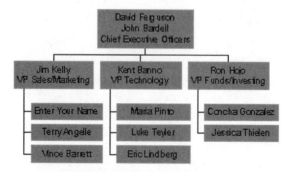

Edit the chart's title text

For the company presentation, change the sample title text to the company name. To edit text, click to place the insertion point and make your changes.

I-Beam Cursor

1. Position the pointer (which changes to an I-beam cursor) to the left of the "Chart Title" text.

2. Drag to select the "Chart Title" text.

   The chart title appears selected or highlighted.

3. Type **Ferguson & Bardell**

4. Click a blank area of the organization chart window to deselect the title.

Rearrange organization chart boxes

After reviewing your organization chart, you remember that Eric Lindberg changed jobs. Rearrange a chart box to reflect the change. To move chart boxes, drag the box onto another box; to move chart text, drag the object to a new location.

1   Click a blank area of the chart window to ensure that all chart boxes are deselected.

To rearrange a chart box, it must be deselected.

Chart Box

2   Drag the chart box with "Eric Lindberg" to the bottom of the chart box with "Ron Hojo" (the pointer cursor changes to a small chart box).

While you are dragging, the cursor changes to a four-headed arrow. When you place one chart box on another, the four-headed arrow changes to one of the following cursors:

■ A left arrow when positioned over the left side of the chart box.

■ A right arrow when positioned over the right side of the chart box.

■ A chart box when positioned over the bottom of the chart box.

To cancel the operation, release the mouse button when the pointer is not positioned over a chart box.

3   When the four-headed arrow changes to a small chart box, release the mouse button.

The chart box is moved to a new position in the organization chart.

Format organization chart boxes

You can change chart boxes' color, shadow, border style, border color, or border line style by clicking commands on the Boxes menu. For the F&B organization chart, add a shadow to the manager chart boxes.

1   On the Edit menu, click Select Levels.

The Select Levels dialog box appears.

2   Press TAB and type **2**

3   Click the OK button.

The top two levels of the chart are selected.

Shadow Style

4   On the Boxes menu, point to Shadow and then click the top button in the second column, as shown in the margin.

The top two levels of the chart are formatted with a box shadow.

5   Click a blank area of the chart window to deselect the chart boxes.

Exit Organization Chart and update your presentation

When exiting Organization Chart, you can either update your presentation with changes you've made or ignore the changes. Unlike Microsoft Graph, Microsoft Word, or Microsoft Excel, where you deselect the object to exit the program, in Microsoft Organization Chart, you need to click the Exit command on the File menu.

1 On the File menu, click Exit And Return To FB Company Pres 09.

The Microsoft Organization Chart dialog box appears.

2 Click the Yes button to update your presentation.

Organization Chart updates the embedded chart in your slide with your changes.

3 Click a blank area of the slide to deselect the embedded object.

Your presentation window should look like the following illustration:

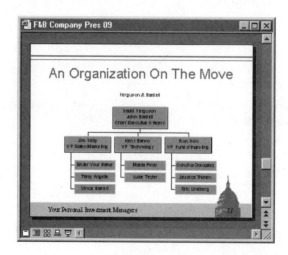

After you have created an organization chart in your PowerPoint slide, you can edit it much like other embedded objects. You can edit the chart from PowerPoint by double-clicking the organization chart object.

Inserting a Picture

If you have pictures—scanned photographs and line art, photos and artwork from CDs or other applications—you can insert them into PowerPoint. Using the Picture submenu on the Insert menu, you can insert pictures from a file, Microsoft Clip Gallery, or scanner in your slides. Using the Clip Art command, you can insert a picture from the Clip Gallery that comes with PowerPoint. If you have a scanner connected to your computer, you can scan and insert a picture using the From Scanner command (which uses Microsoft Photo Editor).

Insert a picture

Next Slide

1 Click the Next Slide button to advance to slide 11.

2 On the Insert menu, point to Picture, and then click From File.

The Insert Picture dialog box appears.

3 In the Look In box, ensure that the PowerPoint SBS Practice folder is open. If it is not, select the hard drive and folder where the Step by Step practice files are stored. Typically, you'll find the PowerPoint SBS Practice folder in the My Documents folder.

4 In the list of file and folder names, click 09 Service Picture.

5 Click the Insert button.

The picture and the Picture toolbar appear.

6 Drag the picture to the right side of the slide, as shown in the following illustration:

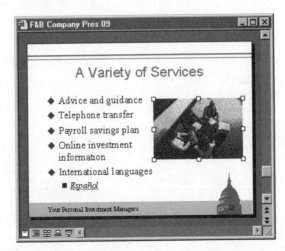

Enhance the picture in PowerPoint

If you insert a photograph or scanned image, you can enhance the image with brightness, contrast, and conversion controls. Convert the picture to grayscale and change the brightness and contrast. After you make changes, you can click the Reset Picture button on the Picture toolbar to reverse all changes.

Image Control

More Brightness

1 On the Picture toolbar, click the Image Control button, and then click Grayscale.

2 On the Picture toolbar, click the More Brightness button.

3 On the Picture toolbar, click the More Contrast button.

The picture brightness and contract increase to enhance the look.

Cropping a Picture

Sometimes you need only a portion of a picture in your presentation. With the Crop Picture command, you can cover portions of a picture so you don't see all of it on the screen. The picture is not altered, just covered up.

Crop a picture

Crop

Cropping Tool

Constrain Cursor

1 Click the Service Picture object, if it's not already selected.

2 On the Picture toolbar, click the Crop button.

The pointer changes to the cropping tool.

3 Position the center of the cropping tool over the left middle resize handle and drag to the right to crop the left side of the picture.

While you're dragging, a dotted outline appears to show you the area that remains after cropping. The cropping tool also changes to a constrain cursor, indicating the direction that you're cropping.

4 Position the center of the cropping tool over the right middle resize handle and drag to the left to crop the right side of the picture.

5 Click a blank area of the slide to deselect the picture.

The cropping tool changes to the pointer. Your presentation window should look like the following illustration:

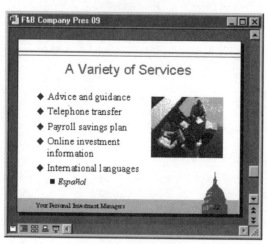

TIP To customize a clip art image, you can ungroup the image into separate objects, deselect the individual objects, add or delete individual objects, and then regroup the objects into an image.

Inserting WordArt

You can insert fancy or stylized text into your presentation with Microsoft WordArt. You do not have to be an artist to create stylized text, WordArt provides you with a gallery of choices. You can insert stylized text by clicking the Insert WordArt button on the Drawing toolbar and selecting a style.

Insert a new slide for the WordArt object

Insert New Slide

Title Only

1 On the Standard toolbar, click the Insert New Slide button.

The New Slide dialog box appears.

2 Click the Title Only layout.

3 Click the OK button.

A blank new slide appears.

4 Click the title placeholder and type **Ferguson & Bardell**

The new title appears in the text object.

5 Click a blank area of the slide to deselect the title text object.

Insert WordArt in a slide

Insert WordArt

1 On the Drawing toolbar, click the Insert WordArt button.

The WordArt Gallery dialog box appears displaying a list of styles.

2 Click the style shown in the following illustration:

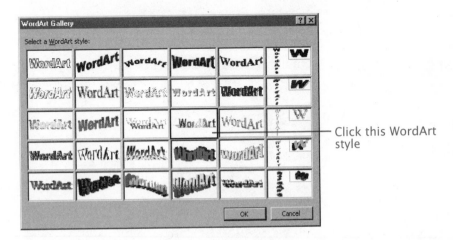

Click this WordArt style

3 Click the OK button.

The Edit WordArt Text dialog box appears.

The WordArt toolbar and menus appear behind the dialog box.

4 In the Text box, type **Investing** and press ENTER.

5 Type **in your** and press ENTER.

6 Type **Future**

The WordArt text defaults to the Times New Roman font at 36 points.

7 Click the OK button.

The text you typed and the WordArt toolbar appear.

8 Drag the lower right resize handle to the logo to enlarge the text object.

Format the WordArt text

Now that you have entered your text, add some special effects.

WordArt Shape

1 On the WordArt toolbar, click the WordArt Shape button, and then click the Double Wave 2 symbol, as shown in the following illustration:

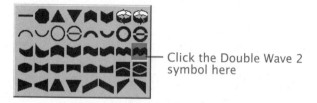

Click the Double Wave 2 symbol here

WordArt Same Letter Heights

2 On the WordArt toolbar, click the WordArt Same Letter Heights button.

The letter heights change to the same size.

WordArt Character Spacing

3 On the WordArt toolbar, click the WordArt Character Spacing button.

A submenu appears with character spacing types.

4 On the Character Spacing submenu, click Loose.

The text spacing changes to very loose.

Exit WordArt

1 Click in a blank area of the presentation window to exit WordArt.

The WordArt toolbar closes.

2 Drag the WordArt text object to the center of the slide as shown in the following illustration:

Save the presentation

Save

➤ On the Standard toolbar, click the Save button.

No dialog box appears because the presentation already has a name. The current information in your presentation is saved with the same name.

One Step Further

You have learned how to insert clip art, a Word table, an Excel chart, a photograph, an organization chart, and a WordArt picture into your slides; scale an object; and crop and recolor a picture.

Add a picture to the Clip Gallery

You might want to add your own pictures and categories to the Clip Gallery. Try adding the company logo to the Clip Gallery.

Insert Clip Art

1   On the Standard toolbar, click the Insert Clip Art button.

The Microsoft Clip Gallery dialog box appears.

2   Click the Import Clips button.

The Add Clip Art To Clip Gallery dialog box appears.

3   In the Look In box, ensure that the PowerPoint SBS Practice folder is open. If it is not, select the hard drive and folder where the Step by Step practice files are stored. Typically, you'll find the PowerPoint SBS Practice folder in the My Documents folder.

4   In the list of file and folder names, click 09 Logo Picture.

5   Click the Open button.

The Picture Properties dialog box appears.

6   In the Keywords text box, type **F&B Logo**

7   Click the New Category button.

The New Category dialog box appears.

8   Type **Ferguson & Bardell**

9   Click the OK button.

10   Click the OK button to close the Picture Properties dialog box.

The new category and picture appear in the dialog box.

11   Click the Insert button.

The new clip art image inserts in the slide.

Customize a clip art image

You might want to customize a clip art image, such as deleting parts of a picture. Try deleting the names on either side of the company logo.

1   On the Drawing toolbar, click the Draw and then click Ungroup.

A message dialog box appears.

2   Click the Yes button to convert the clip art image to PowerPoint objects.

The clip art image appears as individually selected objects.

3   Click a black area of the slide to deselect the objects.

4   Hold down the SHIFT key, click the Ferguson object, click the Bardell object, and then press the DELETE key.

5   Drag to select the capital image object.

6   On the Drawing toolbar, click the Draw menu button, click Regroup.

If you want to continue to the next lesson

1   On the File menu, click Close (CTRL+W).

2   If a dialog box appears asking whether you want to save the changes to your presentation, click the Yes button.

If you want to quit PowerPoint for now

1   On the File menu, click Exit (CTRL+Q).

2   If a dialog box appears asking whether you want to save the changes to your presentation, click the Yes button.

Lesson Summary

To	Do this	Button
Insert clip art using AutoClipArt	On the Tools menu, click AutoClipArt. From the drop-down list, click a keyword. Click the View Clip Art button. Click an image from the Clip Gallery.	
Insert clip art	On the Standard toolbar, click the Insert Clip Art button or double-click a clip art placeholder. Click an image from the Clip Gallery and click the Insert button.	
Scale an object	Click the object. On the Format menu, click Object. Click the Size tab. Type a percentage in height or width.	
Recolor a picture	On the Picture toolbar, click the Recolor button. Click the drop-down arrow for each color and select a new one from the list.	
Insert a Microsoft Word table	On the Insert menu, click Microsoft Word Table, click the Insert Microsoft Word Table button, or double-click a table placeholder.	
Insert a Microsoft Excel chart	On the Insert menu, click Object. Click the Create From File option button. Click the Browse button to select a file and then click the OK button.	

To	Do this	Button
Insert an organization chart	Double-click an org chart placeholder or on the Insert menu, click Object. Double-click Microsoft Organization Chart. Fill in the chart and click Exit.	
Insert a picture	On the Insert menu, point to Picture, and click From File. Click a picture file, and then click the Insert button.	
Convert a picture	On the Picture toolbar, click the Image Control button.	
Change picture brightness	On the Picture toolbar, click the More or Less Brightness button.	
Change picture contrast	On the Picture toolbar, click the More or Less Contrast button.	
Crop a picture	On the Picture toolbar, click the Crop button. Drag a resize handle.	
Insert WordArt	On the Drawing toolbar, click the WordArt button. Type and format your text and click a blank area to exit.	

For online information about	Use the Office Assistant to search for
Inserting clip art	**Clip art**, and then click Insert Clip Art Or A Picture From The Clip Gallery
Scaling a picture	**Resize**, and then click Resize Or Crop An Object
Inserting or editing a table	**Table**, and then click Insert A Word Table Or Edit A Word Table
Inserting a Microsoft	**Excel**, and then click Ways To Share Information Between PowerPoint And Another Office Program
Inserting an organization chart	**Org chart**, and then click Insert An Organization Chart
Inserting a picture	**Insert picture**, and then click Insert And Edit A Picture

To use the Office Assistant, see Appendix A, in the back of this book.

Preview of the Next Lesson

In the next lesson, you'll create and edit a graph, work with graph data, change a graph format, work with a legend, and add title text.

10

Creating and Editing a Graph

In this lesson you will learn how to:

- Use Microsoft Graph.
- Import data from Microsoft Excel.
- Enter and edit data in a datasheet.
- Modify a data series.
- Format a data series.
- Change and format a chart.
- Modify a legend.
- Add text to a chart.

Estimated time

45 min.

To create graphs for your slides, PowerPoint uses an embedded application called Microsoft Graph. Graph offers many of the same features as Microsoft Excel. Adding graphs to a presentation can help communicate your ideas in an effective manner.

As Director of Communications at Ferguson & Bardell, you have been working on a company presentation. Since it is important for stockholders to understand the profitability of the company, add a graph to make the information easier to comprehend.

In this lesson, you'll learn how to start Graph from PowerPoint, select individual cells and groups of cells for editing, import data from a Microsoft Excel worksheet, move through a datasheet, enter and edit data in a datasheet, modify and format a data series, format a legend, and add a chart title and a text label.

Start the lesson

Follow the steps below to open the practice file called 10 PPT Lesson, and then save it with the new name F&B Company Pres 10. If you haven't already started PowerPoint, do so now.

Open

For information about opening a presentation, see Lesson 3.

1   On the Standard toolbar, click the Open button or click the Open An Existing Presentation option button on the Start-up dialog box and click OK.

2   In the Look In box, ensure that the PowerPoint SBS Practice folder is open. If it is not, select the hard drive and folder where the Step by Step practice files are stored.

3   In the file list box, double-click the file named 10 PPT Lesson to open it.

4   On the File menu, click Save As.

The Save As dialog box opens. Be sure the PowerPoint SBS Practice folder appears in the Save In box.

5   In the File Name box, type **F&B Company Pres 10**

6   Click the Save button.

The presentation is saved and the title bar changes to the new name.

Using Microsoft Graph

Microsoft Graph is an application that PowerPoint uses to insert a chart in your presentation slide. When you start Microsoft Graph, create a chart, and return to your presentation slide, the chart becomes an embedded object in the slide. You can start Graph by double-clicking a chart placeholder, clicking the Insert Chart button on the Standard toolbar, or clicking Insert Chart on the Insert menu.

Insert a new slide for a chart

For the company presentation, insert a new slide for your graph.

1   Drag the scroll box to slide 7.

Slide 7 appears in Slide view.

Insert New Slide

2   On the Formatting toolbar, click the Insert New Slide button.

The New Slide dialog box appears.

3   Click the Chart layout.

4   Click the OK button.

A blank new slide appears.

Chart

5   Click the title placeholder and type **Funds That Produce Returns**

The new title appears in the text object. Now use the chart placeholder below the title to insert a chart.

Insert a chart using a layout

Data is displayed in a datasheet and represented in a chart. The *datasheet* is composed of individual cells that form rows and columns, which in turn make up a group of related data points called a *data series*. The *chart* is a graphical representation of the information in the data series.

➤ Double-click the chart placeholder.

PowerPoint launches Microsoft Graph. The Graph Standard toolbar and menus replace the PowerPoint toolbars and menus. The datasheet and chart windows appear with default data that you replace with your own data.

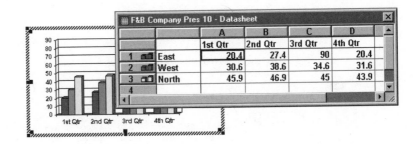

Viewing the Chart

To view the chart, move the datasheet window out of the way by dragging its title bar or clicking its Close button. The data entered in the datasheet is plotted on your chart.

Close the datasheet window

View Datasheet

➤ On the Graph Standard toolbar, click the View Datasheet button or click the datasheet window Close button.

The datasheet window closes and the chart appears in full view.

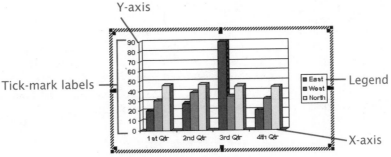

183

Notice that the chart is made up of different elements which help display the data from the datasheet. The chart shown above has an x-axis (horizontal axis) and a y-axis (vertical axis) which serve as reference lines for the plotted data. Along each axis there are labels, called *tick-mark labels*, that identify the data plotted in the chart. There is also a *legend* in the chart that identifies each data series in the datasheet.

Viewing the Datasheet

To view the datasheet, click the View Datasheet button on the Graph Standard toolbar. The data entered in the Graph datasheet is plotted on your Graph chart.

Open the datasheet window

View Datasheet

➤ On the Graph Standard toolbar, click the View Datasheet button. The datasheet window opens again.

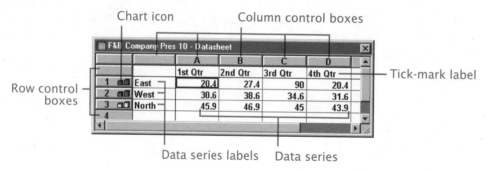

Along the left and top edges of the datasheet are gray boxes called control boxes. *Control boxes* correspond to the different data series in the datasheet. The chart icons on the control boxes indicate the current chart type. The first row and column of the datasheet contain names or labels for each data series. The data series labels appear in the chart.

Selecting Items in a Datasheet

In a datasheet, using the mouse or keyboard commands, you can select an individual cell, a range of cells, or an entire row or column to work with selected data. A selected cell, called an *active cell*, has a heavy border around it. When more than one cell is selected, the active cell is highlighted with a heavy border and all other selected cells are highlighted in black. To perform most tasks on the datasheet, you must select a specific cell or range of cells.

Select a cell

➤ Position the pointer over any cell and click.

A cell is identified by its row and column location in the datasheet. For example, the number 38.6 in the datasheet above is located in cell B2.

Select a range

Select a range of cells by holding down the SHIFT key and clicking the first and last cells you want to select.

1 Click cell A1, the cell containing "20.4" in the datasheet.

2 Hold down the SHIFT key and click cell C3, the cell containing "45."

Active cell
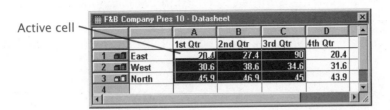

A range of cells, 3 x 3, is selected. If you select the wrong range, click any cell to deselect the cells and try again. You can also drag to select a range.

Select a row or column

Select a row or column by clicking the row or column control box.

1 Click the row 2 control box to the left of the data label "West."

The entire row is selected.

Click the row
control box here
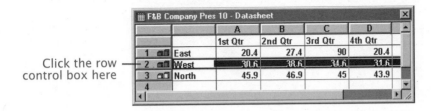

2 Click the column B control box above the data label "2nd Qtr."

The entire column is selected.

185

Select the entire datasheet

1   Click the upper left corner control box.

The entire datasheet is selected.

2   Click any cell to deselect the datasheet.

Exit Graph and embed a chart

To exit Graph, simply deselect the embedded Graph chart object.

1   Position the pointer in a blank area of the presentation window outside the Graph chart and click.

The PowerPoint toolbars and menus replace the Graph toolbar and menus, and the chart is embedded in the presentation slide.

2   Click a blank area of the slide to deselect the graph object.

Your presentation window should look like the following illustration:

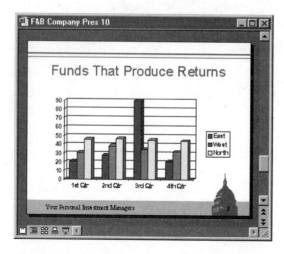

Edit the chart object

You can edit an embedded graph object by double-clicking the object. The embedded graph object opens in Microsoft Graph so you can make any changes you want.

➤   Double-click the chart object.

The Graph Standard toolbar and menu appear.

Importing Data

To enter data into the datasheet, you can do one of three things: type your own data into the datasheet, import information directly from Microsoft Excel, or copy and paste a specified range of data or a complete worksheet into Graph.

Import data from Microsoft Excel

You have mutual fund data in an Excel worksheet. Instead of retyping the information, import the data into the open datasheet.

1 Click the blank cell above the data label "East."

Graph imports the data starting at the currently selected cell.

Import File

2 On the Graph Standard toolbar, click the Import File button.

The Import File dialog box appears. (This dialog box functions just like the Open dialog box.)

3 In the File Name box, click 10 Funds Data.

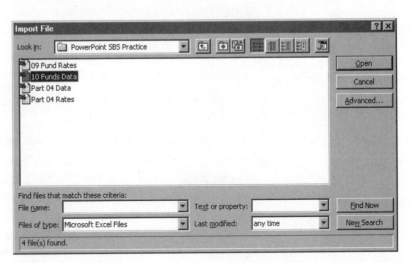

4 Click the Open button.

The Import Data Options dialog box appears. Sheet1 from the Excel file is selected by default for import into the Graph chart.

5 Click the OK button.

The existing data to the right and below the active cell is overwritten by the data from your Microsoft Excel worksheet. Once the datasheet is updated, the chart is automatically updated.

Scroll in the datasheet

After importing the data, you are unable to see all the data at once. Graph allows you to scroll through the datasheet window to view different areas of the datasheet. Use the scroll bars, found on the right and bottom edges of the datasheet window, to move around the datasheet. As you scroll through the datasheet, only the window view changes; an active cell or current selection is not affected by scrolling.

The following table explains how to scroll in a datasheet to view different cells:

To	Do this
Scroll a row or column at a time	Click a scroll arrow at either end of a scroll bar.
Scroll a window up or down, left or right	Click to either side of the scroll box.
Scroll to a location	Drag the scroll box to the location.

1 Click the scroll arrows to view sections of the datasheet.

2 Drag the scroll boxes to reposition the datasheet window back to the upper left corner of the datasheet.

Resize the datasheet

When you can't see all the data in the datasheet window, you can resize the window to see all the data in the datasheet.

1 Position the pointer over the bottom right corner of the datasheet window.

The cursor changes to the diagonal arrow.

Diagonal Arrow

2 Drag the lower right corner of the datasheet window to display column E and row 6.

3 Position the pointer (which changes to the width resize arrow) over the column border to the left of the column A control box and drag to the right until you can see all the text in the first column.

Width Resize Arrow

TIP You can double-click the column borders to automatically adjust the width of the datasheet columns to fit your data.

Your datasheet window should look like the following illustration:

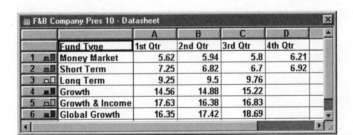

Entering and Editing Data

Now that you've imported the data into the datasheet, you can enter new data and edit existing data that will be used to plot data points on your chart. The chart is updated automatically after you enter the data.

Enter data in the datasheet

1   Click the empty cell D3.

2   Type **10.08** and press the ENTER key.

   Graph accepts your entry and moves the selection box down to cell D4. Graph updates the chart after you press the ENTER key.

3   Type **15.66** and press the UP ARROW key.

   Graph accepts your entry and moves the selection back up to cell D3.

Edit data in the datasheet

You can edit data in a cell two different ways: replace the data or change the data. To replace the data in a cell, select the cell and type new information. To change the data in a cell, double-click the cell, move the insertion point, and make the change. After entering data in cell D4, you realize that you entered the wrong number. Edit the cell to correct the error.

1   Double-click cell D4.

   The insertion point appears in the text.

2   Press the RIGHT ARROW key until the insertion point reaches the right side of the cell.

3   Press the BACKSPACE key, type **7** to change the entry from 15.66 to 15.67, and press ENTER.

   Graph accepts your new entry and moves the selection down to cell D5.

Your datasheet window should look like the following illustration:

		A	B	C	D	
	Fund Type	1st Qtr	2nd Qtr	3rd Qtr	4th Qtr	
1	Money Market	5.62	5.94	5.8	6.21	
2	Short Term	7.25	6.82	6.7	6.92	
3	Long Term	9.25	9.5	9.76	10.08	
4	Growth	14.56	14.88	15.22	15.67	
5	Growth & Income	17.63	16.38	16.83		
6	Global Growth	16.35	17.42	18.69		

F&B Company Pres 10 - Datasheet

Modifying a Data Series

In Graph, you can move and reposition information within the same datasheet to simplify editing tasks. You can drag and drop, or cut data from a datasheet and paste the information to its new location.

Move data within the datasheet

1 In cell D5, type **19.05**, and press ENTER.

The selection moves down to cell D6.

2 Click cell D5.

3 Position the cursor (which changes to the pointer) over the border of the selection rectangle in the cell.

4 Drag the number to cell D6.

The number moves from D5 to D6.

5 Click cell D5, type **16.77** and press ENTER.

Your datasheet window should look like the following illustration:

		A	B	C	D	
	Fund Type	1st Qtr	2nd Qtr	3rd Qtr	4th Qtr	
1	Money Market	5.62	5.94	5.8	6.21	
2	Short Term	7.25	6.82	6.7	6.92	
3	Long Term	9.25	9.5	9.76	10.08	
4	Growth	14.56	14.88	15.22	15.67	
5	Growth & Income	17.63	16.38	16.83	16.77	
6	Global Growth	16.35	17.42	18.69	19.05	

F&B Company Pres 10 - Datasheet

Formatting a Data Series

In Graph, you can change the format of a number to represent fractions, percentages, monetary currencies, scientific notations, or accounting figures. You can also change the format style and size.

Change the font size

Changing the font characteristics of one cell in your datasheet affects all of the datasheet cells but not the chart text.

1   On the Format menu, click Font.

The Font dialog box appears.

2   In the Size box, click 9.

3   Click the OK button.

The font for all the data in your datasheet changes to the 9 point size.

 TIP   You can also click the right mouse button to display a shortcut menu to access formatting and related commands.

Change a number format

To give your fund data more emphasis, change the format of the fund data from general to currency. Unlike font changes, to change the number format, you need to select the cells you want to change first.

1   Click the column A control box.

2   Hold down the SHIFT key and click the column D control box.

Column A through column D are selected.

Currency Style

3   On the Graph Formatting toolbar, click the Currency Style button.

The cell format changes from a general format to a currency format.

4   Click any cell in the datasheet.

Your datasheet window should look like the following illustration:

	Fund Type	A 1st Qtr	B 2nd Qtr	C 3rd Qtr	D 4th Qtr	
1	Money Market	$5.62	$5.94	$5.80	$6.21	
2	Short Term	$7.25	$6.82	$6.70	$6.92	
3	Long Term	$9.25	$9.50	$9.76	$10.08	
4	Growth	$14.56	$14.88	$15.22	$15.67	
5	Growth & Income	$17.63	$16.38	$16.83	$16.77	
6	Global Growth	$16.35	$17.42	$18.69	$19.05	
7						

F&B Company Pres 10 - Datasheet

191

Changing and Formatting a Chart

Graph comes with a Graph gallery that lets you change your chart type and then automatically format the chart to help you get the results you want. There are 14 chart categories, including two-dimensional charts and three-dimensional charts, for a total of 103 different formats.

Change the chart type

Currently the fund data appears in bar chart style type, but the chart might appear clearer in a combination chart style type.

View Datasheet

Chart Type

3-D Bar Chart

1 On the Graph Standard toolbar, click the View Datasheet button.

The datasheet window closes and the chart appears.

2 On the Graph Standard toolbar, click the Chart Type drop-down arrow.

The Chart Type menu appears, displaying seven two-dimensional and seven three-dimensional chart formats.

3 Click the 3-D Bar Chart (the second chart down in the center column).

The chart changes to the 3-D Bar Chart type.

TIP You can give your chart a dynamic look by changing the 3-D view. With Graph, you can control the elevation, rotation, position, and perspective for a 3-D chart using the 3-D View command on the Chart menu.

Change the chart format

To take the guesswork out of formatting your chart, you can choose from a gallery of predefined chart formats with the Chart Type command.

1 On the Chart menu, click Chart Type.

The Chart Type dialog box appears with standard and custom chart types and formats.

2 Click the Custom Types tab.

The Custom Types settings appear. Graph displays additional 3-D and 2-D chart types, such as cylinder, pyramid, and cone charts, to provide more options for better visual representation of data. New chart types, such as Bubbles, Blue Pie, and Cones allow you to add another dimension to your data.

3 In the Chart Type area, click Column-Line.

A preview sample of the Column-Line chart appears, as shown in the following illustration:

A preview of your Graph chart appears in the Chart Type dialog box.

4 Click the OK button.

Change the chart's appearance

You change the appearance of your chart by selecting different parts of the chart and choosing a command on the Format menu. On the chart, change the font size, gridlines, and data labels to improve its appearance.

Chart Object

1 Ensure the Chart Area is selected. On the Graph Standard toolbar, click the Chart Object drop-down arrow, and then click Chart Area.

2 On the Graph Formatting toolbar, click the Font Size drop-down arrow and click 18.

The x-axis and y-axis data labels and the legend font size change from 3 to 18 points.

3 On the Chart menu, click Chart Options, and then click the Gridlines tab.

The Chart Options dialog box appears with the Grindlines settings.

4 Click the Major Gridlines check box to turn off the gridlines.

5 Click the OK button.

The gridlines are taken off the chart.

*Decrease
Decimal*

*Angle Text
Upward*

6 Click the y-axis with the currency values.

Black handles appear at the end of the y-axis.

7 On the Graph Formatting toolbar, click the Decrease Decimal button twice to take off the decimal values.

8 Click the x-axis with the category values.

9 On the Graph Formatting toolbar, click the Angle Text Upward button.

The y-axis text angle changes to a 45 degree angle.

 TIP You can double-click almost any object in the chart window to edit its attributes. For example, you can double-click the y-axis to display the Format Axis dialog box.

Add fill effects to the chart

You can add fill effects to chart objects in the same way you do in PowerPoint.

1 Double-click the Growth & Income Series chart bar.

The Format Data Series dialog box appears.

2 Click the Fill Effects button.

The Fill Effects dialog box appears.

3 Click the Granite texture in the second row.

4 Click the OK button.

The Format Data Series dialog box appears.

5 Click the OK button.

Your Graph chart should look like the following illustration:

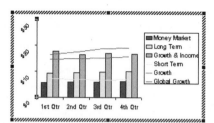

Change the chart plot area

Graph plots a chart by the rows and columns in the datasheet.

➤ On the Graph Standard toolbar, click the By Column button.

The data series changes.

Add a data table

You can add data tables to your charts to emphasize specific data.

1 On the Graph Standard toolbar, click the Data Table button.

The data table appears below the chart, as shown in the following illustration:

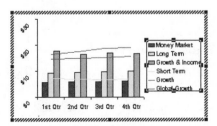

2 Double-click the chart data table.

The Format Data Table dialog box appears.

3 Click the Show Legend Keys check box to turn off the legend display.

4 Click the Font tab, and then click 16 in the Size box.

5 Click the OK button.

The data table legend is removed and the font size is reduced.

Modifying a Legend

Legends represent the data series in a graph using color or patterns. Each color or pattern corresponds to a specific data series name in the chart. Graph legends can be positioned automatically or manually. You can also change the colors, font styles, and patterns of a legend just like you do for PowerPoint objects. The data series supplies the text for the legend.

Format a legend

1 Double-click the chart legend.

The Format Legend dialog box appears.

2 Click the Placement tab.

The Pattern settings appear.

3 In the Type area, click the Bottom option button.

4 Click the Patterns tab, and then click the Shadow check box.

5 Click the OK button.

The legend moves to the bottom of the chart area and appears with a shadow.

Adding Text

You can add text boxes to your chart to call out important information or emphasize data. In Graph, you can add a text box to your chart by simply typing. Graph knows when you type text that you want to create a text box. Graph text boxes are objects that you can move or modify just as you would any other PowerPoint object.

Add a text box

1 Type **Mutual Funds by Quarter**
2 Drag the text box with the selection cursor to the top inside edge of the y-axis.
3 Click a blank area of the chart to deselect the text box.

 TIP In Graph, you can add title text to the chart, x-axis, and y-axis by clicking Chart Options on the Chart menu, clicking the Titles tab, and entering title information.

Your Graph chart should look like the following illustration:

Exit Graph

➤ Click a blank area of the presentation window to exit Graph.

The PowerPoint toolbars and menu appear.

Save the presentation

Save

➤ On the Standard toolbar, click the Save button.

No dialog box appears because the presentation already has a name. The current information in your presentation is saved with the same name.

One Step Further

You have learned to select, edit and move data in a datasheet, import data from a Microsoft Excel worksheet, modify and format a data series, change and format a chart, and add text.

When you create a chart, sometimes you don't want to look at all the data from a datasheet in your chart. You can exclude data from your chart without deleting it from the datasheet by clicking the Exclude Row/Col command. When you want to include the data again, click the Include Row/Col command.

Exclude data from a chart

View Datasheet

1 Double-click the graph object, if necessary.

2 On the Graph Standard toolbar, click the View Datasheet button.

3 Drag the datasheet window to the upper right corner of the presentation window to view the chart.

4 Click the row 2 control box.

5 On the Data menu, click Exclude Row/Col.

The row turns gray in the datasheet and the data series is excluded from the chart.

6 Double-click the row 2 control box to include the row again.

7 Click a blank area of the presentation window to exit Microsoft Graph.

If you want to continue to the next lesson

1 On the File menu, click Close (CTRL+W).

2 If a dialog box appears asking whether you want to save the changes to your presentation, click the No button.

If you want to quit PowerPoint for now

1 On the File menu, click Exit (CTRL+Q).

2 If a dialog box appears asking whether you want to save the changes to your presentation, click the No button.

Lesson Summary

To	Do this	Button
Start Graph using a slide layout	Click the Layout button and click Chart Layout. Double-click the chart placeholder.	

To	Do this	Button
Select a cell	Click the cell.	
Select a row or column	Click the row or column control box.	
Import data	On the Graph Standard toolbar, click the Import File button.	
Enter or edit data	Click the cell, type the data, and press ENTER or TAB.	
Format data	Click the cell. On the Format menu, click Font or Number.	
Format a chart	On the Graph Standard toolbar, click the Chart Type drop-down arrow and click a chart type.	
Modify a legend	Double-click the legend or click the legend and click Selected Legend on the Format menu.	
Exit Graph	Deselect the graph object.	

For online information about	Use the Office Assistant to search for
Creating and editing a graph	**Insert Graph**, and then click Add A Chart To A Presentation
Editing Graph data	**Datasheet**, and then click Change Text And Data In A Chart
Formatting Graph data	**Format chart**, and then click Change Colors, Patterns, Lines, Fills, And Borders In Charts

To use the Office Assistant, see Appendix A, in the back of this book.

Preview of the Next Lesson

In the next lesson, you'll learn how to produce and navigate through an on-screen presentation by adding slide transitions, animating slide text and objects. You'll also learn how to draw freehand in a slide show, hide a slide during a slide show, and create a custom slide show.

Review & Practice

In the lessons in Part 4, you learned skills to insert and modify clip art, a table, a chart, a picture, a graph, and an organization chart. If you want to practice these skills and test your understanding before you proceed with the lessons in Part 5, you can work through the Review & Practice section following this lesson.

Review & Practice

You will review and practice how to:

Estimated time
40 min.

- Insert clip art.
- Recolor and crop a picture.
- Insert a Microsoft Word table.
- Insert a Microsoft Excel chart.
- Insert a Graph chart.
- Create an organization chart.
- Insert WordArt.

Practice the skills you learned in the Part 4 lessons by working through this Review & Practice section. You'll use PowerPoint to insert and modify objects in a presentation.

Scenario

As the account manager at Ferguson & Bardell, continue to work on the investment presentation you worked on in the previous Review & Practice by inserting clip art, a table, a chart, a Graph chart, an organization chart, and WordArt.

In this section, you'll open a presentation, insert clip art using the AutoClipArt command, insert a blank Microsoft Word table and enter text, insert a Microsoft Excel chart, insert and crop a picture, insert and modify a graph using imported data, create and edit an organization chart, and insert WordArt.

199

Step 1: *Insert clip art and modify the picture*

Now that you have finalized your presentation template and color scheme, insert a clip art image with PowerPoint's help using AutoClipArt.

1 From the PowerPoint SBS Practice folder, open the presentation called Part 04 Review.

2 Save the presentation with the name **R&P Investment Pres 04** in the PowerPoint SBS Practice folder.

3 Use AutoClipArt to insert a clip art image in slide 6 using the keyword "Guideline."

4 Insert the Progress Guideline Leadership clip art picture.

5 Recolor the Progress Guideline Leadership clip art to complement the color scheme.

6 Crop the image from left to right until three figures appear.

For more information on	See
Inserting clip art using AutoClipArt	Lesson 9
Recoloring and cropping a picture	Lesson 9

Step 2: *Insert a Microsoft Word table*

A table can help organize your text on a slide. Insert a table, enter text, and format the result.

1 Switch to slide 7 in Slide view.

2 Change the slide AutoLayout to Table.

3 Create a table, enter information, and format the table using AutoFormat with the List 4 style to match the following illustration:

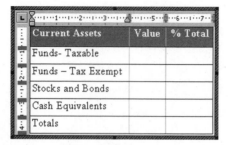

Current Assets	Value	% Total
Funds- Taxable		
Funds – Tax Exempt		
Stocks and Bonds		
Cash Equivalents		
Totals		

For more information on	See
Inserting a Microsoft Word table	Lesson 9

Step 3: *Insert a Microsoft Excel chart*

To take advantage of work you have already done in Microsoft Excel, insert a fund rate chart directly into PowerPoint.

1 Switch to slide 8 in Slide view.

2 Delete the bottom placeholder and insert the Microsoft Excel chart in the slide called Part 04 Rates from the PowerPoint SBS Practice folder. Use the Object command on the Insert menu, the Create From File option, and the Browse command to complete the action.

3 Edit the chart object, change to Chart2, and return to PowerPoint.

4 Resize the chart in PowerPoint to fit in the slide.

For more information on	See
Inserting a Microsoft Excel chart	Lesson 9

Step 4: *Insert a Graph chart*

Investment trends are important information to track for a financial company. Create a Graph chart using data from a Microsoft Excel worksheet and then format the chart.

1 Switch to slide 9 in Slide view.

2 Change the slide AutoLayout to Chart and then start Microsoft Graph.

3 Select the entire datasheet, delete all the contents, and click the upper corner cell.

4 Import the Microsoft Excel data called Part 04 Data into the datasheet.

5 Adjust the column widths to fit the data in the datasheet.

6 Format the datasheet numbers as currency.

7 Change the chart type to Column-Line.

8 Remove the decimal points from the x-axis tick labels.

9 Change the legend and axis font size to 18 point and move the legend to the bottom of the chart.

10 Add the chart text box with **Int'l Exchange Rate**

For more information on	See
Editing a graph	Lesson 10
Importing Microsoft Excel data	Lesson 10
Formatting a datasheet and chart	Lesson 10
Adding text	Lesson 10

Step 5: **_Insert an organization chart_**

Insert an organization chart to illustrate the investment selection process.

1 Switch to slide 11 in Slide view.

2 Change the slide AutoLayout to Organization Chart.

3 Create an organization chart to match the following illustration:

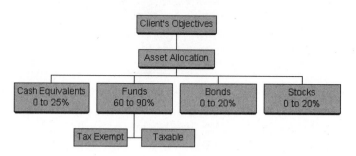

For more information on	See
Creating an organization chart	Lesson 9

Step 6: **_Insert WordArt_**

To complete the last slide in your presentation, insert a WordArt object.

1 Switch to slide 13 in Slide view.

2 Change the slide AutoLayout to Object, and stylize the text **Any Questions** with WordArt.

For more information on	See
Inserting WordArt	Lesson 9

If you want to continue to the next lesson

1 On the File menu, click Close (CTRL+W).

2 If a dialog box appears asking whether you want to save the changes to your presentation, click the Yes button.

If you want to quit PowerPoint for now

1 On the File menu, click Exit (CTRL+Q).

2 If a dialog box appears asking whether you want to save the changes to your presentation, click the Yes button.

Producing and Reviewing a Presentation

Producing a Slide Show

Estimated time
25 min.

In this lesson you will learn how to:

- Navigate in slide show.
- Draw freehand in a slide show.
- Set slide transitions.
- Animate slide text.
- Animate slide objects.
- Hide a slide during a slide show.
- Create and edit a custom show.

In PowerPoint you can display your presentations on your computer monitor using slide show. The Slide Show feature turns your computer into a projector that displays your presentation on your monitor's full screen or, using special hardware, on an overhead screen. A slide show can also operate continuously, unattended, to show a presentation.

As Director of Communications at Ferguson & Bardell, you have been working on a company presentation. With your slides in place, you are ready to set up your slide show for Ferguson, one of the partners, who plans to give the presentation at next month's stockholders' meeting.

In this lesson, you'll learn how to give a slide show, draw on a slide during a slide show, add slide transitions, add text and object slide animation, hide a slide from a slide show, and create and edit a custom slide show.

Start the lesson

Follow the steps below to open the practice file called 11 PPT Lesson, and then save it with the new name F&B Company Pres 11. If you haven't already started PowerPoint, do so now.

Open

1   On the Standard toolbar, click the Open button or click the Open An Existing Presentation option button on the Start-up dialog box and click OK.

2   In the Look In box, ensure that the PowerPoint SBS Practice folder is open. If it is not, select the hard drive and folder where the Step by Step practice files are stored.

For information about opening a presentation, see Lesson 3.

3   In the file list box, double-click the file named 11 PPT Lesson to open it.

4   On the File menu, click Save As.

The Save As dialog box opens. Be sure the PowerPoint SBS Practice folder appears in the Save In box.

5   In the File Name box, type **F&B Company Pres 11**

6   Click the Save button.

The presentation is saved and the title bar changes to the new name.

Navigating in Slide Show

In earlier lessons, you learned to click the mouse button to advance to the next slide in slide show. Besides clicking the mouse to advance to each slide, PowerPoint gives you several different ways to navigate through your slide show presentation. You can press keys on the keyboard or use commands on the Show Popup menu in Slide Show view to move from slide to slide. With the Slide Navigator, you can jump to slides out of sequence.

Navigate through your slide show presentation

Use the Slide Navigator on the Show Popup menu to navigate through your presentation in slide show.

Slide Show

1   Click the Slide Show button.

PowerPoint displays the first slide in the presentation.

2   Move the mouse to display the pointer.

Show Popup Menu

The Show Popup menu button appears in the lower left corner of the screen, as shown in the margin.

3   Click the Show Popup menu button.

The Show Popup menu appears, showing different slide show navigation controls.

4   On the Show Popup menu, click Next.

Slide 2 appears in Slide Show view. You can also press the N key to advance to the next slide.

5   Move the mouse pointer, click the Show Popup menu button, and then click Previous.

Slide 1 appears in Slide Show view. You can also press the P key to return to the previous slide. Besides clicking the Show Popup menu button to access the menu, you can also click the right mouse button to display the menu.

 TIP   You can press the RIGHT ARROW key or the PAGE DOWN key to advance to the next slide and you can press the LEFT ARROW key or the PAGE UP key to return to the previous slide.

---

6   Click the right mouse button, point to Go, and then click Slide Navigator.

The Slide Navigator dialog box appears, showing a list of slides in your presentation with the current slide selected.

7   In the list of slide names, click slide 9.

The Slide Navigator dialog box should look like the following illustration:

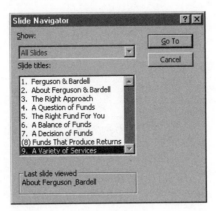

8   Click the Go To button.

Slide 9 appears in Slide Show view.

9   Click the mouse button to advance to the next slide.

Advancing to the next slide when you are viewing the last slide in your presentation exits slide show or displays a black slide depending on your slide show setting in the Options dialog box.

Slide 1 appears in Slide view.

Drawing Freehand in a Slide Show

During a slide show presentation, you can draw freehand lines, circles, and arrows to emphasize your message. You simply move the mouse to display the pointer, click the annotation icon, and then draw. When you finish drawing, you click the annotation icon again to continue the presentation.

Draw a freehand line

Try underlining your slide title during a slide show using the Pen tool.

Slide Show

1 Click the Slide Show button.

PowerPoint displays the current slide in the presentation.

2 Click the right mouse button and click Pen (CTRL+P).

The pointer changes to the pen cursor. Now you are ready to draw on the slide.

Pen Cursor

NOTE When the cursor changes from the pointer to the pen in Slide Show view, clicking the mouse button doesn't advance to the next slide. You need to change the pen cursor back to the pointer to advance using the mouse button.

3 Draw a line under the phrase "Your Personal Investment Managers."

Now erase the line.

4 Click the right mouse button, point to Screen, and then click Erase Pen.

The annotation erases so you can drawing something else. You can also press the E key to erase the annotation drawing.

Change the pen color

You can change the freehand drawing pen color at any time during the presentation by choosing a new color from the Show Popup menu.

1 Click the Show Popup menu button, point to Pointer Options, and then point to Pen Color.

The Pen Color menu appears, showing a selection of different colors.

2 On the Pen Color menu, click Magenta.

3 Draw a line under the phrase "Ferguson & Bardell."

4 Press the E key to erase the annotation drawing.

5 Click the right mouse button and click Arrow (CTRL+A).

The pen cursor changes back to the pointer. With the pointer, you can click the mouse button to advance to the next slide.

Exit Slide Show

You can exit slide show at any time by clicking the End Show command on the Show Popup menu or pressing the ESC key.

➤ Click the right mouse button and click End Show.

The current slide in slide show appears in Slide view.

Setting Slide Transitions

A slide transition is the visual effect given to a slide as it moves on and off the screen during a slide show. Slide transitions include such effects as Checkerboard Across, Cover Down, Cut, and Split Vertical Out; there are a total of 46 slide transition effects. You can set a transition for one slide or a group of slides by selecting the slides in Slide Sorter view and applying the transition.

Apply a slide transition effect

Slide Sorter View

1 Click the Slide Sorter View button.

2 On the Slide Sorter toolbar, click the Slide Transition Effects drop-down arrow, click the down scroll arrow several times, and click Dissolve.

PowerPoint places a transition symbol below the lower left corner of slide 1. This tells you a slide transition effect has been applied to this slide.

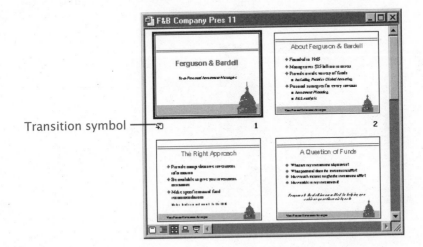

Transition symbol ─────

 TIP You can click the transition symbol below the slide to display the slide transition in the slide miniature.

Slide Show

3   Click the Slide Show button.

Slide Show displays slide 1 with the Dissolve transition effect.

4   Press the ESC key to stop the slide show.

Apply multiple transitions and change transition speed

The Slide Transition button on the toolbar is the fastest and easiest way to apply a slide transition effect. To apply other transition effects to a slide, you need to use the Slide Transition dialog box. Try applying a transition effect to the rest of the slides and then changing the transition speed.

1   On the Edit menu, click Select All (CTRL+A).

All the slides in the presentation appear selected. Deselect slide 1 since it already has a slide transition.

2   Hold down the SHIFT key and click slide 1 to deselect the slide.

3   On the Slide Sorter toolbar, click the Slide Transition button or on the Tools menu, click Slide Transition.

Slide Transition

The Slide Transition dialog box appears.

4   Click the Effect drop-down arrow, click the down scroll arrow, and then click Random Bars Horizontal.

The preview box demonstrates the transition effect.

5   Click the Medium option button to set the transition speed.

The Slide Transition dialog box should look like the following illustration:

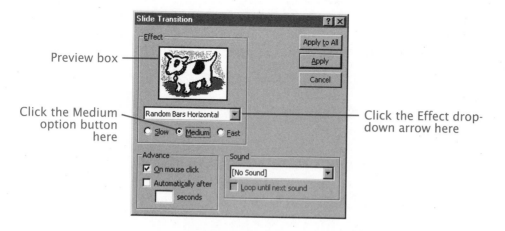

6   Click the Apply button.

The transition effect is applied to the selected slides. Notice that all the slides now have a transition symbol below their left corners.

Slide Show

7 Click the Slide Show button.

Slide Show displays slide 2 with the Random Bars Horizontal effect.

8 Click the mouse button several times to advance through the slides, watch the transition effect, and then press the ESC key to end the slide show.

PowerPoint returns you to Slide Sorter view with the last slide presented in slide show selected.

Animating Slide Text

In a slide show, you can have slide text appear one paragraph, word, or letter at a time on the screen. A slide with text that you set to appear incrementally (a paragraph at a time in slide show) is called a text animation slide. You can apply the Animation feature, which offers 30 different transition effects, in Slide Sorter view and in Slide view.

View the Animation Effects toolbar

With the Animation Effects toolbar, you can apply preset animation effects to your presentation slides.

➤ Right-click any toolbar, and click Animation Effects.

The Animation Effects toolbar appears below the Slide Sorter toolbar. The special effects toolbar contains seven predefined effects, such as Laser, Drive-In, Flying, Camera, Typewriter, Drop-In, and Flash Once, that you can use with your presentation objects.

Animate title slide text

You can animate slides with special effects using the Animation Effects toolbar.

Animate Title

1 Drag the vertical scroll bar scroll box to the top and then click slide 1.

2 On the Animation Effects toolbar, click the Animate Title button.

The Animate Title button applys the Drop-In animation effect to the title of the slide. The Drop-In animation effect is the default settings for the Animate Title button.

Camera

3 On the Animation Effects toolbar, click the Camera button.

The Animate Slide Text button on the Animation Effect toolbar is now pushed in. The Text Preset Animation list on the Slide Sorter toolbar changes to Box Out.

Slide Show

4 Click the Slide Show button.

The title slide appears with a Dissolve transition and then the title flies down from the top.

211

5   Click the mouse button.

The subtitle text animation appears.

6   Press the ESC key to end the slide show.

Animate text for multiple slides

Instead of changing text animation slide by slide, you can animate text for more than one slide by selecting multiple slides in Slide Sorter view and applying an animation effect. Besides the preset animations effects found on the Animation Effects toolbar, PowerPoint also provides animation effects in the Text Preset Animation list on the Slide Sorter toolbar.

1   Click slide 2, hold down the SHIFT key, and then click slide 3 and slide 4.

Slides 2, 3, and 4 are selected.

Text Preset Animation

2   On the Slide Sorter toolbar, click the Text Preset Animation drop-down arrow, and then click Fly From Left.

The Text Preset Animation list on the Slide Sorter toolbar changes to Fly From Left.

Slide Show

3   Click the Slide Show button.

Slide 2 appears with a Random Bars Horizontal transition and without the bulleted text.

4   Click the mouse button four times to display the animations.

The bulleted text flies across the screen from the left one at a time.

5   Press the ESC key to end the slide show.

6   Double-click slide 1.

Change text animation slide settings

Instead of animating the entire subtitle text all at once on the first slide, you can animate the text one word at a time. To change this setting, you need to open the Custom Animation dialog box.

Custom Animation

1   On the Animation Settings toolbar, click the Custom Animation button or on the Slide Show menu, click Custom Animation.

The Custom Animation dialog box appears with current animation settings and a preview of the current slide.

2   Click the Effects tab.

The Effects settings appear.

3   In the Animation Order box, click the text "2. Text."

The subtitle text object appears selected in the preview box.

The Custom Animation dialog box should look like the following illustration:

4 In the Introduce Text area, click the top drop-down arrow, and then click By Word.

The option sets the text to animate one word at a time.

5 Click the OK button.

Start the slide show to demonstrate the new animation effect.

6 Click the Slide Show button.

The animation effect displays automatically after the transition effect.

7 Click the mouse button to display the effect and then press the ESC key.

8 Click the Next Slide button to advance to slide 2.

Slide Show

Next Slide

Change text animation levels for a slide

You can determine what text indent levels you want to animate. For example, in slide 2 there are two levels of bulleted text. When the Grouped By 1st Level Paragraphs option is selected, 2nd level paragraph text animates along with the 1st level paragraph text. When the By 2nd Level Paragraph option is selected, the 1st and 2nd level paragraph text animates separately.

1 On the Animation Setting toolbar, click the Custom Animation button.

The Custom Animation dialog box appears with current animation settings and a preview of the current slide.

2 Click the Effects tab.

Custom Animation

213

3   In the Animation Order box, click the text "1. Text 2"

The bulleted text object appears selected in the preview box. In the Introduce Text area, the Grouped By 1st Level Paragraphs animation setting is turned on.

4   In the Introduce Text area, click the Group By drop-down arrow, and then click 2nd.

The option sets the text to animate 1st and 2nd level paragraph text separately.

5   Click the OK button.

Start the slide show to demonstrate the new animation effect.

Slide Show

6   Click the Slide Show button.

7   Click the mouse button seven times to display the animation effects.

The bulleted text flies across the screen from the left one at a time.

8   Press the ESC key to end the slide show.

Animating Slide Objects

In a slide show, you can also have slide objects transition one at a time on the screen just like you did with text. To animate objects on a slide, select the objects you want to animate in Slide view. For objects with text, you can either animate the text in the object or animate the text and object together.

Animate slide object text

When you animate an object and its text the object and text animate all at the same time by default. However, you can animate only the text in an object, while the object remains unaffected by turning off the Animate Attached Shape option button.

1   Drag the scroll box to slide 5.

Slide 5 appears in Slide view.

2   Drag to select the shapes and connectors at the bottom of the slide.

3   On the Animation Settings toolbar, click the Custom Animation button.

Custom Animation

The Custom Animation dialog box appears with all the objects selected in the preview box and in the Animation Order box.

4   In the Entry Animation And Sound area, click the top drop-down arrow, scroll down, and then click Peek From Bottom.

5   Click the Preview button.

The connector objects appear one at a time and then the multidocument objects appear one at a time.

6   Click the OK button.

NOTE If you print a presentation that contains slides with animation, the Print What option changes to Slides (with Animations) and Slides (without Animations). The Slides (with Animations) option prints each bullet point on a separate page. The Slides (without Animations) option prints the complete slide on one page.

Change the animation order

To customize object animation on a slide, you can change the order of appearance for text or shapes on the screen during a slide show.

Custom Animation

1 On the Animation Settings toolbar, click the Custom Animation button.

The Custom Animation dialog box appears.

2 In the Animation Order box, click "4. Curved connector 6"

The left connector appears selected in the preview box.

3 Click the Down Arrow button.

The left connector animation order changes from fourth to third.

For a demonstration of how to animate objects, double-click the Camcorder Files On The Internet shorcut on your Desktop or connect to the Internet address listed on p. xxiii.

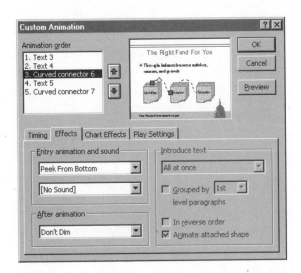

4 Click the Preview button.

The left and center objects appear and then the connector appears.

5 Click the OK button.

Now start slide show to see the order changes.

6 Click the Slide Show button.

7 Click the mouse button five times to display the animation effects.

Slide Show

8 Press the ESC key to end the slide show.

After completing the animation effects, close the Animation Effects toolbar.

9 Click the Close button on the Animation Effects toolbar.

Hiding a Slide During a Slide Show

You might want to customize an on-screen presentation for a specific audience. With PowerPoint, you can hide the slides you don't want to use during a slide show by using the Hide Slide command.

Hide a slide during a slide show

*Slide Sorter
View*

Hide Slide

1 Click the Slide Sorter View button.

2 Drag the scroll box down and click slide 8 to select it.

3 On the Slide Sorter toolbar, click the Hide Slide button.

A hide symbol appears over the slide number, as shown in the following illustration:

Hide symbol

4 Click slide 7 to select it.

5 Click the Slide Show button and then click the mouse button.

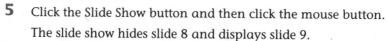

Slide Show

The slide show hides slide 8 and displays slide 9.

6 Press P to go back to slide 7.

7 Click the right mouse button, point to Go and click Hidden Slide or press the H key to show the hidden slide.

The hidden slide appears in Slide Show view.

8 Click the mouse button to complete the slide show.

Switch to Slide view so PowerPoint can save your presentation in Slide view instead of Slide Sorter view.

Slide View

9 Click the Slide View button.

Creating and Editing a Custom Show

With PowerPoint you can create a presentation within a presentation. Instead of creating multiple, nearly identical presentations for different audiences, you can group together and name the slides that differ and then jump to these slides during your presentation.

Create a custom show

1   On the Slide Show menu, click Custom Shows.

The Custom Shows dialog box appears.

2   Click the New button.

The Define Custom Show dialog box appears.

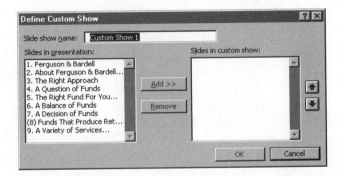

The default custom show name appears selected in the Slide Show Name box. To give the custom show a name, you can type a name.

3   In the Slide Show Name box, type **F&B Custom Show 11**

4   In the Slides In Presentation box, click Slide 1, and then click the Add button.

Slide 1 appears in the Slides In Custom Show box to the right.

5   Select and add slides 2, 3, 4, 7, 8, and 9 to the custom slide show to match to the following illustration:

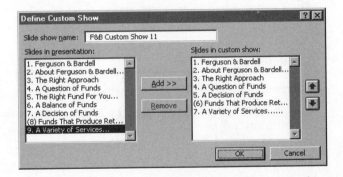

6 Click the OK button.

The Custom Show dialog box appears.

7 Click the Show button.

8 Click the mouse button to complete the slide show.

The Custom Show dialog box appears.

9 Click the Close button.

Edit a custom show

1 On the Slide Show menu, click Custom Shows.

The Custom Shows dialog box appears.

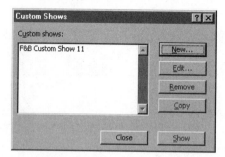

2 Click F&B Custom Show 11 and then click the Edit button.

The Define Custom Show dialog box appears.

3 In the Slides In Custom Show box, click Slide 8.

The Up Arrow button, Down Arrow button, and Remove button appear for use. To change the order of the selected slide, you click the Up Arrow button or the Down Arrow button. To remove the selected slide, you click the Remove button.

4 Click the Remove button.

Slide 8 is removed from the custom show.

5 Click the OK button.

The Custom Show dialog box appears.

6 Click the Close button.

Save the presentation

➤ On the Standard toolbar, click the Save button.

No dialog box appears because the presentation already has a name. The current information in your presentation is saved with the same name.

Save

One Step Further

You have learned to produce and present a slide show in PowerPoint using Slide Navigator, transitions, and text and object animations. You also learned to hide a slide and create and edit a custom slide show.

You practiced using several animation slide settings, including animating 1st level paragraph text, 2nd level paragraph text, and individual words. You can also dim out or hide animation text after displaying it.

Dim out animated text

PowerPoint dims out animation text by changing its color. For the company presentation, set your animation text so that each animated text paragraph dims out once you've shown it.

Custom Animation

1   Ensure slide 9 appears in Slide view.

2   Click a word in the bulleted text to place the insertion point.

3   On the Animation Settings toolbar, click the Custom Animation button.

    The Custom Animation dialog box appears.

4   Click the No Effect drop-down arrow and click Fly From Left.

5   Click the After Animation drop-down arrow and click the dark gray color.

    After an animated text paragraph transition, the previous animated text is grayed out.

6   Click the OK button.

    Start slide show to demonstrate the animation effect.

Slide Show

7   Click the Slide Show button.

8   Click the mouse button five times to display the animation effect.

9   Press the ESC key to end the slide show.

If you want to continue to the next lesson

1   On the File menu, click Close (CTRL+W).

2   If a dialog box appears asking whether you want to save the changes to your presentation, click the Yes button.

If you want to quit PowerPoint for now

1   On the File menu, click Exit (CTRL+Q).

2   If a dialog box appears asking whether you want to save the changes to your presentation, click the Yes button.

Lesson Summary

To	Do this	Button
Run a slide show	Click the Slide Show button.	
Stop a slide show	Press the ESC key.	
Navigate in a slide show	Click the Slide Show button. Right-click the screen and click Next, Previous, or Go To.	
Draw freehand in a slide show	Click the Slide Show button. Right-click the screen, click Pen, and then draw. Right-click the screen and click Arrow to stop.	
Set slide transitions	Select the slides in Slide Sorter view. On the Slide Sorter toolbar, click the Slide Transition button.	
Apply text animations to slides	In Slide Sorter view, select one or more slides. On the Animation Effects toolbar, click the Custom Animation button.	
Apply object animations to slides	On the Animation Effects toolbar, click the Custom Animation button.	
Hide a slide	In Slide Sorter view, select one or more slides. On the Slide Sorter toolbar, click the Hide Slide button.	
Create a new custom slide show	On the Slide Show menu, click Custom Shows, and then click the New button.	

For online information about	Use the Office Assistant to search for
Freehand drawing	**Annotate**, and then click Write Or Draw (Annotate) On Slides During A Slide Show
Adding a slide transition	**Transition**, and then click Add Transitions To A Slide Show
Animating a slide	**Animate**, and then click Create Animated Slides

To use the Office Assistant, see Appendix A, in the back of this book.

Preview of the Next Lesson

In the next lesson, you'll learn to use the multimedia compact disc that comes with the PowerPoint package, insert sounds and movies, play sounds and movies, set and rehearse slide timings, and record a narration.

Creating a Multimedia Presentation

Estimated time
40 min.

In this lesson you will learn how to:

- Use the Microsoft Office multimedia files.
- Insert sounds and movies.
- Play sounds or movies in Slide Show.
- Set slide timings and rehearsed slide timings.
- Record narration in Slide Show.
- Creating a self-navigating presentation.

With PowerPoint you can transform a slide show into a self-running multimedia presentation by adding sounds and movies, creating links to other slides, and setting slide timings. You can have PowerPoint automatically play the sounds and movies or you can play them at your command.

As Director of Communications at Ferguson & Bardell, you have been working on a company presentation. After adding transitions and animations in the previous lesson, you decide to add sounds and movies, set slide timings, and rehearse the presentation for the stockholders' meeting.

In this lesson, you'll learn how to use the multimedia files that come with the CD-ROM version of Microsoft Office, insert a sound and a movie, adjust the play settings, add slide timings, rehearse slide timings, record narration, and set up a self-navigating presentation.

Start the lesson

Follow the steps below to open the practice file called 12 PPT Lesson, and then save it with the new name F&B Company Pres 12. If you haven't already started PowerPoint, do so now.

Open

1 On the Standard toolbar, click the Open button or click the Open An Existing Presentation option button on the Start-up dialog box and click OK.

2 In the Look In box, ensure that the PowerPoint SBS Practice folder is open. If it is not, select the hard drive and folder where the Step by Step practice files are stored.

For information about opening a presentation, see Lesson 3.

3 In the file list box, double-click the file named 12 PPT Lesson to open it.

4 On the File menu, click Save As.

The Save As dialog box opens. Be sure the PowerPoint SBS Practice folder appears in the Save In box.

5 In the File Name box, type **F&B Company Pres 12**

6 Click the Save button.

The presentation is saved and the title bar changes to the new name.

Using the Microsoft Office Multimedia Files

The Microsoft Office CD-ROM contains a Valupack folder with photographs, clip art, presentation templates, sample presentations, sounds, movie and animation clips, and an overview presentation of the Valupack folder. If you don't have a CD-ROM drive or Microsoft Office on CD-ROM, you can skip this section or you can read through it to learn the concepts.

Open a sample presentation on the CD-ROM

Try running the overview presentation on the CD to get some ideas of what you can do with the Valupack folder contents.

Open

1 Insert the Microsoft Office CD into your CD-ROM drive.

2 On the Standard toolbar, click the Open button.

The Open dialog box appears.

3 Click the Look In drop-down arrow and click your CD-ROM drive.

Typically, your CD-ROM drive is (D:). A list of file and folder names appears.

4 Scroll down and double-click the Valupack folder.

A list of Valupack folder names appear. The Overview presentation appears at the bottom of the list.

5   In the list of file and folder names, click Overview.

6   Click the Open button.

PowerPoint displays the presentation.

Slide Show

7   Click the Slide Show button and click the mouse button to advance through the presentation.

8   On the File menu, click Close.

The Overview presentation closes.

Inserting Sounds and Movies

With PowerPoint, you can play sounds and movies during your presentation. You can insert a sound or movie by clicking the Sound or Movie command on the Insert menu or double-clicking a media placeholder. PowerPoint inserts sounds and movies as objects, which you can change and edit. To play sounds, you'll need sound hardware installed on your computer.

Add a sound to a slide transition

You can insert sounds in a slide that plays during a slide show or you can insert a movie to play during a slide transition.

1   On the Slide Show menu, click Slide Transition.

The Slide Transition dialog box appears.

2   Click the Sound drop-down arrow, click the down scroll arrow, and then click Applause.

TIP   For an additional selection of sounds, you can click Other Sound from the Sound drop-down list. Office 97 comes with additional sounds on the Office 97 CD-ROM.

3 Click the Apply button.

The sound is applied to the first slide.

Slide Show

4 Click the Slide Show button.

The sound plays during the transtion of the first slide.

5 Press the ESC key.

Insert a sound

Now insert a sound in slide 9 of your company presentation to play during a slide show.

1 Drag the scroll bar to slide 9.

2 On the Insert menu, point to Movies And Sounds, and click Sound From Gallery.

The Microsoft Clip Gallery dialog box appears with the Sound tab. Sound icons appear from the Sounds And Videos category. The sound icons appear in alphabetical order.

SUSPENSE
3.6 secs

3 In the Sounds list box, scroll down and click SUSPENSE.

TIP If you are connected to the World Wide Web, you can click the Connect To Web For Additional Clips button in the Microsoft Clip Gallery dialog box to access more clip art, photos, sounds, and movies.

---

4 Click the Insert button.

A small sound icon appears on your slide. The sound icon appears small, but you can resize or scale it to a bigger size for better access.

5 Drag the sound icon to the lower left corner of the slide.

TIP You can add Custom Soundtracks to your presentation. Double-click the Setup icon in the Musictrk folder on the Office 97 CD-ROM to install the Custom Soundtracks add-in. In PowerPoint, click Custom Soundtracks on the Slide Show menu, and select the sound tracks you want to accompany your slides.

Play the sound

You can play the sound in Slide view or Slide Show view. To play the sound in Slide view, simply double-click the sound icon.

 Double-click the sound icon.

The sound plays.

Insert a movie

You can insert a movie by clicking one of the Movie commands on the Insert menu or double-clicking a media placeholder. You can insert a movie from the Microsoft Clip Gallery or from a file.

1   On the Insert menu, point to Movies And Sounds and then click Movie From Gallery.

The Microsoft Clip Gallery dialog box appears with the Videos tab.

2   In the list of files names, scroll down and click Money.

The money movie appears selected. To preview the movie, you can click the Play button.

3   Click the Play button.

The money movie plays in a separate window. The window closes after the movie finishes.

4   Click the Insert button.

The money movie appears, as shown in the margin.

5   Drag the money movie to the blank area on the right side of the slide.

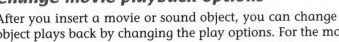

TIP   Office 97 comes with additional movies and animations in the Valupack folder on the Office 97 CD-ROM. To insert a movie from the Office 97 CD-ROM or another location on your hard disk, point to Movies And Sounds and then click Movie From File.

Play a movie

You can play a movie simply by double-clicking the movie object. To pause the movie, click the movie object again.

1   Double-click the movie object.

The movie object starts to play.

2   Position the mouse pointer (which changes to the hand pointer, shown in the margin) and click the movie object.

The movie object pauses.

Hand Pointer

3   Click the movie object again to play the rest of the movie.

Change movie playback options

After you insert a movie or sound object, you can change the way the media object plays back by changing the play options. For the money movie, set the movie object to play continuously until you stop it.

225

1   On the movie object, click the right mouse button, and then click Edit Movie Object.

The Play Options dialog box appears.

2   Click the Loop Until Stopped check box.

A check mark appears. Now when the money movie object plays, the media clip automatically repeats.

3   Click the OK button.

4   Double-click the movie object.

The money movie runs continuously. To stop the movie object from playing, right-click the movie object.

5   Right-click the movie object to stop the movie.

Mscam

Create a Movie with Microsoft Camcorder

If you installed Office from a CD-ROM, you can install and use Microsoft Camcorder to record actions, procedures, and sounds you perform on your computer. See Microsoft Camcorder Help for more information.

Install and start Microsoft Camcorder

■   Double-click the Office 97 Valupack folder on the CD-ROM, double-click the MSCam folder, and then double-click Camcordr.exe to install the program.

■   Click the Start button, point to Programs, and then click Microsoft Camcorder.

Playing Sound or Movies in Slide Show

To play a movie in Slide Show view, you need to set the play options in PowerPoint. Setting the play options tells PowerPoint to play the movie with the current playback options you set in the previous section in the Play Options dialog box.

Change the play settings

For the company presentation, change the play setting to show the movie in slide show.

1 Click the movie object, if it is not already selected.

2 On the Slide Show menu, click Custom Animation.

The Custom Animation dialog box appears with the Play Settings tab.

3 Click the Play Using Animation Order check box.

The media object appears in the Animation Order list. Since you have other animation objects on the slide, set the movie to play while the other objects move across the screen.

4 Click the Continue Slide Show option button.

Now you need to tell PowerPoint when to stop playing the movie.

5 Click the After Current Slide option button.

The Custom Animation dialog box should look like the following illustration:

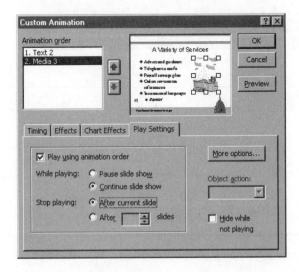

To be consistent with the other objects on the slide, set the movie object to animate on the slide during a slide show.

6   Click the Effects tab.

The Effects settings appear.

7   In the Entry Animation And Sound area, click the top drop-down arrow and then click Dissolve.

Change the animation order so the movie plays before the text animates.

8   In the Animation Order box, click "3. Media3" and then click the Up Arrow.

This setting sets the money movie to animate second during the slide show. The Custom Animation dialog box should look like the following illustration:

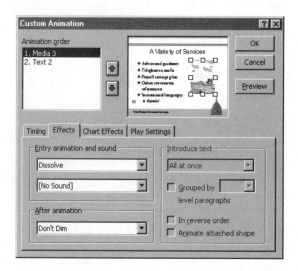

9   Click the OK button.

Change action settings to play in Slide Show view

Instead of clicking an object to perform an action, you can also change the action settings to perform an action by moving the mouse pointer over it.

1   Click the sound icon to select the object.

2   On the Slide Show menu, click Action Settings.

The Action Settings dialog box appears.

3   Click the Mouse Over tab.

The Mouse Over settings appear.

4   In the Action On Click area, click the Object Action option button.

The Play option appears in the drop-down list.

5 Click the OK button.

6 Click the Slide Show button.

Slide Show

7 Move the mouse over the sound icon to play the sound and click the mouse button to advance through the slide animations.

8 Press the ESC key twice to stop the movie and slide show.

Setting Slide Timings

Slide timing refers to the length of time a slide appears on the screen. As with transitions, you can set slide timings for one slide or a group of slides depending on how many slides are selected when you apply the slide timing.

Apply slide timings

Slide Sorter View

1 Click the Slide Sorter View button.

2 On the Slide Sorter toolbar, click the Slide Transition button, or click Slide Transition on the Tools menu.

The Slide Transition dialog box appears.

Slide Transition

3 In the Advance area, click the Automatically After X Seconds check box and then type **2**

There are two ways to advance your slide show, automatically or by mouse click.

- The mouse click timing feature manually moves your slides through the slide show.

- The automatic advance timing feature moves your slides through the slide show automatically, keeping each slide on the screen for the length of time designated in the Seconds box.

229

TIP In Slide Show, a mouse click always advances a slide, even if the timing set in the Slide Transition dialog box has not elapsed. Conversely, holding down the mouse button prevents a timed transition from occurring until you release the mouse button, even if the set timing has elapsed.

4 Click the Apply To All button.

The slide timing is applied to all the slides.

5 Scroll up and click Slide 1.

6 Click the Slide Show button.

Slide Show

PowerPoint runs through your slide show in the presentation window, using the slide timing you set using the Slide Transition dialog box.

NOTE Applying animations to multiple slides might affect how long you want the slide to stay on the screen during a slide show. Slide timings are divided equally among the animations for each slide, and you might need to adjust the slide timing to adequately show your animation points.

Setting Rehearsed Slide Timings

Since you are likely to want to spend more time on some slides than others, you can also set slide timings using the Rehearse Timings button. If you are unsure of how fast to set the slide timings of your presentation, you can rehearse your slide show and adjust your timings appropriately for each slide.

WARNING Before you begin this section, read all the steps carefully so you understand what happens when you click the Rehearse Timings button.

Rehearse Timings

1 On the Slide Sorter toolbar, click the Rehearse Timings button.

Slide Show begins and displays the Rehearsal dialog box in the lower right corner of the screen, as shown in the following illustration:

Close button

Forward button

The slide time begins running as soon as the first slide appears. As soon as you feel enough time has passed to adequately view or discuss the information on the slide, click your mouse button or the Forward button in the Rehearsal dialog box to move to the next slide or animation point. If you don't like the time, you can click the Repeat button and then rehearse the slide again. You can stop the slide rehearsal at any time by clicking the Rehearsal dialog box Close button.

2   Click the Forward button to select a new slide timing or press the O key to use the original timings for each slide in the presentation.

At the end of the slide rehearsal, a confirmation dialog box appears with the total time for the slide show.

3   Click the Yes button to save the new slide timings.

Your slides now display the new slide time settings.

4   Click the Yes button to review the slides in Slide Sorter view.

After setting rehearse timings, try displaying the slide show in a window.

Slide Show

5   Click the Slide Show button.

PowerPoint runs through your slide show in the presentation window, using the slide timings you set during the slide show rehearsal.

Recording a Narration in Slide Show

When creating a slide show for individuals who can't attend a presentation, or for archiving a meeting so presenters can review it later and hear comments made during the presentation, you can add voice narration or sound in a slide show. To record a narration, your computer needs a sound card and a microphone. You can record a narration before you run a slide show, or you can record it during the presentation and include audience comments.

Record a sound or comment on a single slide

If you don't have sound recording or playing hardware installed on your computer, the Record Sound command is grayed out. If so, skip this section.

1   Double-click slide 1.

2   On the Insert menu, point to Movies And Sounds, and click Record Sound.

The Record Sound dialog box appears.

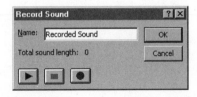

3 Select the text in the Name box and type **Slide 1 Welcome**

4 Click the Record button (red circle).

The Record Sound dialog box appears.

5 Say "Welcome to Ferguson and Bardell! Your Personal Investment Managers."

6 Click the Stop button (black square).

7 Click the Play button (black forward arrow).

8 Click the OK button.

A sound icon appears on the slide.

Delete voice narration from a slide

You can delete a voice narration like any other PowerPoint object.

1 Click the sound icon.

2 Press the DELETE key.

Record a voice narration through a presentation

If you don't have sound recording or playing hardware installed on your computer, the Record Narration command is grayed out. If so, skip this section.

For a demonstration of how to record a narration, double-click the Camcorder Files On The Internet shortcut on your Desktop or connect to the Internet address listed on p. xxiii.

1 On the Slide Show menu, click Record Narration.

The Record Narration dialog box appears showing the amount of free disk space and the number of minutes you can record.

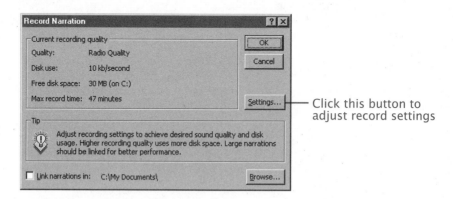

Click this button to adjust record settings

To insert the narration sound in your slides as an embedded object and to begin recording, click OK. To insert the narration as a linked object, click the Link Narrations In check box, and then click OK to begin recording. Embedding the narration adds the sound objects to the presentation, while linking stores the sound objects in separate files.

2   Click the OK button.

3   Advance through the slide show and add narration as you go.

    While you are recording you won't hear other sounds you inserted in the slide show. You can pause or stop voice narration during recording.

4   Right-click the screen, and then click Pause Narration.

    The voice narration pauses during the recording.

5   Right-click the screen, and then click Resume Recording.

    At the end of the slide show, a message appears to save the timings along with the narration.

6   Click the Yes button.

    A sound icon appears in the lower right corner of each slide that has narration.

NOTE To show a presentation with narration on a computer without sound hardware installed, click Set Up Show on the Slide Show menu and then click the Show Without Narration check box to avoid problems.

7   Click the No button to decline to review the slide timings in the Slide Sorter view.

Slide Show

8   Click the Slide Show button.

    The narration automatically plays with the slide show.

Creating a Self-Navigating Presentation

Self-running slide shows are a great way to communicate information without having to have someone available to run the show. You might want to set up a presentation to run unattended in a booth or kiosk at a trade show or convention. A self-navigating show turns off all navigation tools except Action buttons and other Action settings available to the user. To set up a self-navigating show, click Set Up Show on the Slide Show menu.

Set up a self-running slide show

1   On the Slide Show menu, click Set Up Show.

    The Set Up Show dialog box appears.

TIP You can also hold down the Shift key and click the Slide View button to display the Set Up Show dialog box.

233

2   Click the Browsed At A Kiosk (Full Screen) option button.

When you click this option, the Loop Continuously Until "Esc" check box turns on and grays out.

The narration automatically plays with the slide show.

Click this option button —

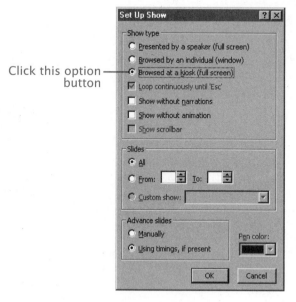

3   Click the OK button.

4   Click the Slide Show button.

Slide Show

Slide show runs through your presentation, using the slide time you set in the previous section. The transitions you set in the previous lesson are not changed.

5   Press the ESC key to stop the slide show.

TIP   You can save a presentation as a PowerPoint show to launch directly into slide show when activated, skipping the editing view. Open the presentation you want to save as a PowerPoint show, click the Save As command on the File menu, click the Save As Type drop-down arrow and click PowerPoint Show and click Save.

Save the presentation

Save

➤   On the Standard toolbar, click the Save button.

No dialog box appears because the presentation already has a name. The current information in your presentation is saved with the same name.

One Step Further

In this lesson you have learned how to use the multimedia CD files, add sound and movies, set slide timings, rehearse slide timings, record a narration, and create a self-navigating presentation. In Slide Show view, you can also use the slide meter to determine if your slide timings are too slow or too long.

Use the slide meter in Slide Show view

Slide Show

1   Click the Slide Show button.

   The slide show starts with slide 1.

2   Click the right mouse button, and then click Slide Meter.

   The Slide Meter dialog box appears, as shown in the following illustration:

As the slide show runs, the Slide Meter dialog box displays a visual meter for each slide to determine if the current slide time is too slow, too fast, or just right. If you want to make any slide timing changes you can reset slide times with the Slide Transition dialog box or the Rehearse Timings command. When the slide show completes, the Slide Meter dialog box closes.

If you want to continue to the next lesson

1   On the File menu, click Close (CTRL+W).

2   If a dialog box appears asking whether you want to save the changes to your presentation, click the No button.

If you want to quit PowerPoint for now

1   On the File menu, click Exit (CTRL+Q).

2   If a dialog box appears asking whether you want to save the changes to your presentation, click the No button.

Lesson Summary

To	Do this	Button
Insert a sound or movie	On the Insert menu, point to Movies And Sounds, and click a Sound or Movie command.	
Play sounds or movies	Double-click the sound or movie.	
Change movie playback options	Right-click the movie object, and then click Edit Movie Object.	
Play sounds or movies in slide show	Click the object. On the Slide Show menu, click Custom Animation. Click the Play Using Animation Order check box.	
Change action settings for sounds or movies	Select the object. On the Slide Show menu, click Action Settings. Click the Object Action option button.	
Set slide timings	Select the slides in Slide Sorter view. On the Slide Sorter toolbar, click the Slide Transition button. Set the slide timings.	
Rehearse slide timings	On the Slide Sorter toolbar, click the Rehearse Timings button.	
Record a narration	On the Slide Show menu, click Record Narration. Click OK and add narration.	
Create a self-navigating presentation	On the Slide Show menu, click Set Up Show. Click the Browsed At A Kiosk option button and click OK.	

For online information about	Use the Office Assistant to search for
Inserting a sound	**Sound**, and then click Insert Music Or Sound
Inserting a movie	**Movie**, and then click Insert A Video
Record a narration	**Sound**, and then click Record A Voice Narration Or Sound In A Slide

To use the Office Assistant, see Appendix A, in the back of this book.

Preview of the Next Lesson

In the next lesson, you'll create an agenda slide or home page; create a hyperlink to a slide, a file, and the Internet; create an action button; save a presentation for the Internet; and access the Internet from PowerPoint.

Creating an Internet Presentation

In this lesson you will learn how to:

Estimated time
25 min.

- Create an agenda slide or home page.
- Create a hyperlink to a slide and a file.
- Create a hyperlink to the Internet.
- Create an action button.
- Save a presentation for the Internet.
- Access the Internet from PowerPoint.

With PowerPoint, you can publish a presentation on the World Wide Web. PowerPoint comes with online templates that help you design your presentation for Internet viewing and with tools that help you create jumps, known as *hyperlinks*, to slides and files, save your presentation for the Internet, and access the Internet.

As Director of Communications at Ferguson & Bardell, you decide to create an Internet and Intranet presentation for the corporate web site and network site. After creating a basic presentation, you're ready to modify the presentation for use on the Internet.

In this lesson, you'll learn how to create a home page; create a hyperlink to a slide, a file and the Internet; create an action button; save a presentation for the Internet; and access the Internet from PowerPoint.

Start the lesson

Follow the steps below to open the practice file called 13 PPT Lesson, and then save it with the new name F&B Internet Pres 13. If you haven't already started PowerPoint, do so now.

Open

1 On the Standard toolbar, click the Open button or click the Open An Existing Presentation option button on the Start-up dialog box and click OK.

2 In the Look In box, ensure that the PowerPoint SBS Practice folder is open. If it is not, select the hard drive and folder where the Step by Step practice files are stored.

For information about opening a presentation, see Lesson 3.

3 In the file list box, double-click the file named 13 PPT Lesson to open it.

4 On the File menu, click Save As.

The Save As dialog box opens. Be sure the PowerPoint SBS Practice folder appears in the Save In box.

5 In the File Name box, type **F&B Internet Pres 13**

6 Click the Save button.

The presentation is saved and the title bar changes to the new name.

Creating an Internet Presentation

PowerPoint comes with online presentation and Web page banner templates that help you create and design your presentation for Internet viewing.

Using the AutoContent Wizard

■ In the PowerPoint Startup dialog box, click the AutoContent Wizard option button and then click the OK button.

■ After reading the introduction, click the Next button.

■ Select a presentation type and then click the Next button.

■ Click the Internet, Kiosk option button and then click the Next button.

■ Click any extra item check boxes for your Internet presentation.

■ Click the Next button and then click the Finish button.

Using an online presentation or Web page template

■ In the PowerPoint Startup dialog box, click the Template option button and then click the OK button.

■ Click the Presentations tab and click an online template, or click the Web Pages tab and click a sample banner template.

■ Click the OK button.

Creating an Agenda Slide or Home Page

Using the Summary Slide feature, you can create a summary slide to use as an agenda slide or home page. With the agenda slide, you can jump to a related slide in your presentation and then return to the agenda slide when you're done.

Create a home page

Slide Sorter View

Summary Slide

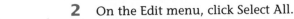

1 Click the Slide Sorter View button.

Slide 1 appears selected in Slide Sorter view. To create an agenda slide or home page, select the slides you want to include on the agenda or home page slide.

2 On the Edit menu, click Select All.

3 On the Slide Sorter toolbar, click the Summary Slide button.

A new slide with bulleted titles from the selected slides appears in front of the first selected slide.

4 Double-click Slide 1.

Slide 1 appears in Slide view.

5 Drag to select the title text "Summary Slide."

6 Type **Ferguson & Bardell** and press TAB.

7 On the Formatting toolbar, click the Font Size drop-down arrow and click 28 point.

8 On the Formatting toolbar, click the Italic button.

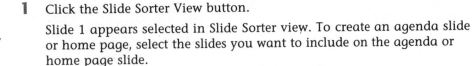

Italic

9 Type **Home Page** and then click in a blank area to deselect the object.

Your presentation window should look like the following illustration:

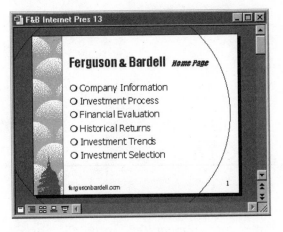

Creating a Hyperlink

The power of an Internet presentation is its ability to jump to different places in your presentation, on your computer, and over the World Wide Web. In PowerPoint, you can create a hyperlink that jumps to another slide, a different presentation, or a web site during a slide show. Using the Action Settings command, you can add a hyperlink to any text or object, including a shape, a table, a graph, or a picture, to hyperlink to another location when you click the object or hold the mouse over it to start its action. If you have text within a shape, you can set up separate hyperlinks for the shape and the text.

For a demonstration of how to create a hyperlink, double-click the Camcorder Files On The Internet shorcut on your Desktop or connect to the Internet address listed on p. xxiii.

Create a hyperlink to a slide

1 Drag to select the second item in the bulleted list, "Investment Process."

2 On the Slide Show menu, click Action Settings.

   The Action Settings dialog box appears with the Mouse Click tab.

3 In the Action On Click area, click the Hyperlink To option button.

   The Hyperlink To drop-down list becomes available.

4 In the Action On Click area, click the Hyperlink To drop-down arrow button.

   The Action Settings dialog box should look like the following illustration:

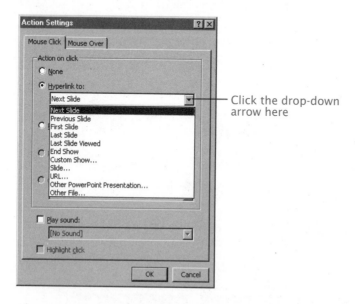

Within a PowerPoint presentation, you can create a hyperlink to slides, slide shows, other presentations, other files, and Web site addresses (called URLs).

5   Click Slide.

The Hyperlink To Slide dialog box appears. Now select a slide to link to.

6   In the Slide Title list, click "3. Investment Process," as shown in the following illustration:

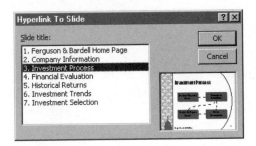

7   Click the OK button.

The Action Settings dialog box appears.

8   Click the OK button.

The hyperlink text appears underlined and in the color teal, which coordinates with the accent and hyperlink color in the color scheme.

9   Click the Slide Show button.

10   Move the mouse to display the pointer and then position the pointer (which changes to the hand pointer) over the text "Investment Process."

11   Click the underlined text.

The slide show branches to slide 3.

12   Press the ESC key to exit the slide show.

Slide Show

Creating a Hyperlink to a File

You can create a hyperlink to a file from another program or another PowerPoint presentation during a slide show. For example, you might jump to a Microsoft Excel chart to provide more detail on a topic. You can create a hyperlink from an object on a slide to a file. You can edit or change an object without losing the hyperlink. However, if you delete all of the text or the entire object, you'll lose the hyperlink.

Create a hyperlink to an Excel chart

1   With the selection cursor, click the rectangle object entitled "Review & Report Status."

2   On the Slide Show menu, click Action Settings.

The Action Settings dialog box appears with the Mouse Click tab.

3   Click the Hyperlink To option button.

241

4 Click the Hyperlink To drop-down arrow button and click Other File.

The Hyperlink To Other File dialog box appears.

5 In the Look In box, ensure that the PowerPoint SBS Practice folder is open. If it is not, select the hard drive and folder where the Step by Step practice files are stored. Typically, you'll find the PowerPoint SBS Practice folder in the My Documents folder.

6 In the list of file and folder names, click 13 Review Results.

7 Click the OK button.

The Action Settings dialog box appears.

8 Click the OK button.

9 Click the Slide Show button.

Slide Show

10 Move the mouse to display the pointer and then position the pointer (which changes to the hand pointer) over the object "Review & Report Status" and click the rectangle object (not the text).

Excel opens and displays a chart of investment returns.

11 On the File menu, click Exit.

Excel closes and returns you to Slide view.

Creating a Hyperlink to the Internet or Intranet

You can create a hyperlink to an address on the Internet (called a URL) or to a document on your company's Intranet. Hyperlinks to the Internet or Intranet give you easy access to the World Wide Web or to the company network to provide the latest information during a slide show presentation.

Create a hyperlink to a Web site

1 On the View menu, point to Master, and click Slide Master.

The Slide Master appears.

2 With the selection cursor, click the text box "fergusonbardell.com."

A dotted selection rectangle with white resize handles appears.

3 On the Standard toolbar, click the Insert Hyperlink button.

The Insert Hyperlink dialog box appears.

Insert Hyperlink

4 Click the Link To File Or URL drop-down arrow and click Http://.

Http:// appears in the text box. Http:// is a prefix indicating an address on the Internet. Now you're ready to type a web site address. A web site address consists of a network identification, such as www for World Wide Web, and an Internet address, such as perspection.com.

5   Type **www.fergusonbardell.com**

Your Insert Hyperlink dialog box should look like the following illustration:

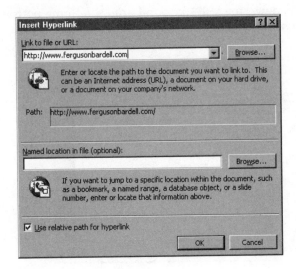

6   Click the OK button.

7   On the Master toolbar, click the Close button.

You'll access an Internet web site later in this lesson.

Creating an Action Button

PowerPoint comes with a set of predefined navigation buttons, such as Home, Help, Information, Back, Next, Beginning, End, and Return, known as Action buttons. *Action buttons* help you navigate to typical parts of a presentation or a file. You create an action button by clicking an Action button from the Action Buttons submenu on the Slide Show menu and dragging to create a button.

Create and link a home page button

1   On the View menu, point to Master, and click Slide Master.

The Slide Master appears.

2   On the Slide Show menu, point to Action Buttons.

The Action Buttons submenu appears.

Home

3 Click the Action Button: Home in the top row, shown in the margin.

The arrow cursor changes into the cross hairs cursor.

4 Position the cross hairs cursor in the upper left corner of the slide.

5 Hold down the SHIFT key and drag the Home button, as shown in the following illustration:

After you drag the Home button, the Action Settings dialog box appears with the Hyperlink To option button set to First Slide and the Highlighted Click check box selected. Before closing the dialog box, add a sound to the Home button when you click it, and then change the button fill color.

6 Click the Play Sound check box to select the option.

The Play Sound option activates the drop-down menu.

7 Click the Play Sound drop-down arrow, and then click Whoosh.

8 Click the OK button.

9 On the Drawing toolbar, click the Fill Color drop-down arrow, and then click No Fill.

Fill Color

10 On the Master toolbar, click the Close button.

Return to the first slide or home page

Slide Show

1 Click the Slide Show button.

The slide entitled "Investment Process" appears.

2 Click the Home button.

Notice that the Home button animates when you click it. The slide show returns to the first slide or home page.

3 Press the ESC key to exit the slide show.

Saving a Presentation for the Internet

PowerPoint comes with an Internet Assistant that creates documents ready to publish to the World Wide Web from your presentations. PowerPoint runs the Internet Assistant when you click Save As HTML on the File menu. The Save As HTML Wizard helps you customize your presentation for the Internet and save your presentation in the Internet-ready HTML format. The Save As HTML Wizard leads you step by step through the Internet publishing process.

Start the Save As HTML Wizard

1 On the File menu, click Save As HTML.

The Save As HTML Wizard displays an introduction dialog box.

2 After reading the introduction, click the Next button.

Choose the layout selection

The Save As HTML Wizard prompts you to create a new layout or select an existing layout (previously saved Save As HMTL Wizard settings). The default appears with the New Layout option selected.

1 Click the Next button.

The Save As HTML Wizard now prompts you to select a page style, either Standard or Browser Frames. Framed layouts require the latest web browsers, which support HTML frames.

2 Click the Browser Frames option button.

The Save As HTML dialog box should look like the following illustration:

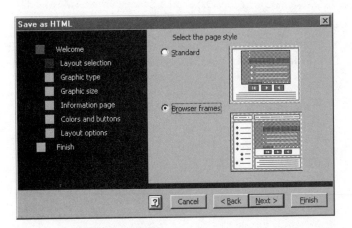

3 Click the Next button.

Choose the graphic type

The Save As HTML Wizard now prompts you to select the graphic type in which you want to save your presentation for the Internet.

Three graphic types are available.

GIF   Use this setting when converting a mostly text presentation you want people on every platform to view. This option strips out all special effects and converts your presentation slides into GIF images (lower file compression, but better screen resolution) linked to an HTML document.

JPEG   Use this setting when converting a graphical presentation you want people on every platform to view. This option strips out all special effects and converts your presentation slides into JPEG compressed images (better file compression, but lower screen resolution) linked to an HTML document.

PowerPoint Animation   Use this setting when converting a presentation to display full animation, transitions, and multimedia effects by the latest browsers with the *PowerPoint Animation Player* installed on your computer with Windows 95 or Windows NT.

 TIP   To install the PowerPoint Animation Player—a free Internet browser extension—on your computer, double-click the AXplayer file on the Office 97 CD-ROM or access Microsoft On The Web Product News. For access information, see the "One Step Further" at the end of this lesson.

1   Click the PowerPoint Animation option button.

2   Click the Next button.

Choose the graphic size

The Save As HTML Wizard now prompts you to select a monitor resolution to display your Internet document. To accomodate the most Internet users, select the smallest monitor resolution option.

1   Click the 640 By 480 option button.

Use the default setting for the Width Of Graphics Setting.

2   Click the Next button.

Enter HTML page information

The Save As HTML Wizard now prompts you to enter information to create a table of contents for your new HTML document.

1   Press TAB and then type **johnb@fergusonbardell.com**

2   Press TAB and then type **fergusonbardell.com**

The Save As HTML Wizard dialog box should look like the following illustration:

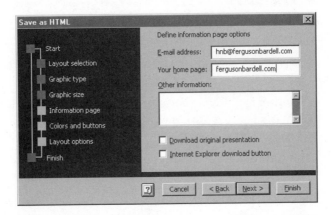

3 Click the Next button.

Choose the colors and buttons

The Save As HTML Wizard now prompts you to select a background, text and link colors, and a button look for the Internet document. To change any of the colors, click a custom color button.

1 Click the Custom Colors option button.
2 Click the Next button.
3 Click the upper right button style option button.
4 Click the Next button.

Choose the layout options

The Save As HTML Wizard now prompts you to select page layout and Internet file saving options.

1 Click the Include Slide Notes In Page check box to select the option.
2 Click the Next button.

Select a location to create an HTML directory to store the Internet files.

3 Click the Browse button.

The Browse dialog box apears.

4 In the Save In box, ensure that the My Documents folder is selected.
5 In the list of file and folder names, double-click the PowerPoint SBS Practice folder.
6 Click the Select button.

The path to the PowerPoint SBS Practice folder appears in the text box.

6   Click the Next button.

Finish the Save As HTML Wizard

If you want to make any changes to the information before the Save As HTML Wizard creates your presentation, you can click the Back button.

1   Click the Finish button.

The Save As HTML dialog box appears asking if you want to save your current HTML layout settings so you can use them later.

2   Click the Don't Save button.

An HTML Export In Progress dialog box appears, giving your status. The Internet-ready documents are saved in a folder named after the presentation filename. In this case, the documents are stored in the F&B Internet Pres 13 folder.

 TIP   You can save a presentation to an FTP site. FTP is a File Transfer Protocol that lets you transfer and save files over the Internet. To save a presentation to a FTP site, click Internet Locations (FTP) in the Save In box, double-click the site you want, and then double-click the location you want to save the presentation to. Type the presentation name and then click the Save button.

FrontPage

Importing an Animation into FrontPage 97

With Internet Web page creation programs like Microsoft FrontPage 97, you can integrate a PowerPoint animation into another Web page. See Microsoft FrontPage online help for more information.

Inserting a PowerPoint Animation into Microsoft FrontPage

- Click the Start button, point to Programs, and click Microsoft FrontPage.
- On the File menu, click Open and then double-click a FrontPage web document.
- On the File menu, click Import.
- Click the Add File button.
- Select a PowerPoint animation file (.ppz).
- Click the Import Now button.
- Integrate the PowerPoint animation into your web page.
- On the File menu, click Save.
- On the File menu, click Exit.

Accessing the Internet from PowerPoint

If you have access to the Internet or to an Intranet through your corporation network, you can browse through Internet presentations and other Office documents on the World Wide Web using the Web toolbar.

Open an Internet presentation

1   Right-click a toolbar, and click Web.

The Web toolbar appears. With the Web toolbar, you can access the Internet using common Microsoft Explorer commands.

2   On the Web toolbar, click the Go button.

The Go submenu appears.

Go

3   On the Go submenu, click Open.

The Open Internet Address dialog box appears.

4   Click the Browse button.

The Browse dialog box appears.

5   In the Look In box, ensure that the My Documents folder is selected.

6   In the list of file and folder names, double-click the PowerPoint SBS Practice folder, and then double-click the F&B Internet Pres 13 folder you created in the previous section.

7   In the list of folder and file names, click **Index**

8   Click the Open button.

The Open Internet Address dialog box appears.

9   Click the OK button.

   TIP   If you know the Internet or hard drive location you want to access, you can click the Address box on the Web toolbar and type in a Web site address, such as http://www.perspection.com, or file name.

Microsoft Explorer starts and displays the Internet page, as shown in the following illustration:

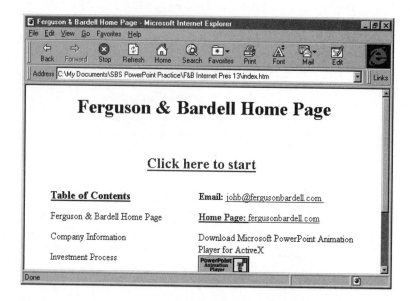

If you do not have the PowerPoint Animation Player installed on your computer, click the hyperlink "download" to install it.

10 Click the Internet hyperlink "Click here to start" to browse the Internet presentation.

11 Click different hyperlinks and buttons to explore the Internet page.

12 On the File menu, click Close.

Microsoft Explorer closes and returns you to PowerPoint.

Connecting to PowerPoint Central

If you have access to the Internet, you can connect to PowerPoint Central for the latest tools and techniques to help you create compelling presentations.

Access PowerPoint Central

1 On the Tools menu, click PowerPoint Central.

Microsoft Explorer starts and connects with the Microsoft home page at www.microsoft.com.

2 Click Yes if you are prompted to check for an update to PowerPoint Central.

3 Click hyperlinks to navigate through the presentation.

4   On the File menu, click End Show.

Microsoft Explorer closes and returns you to PowerPoint.

Save the presentation

Save

➤ On the Standard toolbar, click the Save button.

No dialog box appears because the presentation already has a name. The current information in your presentation is saved with the same name.

One Step Further

You have learned to create a home page; a hyperlink to a slide, a file, and the Internet; create an action button; save a presentation for the Internet; and access the Internet from PowerPoint.

If you have access to the Internet, you can get free stuff, product news, answers to frequently asked questions, and online support for your Microsoft products while working in any of your Microsoft Office programs by using the Microsoft On The Web commands found on the Help menu.

Access free stuff through Microsoft On The Web

1   On the Help menu, point to Microsoft On The Web, and click Free Stuff.

Microsoft Explorer starts and connects with the Microsoft home page at www.microsoft.com.

2   Click hyperlinks to navigate through the Web pages.

After reading the latest Microsoft product news, exit from Microsoft Explorer.

3   On the File menu, click Exit.

Microsoft Explorer closes and returns you to PowerPoint.

If you want to continue to the next lesson

1   On the File menu, click Close (CTRL+W).

2   If a dialog box appears asking whether you want to save the changes to your presentation, click the Yes button.

If you want to quit PowerPoint for now

1   On the File menu, click Exit (CTRL+Q).

2   If a dialog box appears asking whether you want to save the changes to your presentation, click the Yes button.

Lesson Summary

To	Do this	Button
Create an Internet presentation	In the Startup dialog box, click the AutoContent Wizard option button, and follow the instructions.	
Create an agenda slide or home page	Click the Slide Sorter View button. Select the slides you want included. Click the Summary Slide button on the Slide Sorter toolbar.	
Create a hyperlink	Select an object. Click Insert Hyperlink on the Standard toolbar and enter a path to a presentation, a file, or an Internet address (URL).	
Create an action button	On the Slide Show menu, point to Action Buttons, and then click a button. Drag the button, click the Hyperlink To option button, and then click an option.	
Save a presentation for the Internet	On the File menu, click Save As HTML and follow the Internet Assistant instructions.	
Open an Internet presentation	On the Web toolbar, click the Go button and click Open. Click a file.	Go ▼
Connect to PowerPoint Central	On the Tools menu, click PowerPoint Central.	

To use the Office Assistant, see Appendix A, in the back of this book.

For online information about	Use the Office Assistant to search for
Creating an Internet presentation	**Internet**, and then click Presentations On The Internet
Saving a presentation for the Internet	**Save**, and then click Save A Presentation In HTML Format

Preview of the Next Lesson

In the next lesson, you'll review a presentation, send a presentation using electronic mail, use the Presentation Conference Wizard, present the presentation on another computer, take meeting notes during a slide show, use the Pack And Go Wizard, and use the PowerPoint Viewer.

14

Reviewing and Sharing a Presentation

Estimated time
45 min.

In this lesson you will learn how to:

- Review a presentation.
- Send a presentation using electronic mail.
- Use the Presentation Conference Wizard.
- Take notes during a slide show.
- Use the Pack And Go Wizard.
- Use the Microsoft PowerPoint Viewer.

PowerPoint gives you the flexibility to insert comments into your presentation and send your presentation to another person's computer using electronic mail. If your computer is on a network or you have access to the Internet, you can give a slide show presentation on any other computer on the network using PowerPoint's Presentation Conference Wizard. During the slide show, you can also type notes so you don't forget them.

As Director of Communications at Ferguson & Bardell, you have been working on a company presentation. After completing the company presentation, you're ready to send the presentation out for review, and review the slide show over the network with David Ferguson before you pack the presentation for the stockholders' meeting.

In this lesson, you'll learn how to review a presentation, send a presentation using electronic mail, use the Presentation Conference Wizard, run a slide show on a remote computer, take notes during a slide show, use the Pack And Go Wizard, and use the PowerPoint Viewer.

Start the lesson

Follow the steps below to open the practice file called 14 PPT Lesson, and then save it with the new name **F&B Company Pres 14**. If you haven't already started PowerPoint, do so now.

Open

1 On the Standard toolbar, click the Open button or click the Open An Existing Presentation option button on the Start-up dialog box and click OK.

2 In the Look In box, ensure that the PowerPoint SBS Practice folder is open. If it is not, select the hard drive and folder where the Step by Step practice files are stored.

For information about opening a presentation, see Lesson 3.

3 In the file list box, double-click the file named 14 PPT Lesson to open it.

4 On the File menu, click Save As.

The Save As dialog box opens. Be sure the PowerPoint SBS Practice folder appears in the Save In box.

5 In the File Name box, type **F&B Company Pres 14**

6 Click the Save button.

The presentation is saved and the title bar changes to the new name.

Reviewing a Presentation

When you review a presentation, you can insert your comments right on the slides. The comments appear in yellow comment boxes, and you can move, resize, and reformat the text and the comment boxes just as you can any other object. You can also route your presentation and have others add their comments.

Inserting a comment

For the company presentation, insert comments into your presentation for your boss as he reviews it.

1 Right-click a toolbar and click Reviewing.

The Reviewing toolbar appears.

Insert Comment

2 On the Reviewing toolbar, click the Insert Comment button.

A yellow comment text box appears with your name inserted. Since the comment text box appears small, increase the display size to type in a comment.

3 On the Standard toolbar, click the Zoom drop-down arrow and click 66%.

4   Type **David**, press the RETURN key, and type **Please review the presentation by Thursday.**

The text wraps in the comment text box.

5   Click outside the text box to deselect the comment.

Your presentation window should look like the following illustration:

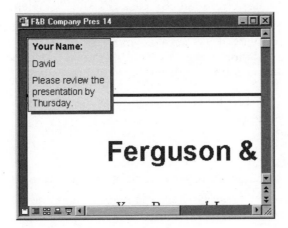

Hiding a comment

If comments in your presentation make it hard to see the slide material, you can hide the comments for viewing later.

Show/Hide Comments

1   On the Reviewing toolbar, click the Show/Hide Comments button.

The comment is hidden.

2   On the Standard toolbar, click the Zoom drop-down arrow and click Fit.

The comment text box appears with your name inserted.

3   Right-click a toolbar and click Reviewing to close the toolbar.

Sending a Presentation Using Electronic Mail

With the Send To commands on the File menu, you can send your presentations to other people using electronic mail, such as Microsoft Outlook or Microsoft Exchange, over a local network or the Internet. With Outlook or Exchange, you can send a presentation to just one person or you can use the Routing Recipient command to route it to any number of recipients.

To send and route presentations, the sender and the receiver must have PowerPoint and Exchange or another compatible mail package installed.

Send a presentation

When you send a presentation directly to another person, the file is saved as an attachment to a mail message. This section assumes you are using Microsoft Outlook or Microsoft Exchange. Now, send the company presentation to your boss for review before the stockholders' meeting.

Mail Recipient

1 On the Reviewing toolbar, click the Mail Recipient button.

The Microsoft Exchange dialog box appears so that you can identify the person who is to receive your presentation. The first time you send a presentation, the Choose Profile dialog box appears. Click the OK button to continue with the Exchange or Outlook Settings.

2 Click the To... button and complete the address information.

The Address Book dialog box appears. Type a name or select one from your list.

3 Click the OK button.

Send

4 On the Standard toolbar, click the Send button.

Microsoft Exchange sends the presentation and returns you to PowerPoint.

Route a presentation

You can send one or more copies of the same presentation to a group for an important review before you give the presentation by using the Routing Recipient command.

1 On the File menu, point to Sent To, and then click Routing Recipient.

The Routing Recipient dialog box appears.

2 Click the Address button.

The Address dialog box appears.

3 Click the recipient names and then click the Add button.

4 Click the OK button.

5 In the Subject and Message text boxes, type the subject and any message you want to send with the presentation.

6 In the Route To Recipients area, click the All At Once option button.

This option routes a copy of the presentation to all recipients at the same time.

7 Click the Route button.

8 Click the Yes button to confirm that you want to route the presentation.

The mail messages are sent.

Outlook

Create a Microsoft Outlook Task

You can send one or more copies of the same presentation to a group for an important review before you give the presentation by using the Routing Slip command. Skip this task if you do not have Microsoft Outlook installed.

Create Microsoft Outlook Task

1 On the Reviewing toolbar, click the Create Microsoft Outlook Task button.

Microsoft Outlook starts and displays a new task with the company presentation attached at the bottom.

2 In the Subject box, type **Review Company Presentation**

3 Click the Due drop-down arrow and click a date.

Outlook task sets the due date.

4 Click the Status drop-down arrow and click In Progress.

Outlook task sets the task status to In Progress.

🖫 Save and Close

Save And Close

5 On the Standard toolbar, click the Save And Close button.

Microsoft Outlook closes and returns to PowerPoint.

Using the Presentation Conference Wizard

For a demonstration of how to run a presentation conference, double-click the Camcorder Files On The Internet shorcut on your Desktop or connect to the Internet address listed on p. xxiii.

The Presentation Conference Wizard helps you give or view a slide show over a computer network, or on the Internet. As the presenter, you can view speakers' notes, take meeting minutes, preview slides, and control the presentation slide sequence. As a member of the slide show conference audience, you are able to watch the slide show on your computer screen just as you would a slide show of your own. To use the Presentation Conference Wizard, you must be connected to a TCP/IP network or an Internet Service Provider. If your network is not compatible, the Presentation Conference command on the Tools menu is not available.

Start a presentation conference as the audience

To participate in a presentation conference as the audience, you need to acknowledge your participation using the Presentation Conference Wizard before the presenter starts the presentation conference slide show. For the company presentation, have David Ferguson participate in a presentation conference as the audience to review the presentation.

1 On the Tools menu, click Presentation Conference.

The Presentation Conference Wizard displays an introduction dialog box.

2 After reading the introduction, click the Next button.

The Presentation Conference Wizard prompts you to select your participation in the conference as the presenter or the audience.

3 Click the Audience option button.

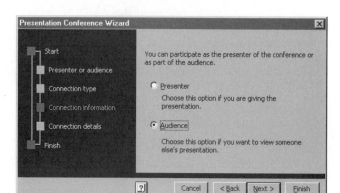

4 Click the Next button.

The Presentation Conference Wizard prompts you to select the type of connection you will use to connect to the presenter. The Local Area Network (LAN) or Corporate Network appears by default.

5 Click the Next button.

The Presentation Conference displays connection information.

6 Click the Next button.

The Presentation Conference Wizard displays a Finish dialog box, indicating you're ready to participate in the presentation conference.

7 Click the Finish button.

The Presentation Conference Wizard now prepares for the connection with the presenter's computer over the network. After the presenter connects to the network and starts the conference slide show, the presenter's slide presentation fills your computer screen and the slide show begins.

Start a presentation conference as the presenter

The Presentation Conference Wizard leads you through the connection and delivery of a slide show over a network as the presenter in an easy step-by-step process.

1 On the Tools menu, click Presentation Conference.

The Presentation Conference Wizard displays an introduction dialog box. Read the instructions carefully before you continue.

2 Click the Next button.

The Presenter option appears by default.

3 Click the Next button.

The Presentation Conference displays slide show details.

4   Click the Next button.

The Presentation Conference displays connection information. If any connections use the Internet, connect to your Internet Service Provider with a modem at this time.

5   Click the Next button.

The Presentation Conference Wizard asks you the name of the computer or Internet address to which you would like to connect. To find the name of a computer, click the Identification tab in the Network dialog box located in the Control Panel.

6   In the text box, type a computer name on *your* network.

For this company presentation, you might type **Ferguson** as the computer name.

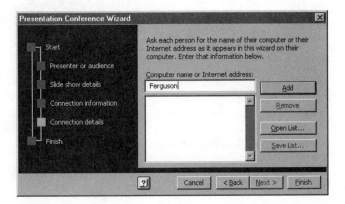

If you are connecting to the Internet, type the Internet address of the computer you want to connect, such as http://www.perpsection.com in the text box.

7   Click the Add button.

The computer name you typed in the previous step appears in the connection list.

8   Click the Next button.

The Finish dialog box appears. If you want to make any changes to your settings before the Presentation Conference Wizard establishes the connection with the other computers, you can click the Back button.

9   Click the Finish button (after all audience members finished setup.)

Once the connections are established, Slide Show In A Window and Stage Manager appear along with the Meeting Minder and Slide Navigator tools you selected in the Presentation Conference Wizard.

Slide Show In A Window allows you to see what your audience sees. The Stage Manager dialog box allows you to control the slide show. With the Meeting Minder dialog box you can view your speaker notes and enter meeting notes during a slide show. With the Slide Navigator dialog box you can branch to a different slide in your presentation.

10   On the Meeting Minder, click the Notes Pages tab.

Your presentation window should look like the following illustration:

Give a slide show on the remote computer

The Presentation Conference Wizard displays the Slide Show In A Window, the Stage Manager, the Meeting Minder, and the Slide Navigator for you to control your on-screen presentation.

Next Slide

Draw

1   On the Stage Manager, click the Next Slide button until slide 3 with full animated text appears.

2   On the Stage Manager, click the Draw button.

The pointer changes to a pen.

3   Draw a line under the phrase "Mutual funds are not insured by the FDIC."

A line appears under the phrase.

4   On the Slide Navigator, double-click "6. A Balance of Funds."

The slide show branches to slide 6.

Continue in the next section by taking notes during the presentation conference slide show.

Taking Notes During a Slide Show

With PowerPoint's Meeting Minder feature, you can view the contents of your speaker's notes pages, take meetings minute, and enter action items during a slide show presentation. You can use the Meeting Minder tool to take notes while you give a conference presentation without the audience noticing. As the presenter of a presentation conference, the Meeting Minder dialog box opens on your computer only. You can also access the Meeting Minder command on the Tools menu or on the Popup menu in Slide Show view.

Enter notes and action items in the Meeting Minder

During a presentation conference slide show, the Meeting Minder dialog box appears, displaying two tabs: Meeting Minutes and Action Items. The Meeting Minutes tab displays a blank text box for you to enter text. The Action Items tab displays a description field and an assigned to field for you to fill in. Now, continue the presentation conference from the previous section and enter notes and action items.

Next Slide

1   On the Stage Manager, click the Next Slide button until slide 9 appears.

2   Click the Meeting Minutes tab.

A text box appears. Now, place the insertion point and type your notes.

3   Click the text box and type the following text:

Growth and global funds met year end projections of a 10% return, while money market and long term funds fell behind by 15%.

4   Click the Action Items tab.

5   In the Description box, type **Verify year end results**

6   Press TAB and type **Ron Hojo**

7   Click the Add button.

The Meeting Minder dialog box should look like the following illustration:

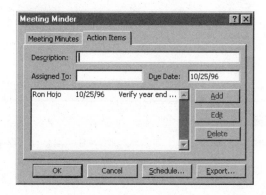

261

Outlook

The action item is posted in the Meeting Minder. At this point, you can click the Export button to set options to send meeting minutes and action items to Microsoft Word or post action items to Microsoft Outlook.

8 Click to advance through the rest of the slide show presentation.

9 Click the End Show button to finish the presentation conference.

Using the Pack And Go Wizard

If you need to take your presentation on the road, you can use the Pack and Go Wizard to help you compress and save your presentation to a diskette or a hard drive so you can easily transport it to another computer.

Start the Pack And Go Wizard

The Pack and Go Wizard leads you through the packaging in an easy step-by-step process.

1 On the File menu, click Pack And Go.

The Pack And Go Wizard displays an introduction dialog box.

2 After reading the introduction, click the Next button.

The Pack And Go Wizard asks you which presentation you would like to package. The current presentation appears selected by default, though you can select any presentation.

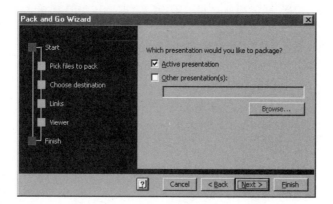

3 Click the Next button.

The Pack And Go Wizard asks you which drive you would like to place the disk in. Drive A appears by default.

4 Insert a blank disk into drive A or B of your computer.

5 If you inserted a blank disk into drive B, click the Drive B option button.

You can also click the Choose Destination option button to select a specific location on your local hard drive or on a network drive to place your file.

6   Click the Next button.

With the Pack And Go Wizard, you can include linked files and fonts used in the presentation that the remote computer might not have access to. The Pack And Go Wizard includes linked files by default.

7   Click the Embed TrueType Fonts check box.

When the Embed TrueType Fonts option is checked, the wizard stores TrueType fonts in your presentation. Then when you open or show your presentation on another computer that doesn't have these TrueType fonts, your presentation displays fine. If you are using special fonts in your presentation, not installed by Windows 95, then it's important to check this option. Including embedded fonts in your presentation increases the file size.

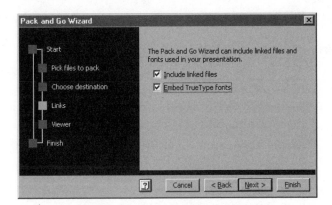

8   Click the Next button.

The Pack And Go Wizard asks you to include the PowerPoint Viewer. The PowerPoint Viewer is a separate application that allows you to show a slide show on a computer that does not have PowerPoint installed. The Pack And Go Wizard doesn't include the Viewer by default.

9   Click the Next button.

The Finish dialog box appears. If you want to make any changes before the Pack And Go Wizard finishes, click the Back button.

10   Click the Finish button.

The Pack And Go Wizard saves and compresses your presentation onto one or more blank disks. If you need more disks, the wizard prompts you to insert a disk.

11   Click the OK button to complete the Pack And Go Wizard.

You are now ready to take your presentation on the road.

Close the presentation file

Now, close your presentation and then view it with the Microsoft PowerPoint Viewer.

1   On the File menu, click Close.

2   If a dialog box appears asking whether you want to save the changes to your presentation, click the Yes button.

3   Click the Minimize button to minimize the PowerPoint application.

Using the PowerPoint Viewer

PowerPoint comes with a special application called the *PowerPoint Viewer* that allows you to show a slide show on a computer that does not have PowerPoint installed. You can freely install the PowerPoint Viewer program on any compatible system.

Showing presentations with the PowerPoint Viewer

Start

1   On the Windows taskbar, click the Start button.

2   Point to Programs and then click Windows Explorer.

The Windows Explorer window appears.

3   Double-click the Programs Files folder, double-click the Microsoft Office folder, and then double-click the Office folder.

A list of applications and files appears to the right.

4   Click the down scroll arrow to the bottom of the list.

If the PowerPoint Viewer is not available, then check your installation.

5   Double-click Pptview32.

The Microsoft PowerPoint Viewer dialog box appears.

6   In the Directories box, ensure that the PowerPoint SBS Practice folder is open. If it is not, click the drive where the Step by Step practice files are stored, and open the appropriate folders to find the PowerPoint SBS Practice folder.

7   In the File Name box, click the down scroll arrow, and then click F&B Company Pres 14.

8   Click the Show button.

PowerPoint shows F&B Company Pres 14.

9   Click the mouse button to advance through the presentation slides.

When the slide show ends, the Microsoft PowerPoint Viewer dialog box reappears on your screen.

10 Click the Exit button to exit the PowerPoint Viewer.

Restore PowerPoint

➤ On the taskbar, click the Microsoft PowerPoint button.

The PowerPoint window appears.

One Step Further

You have learned how to insert comments in a slide, send a presentation with Microsoft Exchange or Outlook, create a task in Microsoft Outlook, use the Presentation Conference Wizard, take meeting notes and action items during a slide show, use the Pack And Go Wizard, and use the PowerPoint Viewer.

Show a presentation on two screens

If you have a computer with two monitors or don't have the capabilities to run a presentation conference, you can view a slide show on one computer while you control it from another with the View On Two Screens command.

1   On the File menu, click F&B Company Pres 14 to open the file.

2   On the Slide Show menu, click View On Two Screens.

The View On Two Screens dialog box appears, showing the four step process to view a slide show on two screens.

3   Click the Presenter option button.

4   Click the Port drop-down arrow and click COM1 or COM2.

5   Plug in the cable to connect the two computers.

6   Open PowerPoint on the other computer and run the View On Two Screens feature and set it up as the audience.

7   Click the OK button.

During the slide show, you can right-click, and then use the same Stage Manager tools you use when you give a presentation conference.

8   Click the mouse button to advance through the presentation slides.

9   On the File menu, click Exit to exit PowerPoint and click No.

Lesson Summary

To	Do this	Button
Insert a comment	On the Reviewing toolbar, click the Insert Comment button, and type comment text.	
Hide a comment	On the Reviewing toolbar, click the Show/Hide Comment button.	

To	Do this	Button
Send a presentation	On the Reviewing toolbar, click the Mail Recipient button, fill out the the Outlook or Exchange window and click the Send button.	
Create a Microsoft Outlook task	On the Reviewing toolbar, click Create Microsoft Outlook Task button, fill out the Outlook window and click the Save And Close button.	
Set up a presentation conference	On the Tools menu, click Presentation Conference. Follow the wizard step-by-step instructions.	
Take notes during a slide show	On the Tools menu, click Meeting Minder. Click the Meeting Minutes tab or the Action Items tab and type your notes or action items.	
Save a presentation onto a disk	On the File menu, click Pack And Go. Follow the wizard instructions.	
Run the PowerPoint Viewer	Double-click the PowerPoint Viewer icon in the Windows Explorer. Select a presentation and click the Show button.	

For online information about	Use the Office Assistant to search for
Sending mail	**Send mail**, and click Distribute Presentations To Other People
Setting up a presentation conference	**Conference**, and then click About Running A Presentation Conference
Taking notes during a slide show	**Meeting**, and then click Record And Print Meeting Minutes And Action Items
Using the PowerPoint Viewer	**Viewer**, and then click The PowerPoint Viewer

To use the Office Assistant, see Appendix A, in the back of this book.

Review & Practice

In the lessons in Part 5, you learned skills to run a slide show, add transition effects, text and object animation effects, and multimedia effects, set slide timings, and run a slide show over a network. If you want to practice these skills and test your understanding, you can work through the Review & Practice section following this lesson.

Review & Practice

You will review and practice how to:

Estimated time
30 min.

- Insert sounds and movies.
- Hyperlink to a slide and another presentation.
- Animate slide text and objects.
- Set slide transitions and timings.
- Present the presentation on another computer.
- Take notes during a slide show.
- Use the Pack And Go Wizard.

Practice the skills you learned in the Part 5 lessons by working through this Review & Practice section. You'll use PowerPoint to create a multimedia presentation.

Scenario

As the account manager at Ferguson & Bardell, continue to work on the investment presentation you worked on in the previous review and practice by creating a self-running multimedia presentation, and then presenting it over the network. When you're done, prepare the presentation to take on the road.

In this section, you'll open a presentation, insert a sound and a movie from the Office CD-ROM, create a hyperlink to another presentation, animate slide text and objects, set slide transitions and timings, use the Presentation Conference Wizard, and use the Pack And Go Wizard.

Step 1: **_Insert a sound and a movie_**

1 From the PowerPoint SBS Practice folder, open the presentation called Part 05 Review.

2 Save the presentation with the name **R&P Investment Pres 05** in the PowerPoint SBS Practice folder.

3 In slide 1, insert the sound called Drumrol4 from the Clip Gallery.

4 Switch to slide 13.

5 Insert the movie called Arrowhit from the Clip Gallery.

For more information on	**See**
Inserting a sound and a movie	Lesson 12

Step 2: **_Create a hyperlink to a slide and another presentation_**

1 Switch to slide 4 in Slide view.

2 Select the object labeled "Formulate Guidelines."

3 Create a hyperlink to slide 6 using action settings.

4 Switch to slide 6 in Slide view.

5 Select the text "Click here for more information" and create a hyperlink to the presentation called Part 05 Pres, and then set action settings to play.

6 Run the slide show from slide 4, hyperlink to slide 6, and then hyperlink to the presentation.

For more information on	**See**
Hyperlinking to a slide and a presentation	Lesson 13

Step 3: **_Apply slide animations_**

1 Switch to slide 13 in Slide view.

2 Select the movie object.

3 Create object animations with the Dissolve effect, the Play Using Animation Order option, and the Continue Slide Show object option.

4 Switch to Slide Sorter view and select all the slides.

5 Create a text animation with the Split Vertical Out effect.

For more information on	**See**
Animating slide text and slide objects	Lesson 11

Step 4: *Hide a slide and create a custom slide show*

1 Hide slide 2.
2 Create a custom slide show with slides 1-5, 7-9, and 11 called R&P Custom Show 05.
3 Run the slide show.

For more information on	See
Hiding a slide	Lesson 11
Creating and editing a custom show	Lesson 11

Step 5: *Set slide transitions and rehearse timings*

1 Apply the Fade Through Black transition to all the slides.
2 Set rehearse slide timings.
3 Run the slide show.

For more information on	See
Setting slide transitions	Lesson 11
Setting rehearse slide timings	Lesson 12

Step 6: *Give a slide show on a remote computer*

1 Connect to a network computer using the Presentation Conference Wizard or View On Two Screens.
2 Start the slide show on the remote computer.
3 Pause the slide show at slide 4.
4 Click the "Formulate Guidelines" object to jump to slide 6.
5 Pause the slide show at slide 7.

For more information on	See
Using the Presentation Conference wizard	Lesson 14
Viewing a presentation on two screens	Lesson 14

Step 7:   *Do freehand drawing and take notes*

1   With a red pen, write sample values in the table.
2   Continue the slide show and pause at slide 9.
3   Type in the following meeting minutes.

The current investing trends show a steady increase over the next five years, but fears of a recession cause these investment numbers to be inaccurate.

4   Type in the following action item.

Have Ron Hojo in the Investing Group investigate these trends in terms of a possible recession.

5   Finish the slide show.

For more information on	See
Freehand drawing	Lesson 11
Taking notes in a slide show	Lesson 14

Step 8:   *Use the Pack And Go Wizard*

1   Compress the presentation to a disk using the Pack And Go Wizard.
2   Run the slide show using the Microsoft PowerPoint Viewer.

For more information on	See
Using the Pack And Go Wizard	Lesson 14
Using the Microsoft PowerPoint Viewer	Lesson 14

If you want to quit PowerPoint for now

1   On the File menu, click Exit (CTRL+Q).
2   If a dialog box appears asking whether you want to save the changes to your presentation, click the Yes button.

Appendixes

If You Are New to Windows or PowerPoint

If you are new to Microsoft Windows 95, Microsoft Windows NT 4.0, or PowerPoint, this appendix will prepare you for your first steps into using this book and finding information when you need it. You'll get an overview of Windows features, and you'll learn how to use online Help to learn more about your operating system. You'll also get an introduction to some terms and concepts that are important to understand as you learn PowerPoint.

If You Are New to Windows

Both Microsoft Windows 95 and Windows NT are easy-to-use work environments that help you handle the daily work that you perform with your computer. You can use either Windows 95 or Windows NT to run PowerPoint—the explanations in this appendix are valid for either operating system. Windows-based programs have a common look and functionality in the way they share data and in the way you use the programs. This makes it easy for you to learn and use different programs. In this section, you'll get an introduction to Windows. If you are already familiar with Windows 95 or Windows NT, you can skip to the section, "What Is Microsoft PowerPoint?"

Start Windows 95 or Windows NT

Starting Windows 95 or Windows NT is as easy as turning on your computer.

If you do not know your username or password, contact your system administrator for assistance.

1 If your computer isn't on, turn it on now.

2 If you are using Windows NT, press CTRL+ALT+DEL to display a dialog box asking for your username and password. If you are using Windows 95, you might see this dialog box, depending on your Windows setup. Type your username and password in the appropriate boxes, and then click OK.

Close

3 If you see the Welcome dialog box, click the Close button.

Your screen should look similar to the following illustration:

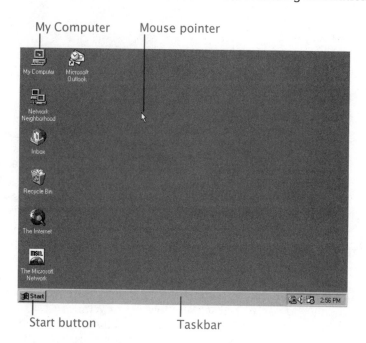

Using the Mouse

Although you can use the keyboard for most actions, many of these actions are easier to perform with a mouse.

The mouse controls a pointer on the screen, as shown in the previous illustration. You move the pointer by sliding the mouse over a flat surface in the direction you want the pointer to move. If you run out of room to move the mouse, lift it up and then put it down in a more comfortable location.

You will use five basic mouse actions throughout the lessons in this book.

NOTE For the purposes of the following table, the primary mouse button is the left button, and the secondary mouse button is the right button. These are the default button settings, though you can change this configuration for left-handed use.

When you are directed to	Do this
Point	Move the mouse to place the pointer on the item.
Click	Point to the item on your screen, and quickly press and release the primary mouse button.
Use the right mouse button to click (Right-click)	Point to the item on your screen, and then quickly press and release the secondary mouse button. Clicking the secondary mouse button displays a shortcut menu from which you can choose from a list of commands pertaining to your current action.
Double-click the	Point to the item, and then quickly press and release primary mouse button twice.
Drag	Point to the item, and then hold down the primary mouse button as you move the pointer.

Using Windows-Based Programs

All Windows-based programs share similar characteristics in how they appear on the screen and how you use them. All the windows in Windows-based programs have common controls that you use to scroll, size, move, and close a window.

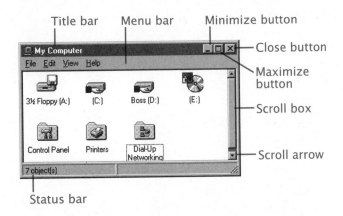

To	Do this	Button
Scroll through a window	Click a scroll bar or scroll arrow, or drag the scroll box. (The previous illustration identifies these controls.)	
Enlarge a window to fill the screen	Click the Maximize button, or double-click the title bar.	
Restore a window to its previous size	Click the Restore button, or double-click the title bar. When a window is maximized, the Maximize button changes to the Restore button.	
Reduce a window to a button on the taskbar	Click the Minimize button. To display a minimized window, click its button on the taskbar.	
Move a window	Drag the title bar.	
Close a window	Click the Close button.	

Using Menus

Just like a restaurant menu, a program menu provides a list of options, called *commands*, from which you can choose. To select a menu or a menu command, you click the item you want. You can also make selections with the keyboard by holding down ALT as you press the underlined letter in a menu or command name.

In the following exercise, you'll open and make selections from a menu.

Open and make selections from a menu

You can also press ALT+E to open the Edit menu.

1 In the My Computer window, click Edit in the menu bar.

The Edit menu appears. Notice which commands are dimmed, indicating that a command is not available.

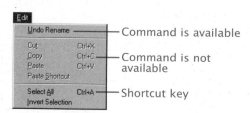

2 Click the Edit menu name to close the menu.

The menu closes.

3 Click View in the menu bar to open the menu.

4 On the View menu, click Toolbar.

The View menu closes, and a toolbar appears below the menu bar.

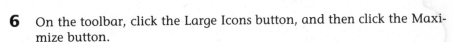

5   On the View menu, click List.

The items in the My Computer window now appear in a list, rather than by icons.

Maximize

6   On the toolbar, click the Large Icons button, and then click the Maximize button.

Clicking a button on a toolbar is a quick way to select a command.

7   On the View menu, point to Arrange Icons.

A cascading menu appears listing additional menu choices. When a right-pointing arrow appears after a command name, it indicates that additional commands are available.

8   Click anywhere outside the menu to close it.

9   On the menu bar, click View, and then click Toolbar again.

The View menu closes and the toolbar is now hidden.

Close

10   Click the Close button in the upper-right corner of the My Computer window to close the window.

Using Dialog Boxes

When you choose a command name that is followed by an ellipsis (...), Windows-based programs display a dialog box in which you can provide more information about how the command should be carried out. Dialog boxes consist of standard features as shown in the following illustration.

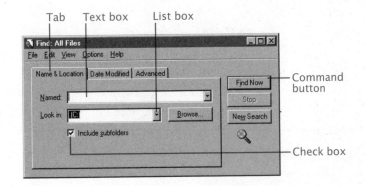

You can press CTRL+TAB to move between dialog box tabs.

To move around in a dialog box, you click the item you want. You can also use the keyboard to select the item by holding down ALT as you press the underlined letter. Or, you can press TAB to move between items.

Display the Taskbar Properties dialog box

Some dialog boxes provide several categories of options displayed on separate tabs. You click the top of an obscured tab to bring it forward and display additional options.

1 On the taskbar, click the Start button. On the Start menu, point to Settings, and then click Taskbar.

2 In the Taskbar Properties dialog box, click the Start Menu Programs tab.

On this tab, you can customize the list of programs that appears on your Start menu.

3 Click the Taskbar Options tab, and then click to select the Show Small Icons In Start Menu check box.

When a check box is selected, it displays a check mark.

4 Click the check box a couple of times, and observe how the display in the dialog box changes.

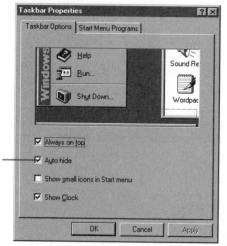

When you click a check box that is selected, you turn the option off.

Clicking any check box or option button will turn the option off or on.

5 Click the Cancel button in the dialog box.

This closes the dialog box without changing any settings.

Getting Help with Windows 95 or Windows NT

When you're at work and you want to find out more information about how to do a project, you might ask a co-worker or consult a reference book. To find out more about functions and features in Windows 95 or Windows NT, you can use online Help. For example, when you need information about how to print, the online Help system is one of the most efficient ways to learn. The Windows Help system is available from the Start menu, and you can choose the type of help you want from the Help Topics dialog box.

For instructions on broad categories, you can look on the Contents tab. Or, you can search the Help index for information on specific topics. The Help information is short and concise, so you can get the exact information you need quickly. There are also shortcut buttons in many Help topics that you can use to directly switch to the task you want.

Viewing Help Contents

The Contents tab is organized like a book's table of contents. As you choose top-level topics, called *chapters*, you see a list of more detailed topics from which to choose. Many of these chapters have Tips and Tricks subsections to help you work more efficiently as well as Troubleshooting subsections to help you resolve problems.

Find Help on general categories

Suppose you want to learn more about using Calculator, a program that comes with Windows. In this exercise, you'll look up information in the online Help system.

1   Click Start. On the Start menu, click Help.

The Help Topics: Windows Help dialog box appears.

2   If necessary, click the Contents tab to make it active.

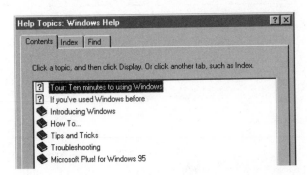

3   Double-click "Introducing Windows" or "Introducing Windows NT."

A set of subtopics appears.

4 Double-click "Using Windows Accessories."

5 Double-click "For General Use."

6 Double-click "Calculator: for making calculations."

A Help topic window appears.

7 Click the Close button to close the Help window.

Close

Finding Help on Specific Topics

You can find specific Help topics by using the Index tab or the Find tab. The Index tab is organized like a book's index. Keywords for topics are organized alphabetically. You can either scroll through the list of keywords, or type the keyword you want to find. You can then select from one or more topic choices.

With the Find tab, you can also enter a keyword. The main difference is that you get a list of all Help topics in which that keyword appears, not just the topics that begin with that word.

Find Help on specific topics using the Help index

In this exercise, you'll use the Help index to learn how to change the background pattern of your Desktop.

1 Click Start. On the Start menu, click Help.

The Help Topics dialog box appears.

2 Click the Index tab to make it active.

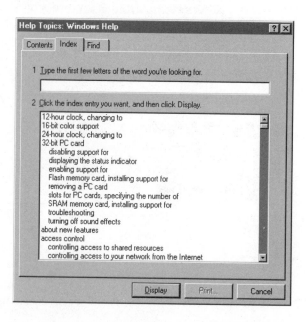

3 In the text box, type **display**

A list of display-related topics appears.

4 Double-click the topic named "background pictures or patterns, changing."

The Topics Found dialog box appears.

5 Double-click the topic named "Changing the background of your desktop."

6 Read the Help topic.

7 Click the shortcut button in step 1 of the Help topic.

The Display Properties dialog box appears. If you want, you can immediately perform the task you are looking up in Help.

8 Click the Close button on the Display Properties dialog box.

9 Click the Close button on the Windows Help window.

Shortcut

Close

Close

NOTE You can print any Help topic. Click the Options button in the upper-left corner of any Help topic window, click Print Topic, and then click OK. To continue searching for additional topics, you can click the Help Topics button in any open Help Topics window.

Find Help on specific topics using the Find tab

In this exercise, you'll use the Find tab to learn how to change your printer's settings.

1 Click Start. On the Start menu, click Help to display the Help dialog box.

2 Click the Find tab to make it active.

3 If you see the Find Setup wizard, accept the default selections by clicking Next, and then click Finish to complete and close the wizard.

The wizard creates a search index for your Help files. This might take a few minutes. The next time you use Find, you won't have to wait for Windows to create the list. The Find tab appears.

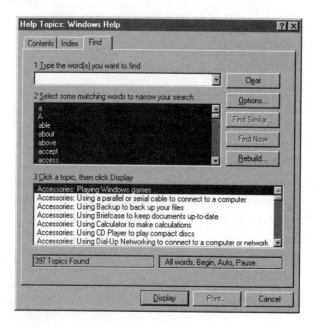

4 In the text box, type **print**

All topics that have to do with printing appear in the list box at the bottom of the tab.

5 In area 3 of the Help Topics dialog box, click the "Changing printer settings" topic, and then click Display.

The Help topic appears.

Close

6 Read the Help topic, and then click the Close button on the Windows Help window.

Find Help on a dialog box

Almost every dialog box includes a question mark button in the upper-right corner of its window. When you click this button, and then click any dialog box control, a Help window appears that explains what the control is and how to use it. In this exercise, you'll get help on specific elements in a dialog box by using context-sensitive Help.

1 Click the Start button, and then click Run.

The Run dialog box appears.

Help

2 Click the Help button.

The mouse pointer changes to an arrow with a question mark.

3 Click the Open text box.

A Help window appears, providing information on how to use the Open text box.

4 Click anywhere on the Desktop, or press ESC to close the Help window. The mouse pointer returns to its previous shape.

5 In the Run dialog box, click Cancel.

TIP You can change the way the Help topics appear on your screen. Click the Options button in any Help Topics window, and then point to Font to change the font size.

What Is Microsoft PowerPoint?

Whether presentations help you deliver company results to a shareholders' meeting or report sales figures at a hastily scheduled business meeting, they play a major role in how business people communicate. Microsoft PowerPoint 97 for Windows, the leader in presentation graphics software, has all the tools you'll need to put together professional, compelling presentations quickly and easily.

Microsoft PowerPoint 97 Step by Step is a comprehensive tutorial that shows you how to use PowerPoint to create professional-looking presentations. Working through this book you'll learn about the different presentation materials PowerPoint helps you create: slides, overheads, audience handouts, presentation outlines, speaker's notes, and electronic presentations that show on your computer. You'll discover the basic building blocks that make up dynamic slides, including eye-catching clip art, easy-to-use text tools that let you create and format text, drawing tools help you create interesting shapes and effects, and special tools that help you import information from other sources, such as charts, graphs, tables, pictures, sounds, and movies. This book also teaches you how to find the help you need from PowerPoint's useful aids, such as online Help, tips, and wizards.

Start Microsoft PowerPoint and put the Office Assistant to work

Now that you are familiar with some of the terms and concepts that are important to your understanding of PowerPoint, you can start PowerPoint and learn how to use online Help. You can obtain PowerPoint online Help by using the Office Assistant to guide you as you work.

1 On the taskbar, click Start, point to Programs, and then click Microsoft PowerPoint.

Microsoft PowerPoint starts.

Close

2 If a dialog box appears, click the Close button, and then on the Help menu, click Microsoft PowerPoint Help.

The Office Assistant appears.

3 In the text box, type **Create A New Presentation** and then click Search.

4 Click the blue bullet next to Create A New Presentation.

A Help window appears.

Close

5 Read the contents of the Help window, and then click the Close button.

The Help window closes.

Create a blank presentation

To get to know PowerPoint and its features, you'll create a blank presentation.

1 Click the Blank Presentation option button.

2 Click the OK button.

The New Slide dialog box appears with the Title Slide layout selected. The New Slide dialog box displays 24 ready-made slide layouts with placeholders for titles, text, and objects such as clip art, graphs, and charts. You'll learn more about this dialog box in Lesson 1.

3　Click the OK button.

A maximized blank presentation appears with the Title Slide layout. Don't worry if your screen is sized differently; PowerPoint automatically fits the PowerPoint window to the maximum size allowed by your monitor.

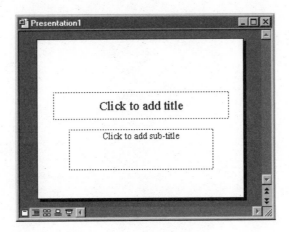

Quit Microsoft PowerPoint

Now that you are familiar with Windows and Microsoft PowerPoint, you can proceed to Lesson 1. You can quit PowerPoint either by clicking the Close button on the Microsoft PowerPoint title bar or by clicking the Exit command on the File menu. Try exiting PowerPoint so that you can start with a new presentation in Lesson 1.

1　On the File menu, click Exit.

To exit PowerPoint, you can also use the keyboard shortcut CTRL+Q.

2　If a dialog box appears asking if you want to save changes to the presentation, click the No button.

Quit Windows 95 or Windows NT

Close

1　Close all open windows by clicking the Close button in each window.

2　Click Start, and then click Shut Down.

3　When you see the Shut Down Windows dialog box, click the Yes button.

 WARNING To avoid loss of data or damage to your operating system, always quit Windows by using the Shut Down command on the Start menu before you turn your computer off.

285

Customizing PowerPoint

PowerPoint has many optional settings that can affect either the screen display or the operation of certain functions. In this appendix, you'll learn how to customize the PowerPoint screen display to meet your needs. You'll learn how to change your toolbars so that the tools you use most often are easy to find. In addition, you'll find out how to customize your default drawing attributes. Finally, you'll learn where to find PowerPoint's option commands.

Customizing PowerPoint Toolbars

PowerPoint comes with several preset toolbars with buttons that can save you time and effort. The toolbars that appear depend on which view is active. In Slide view, for example, you see three default toolbars: Standard, Formatting, and Drawing. You've already used these toolbars, as well as the Outlining, the AutoShapes, and the Animation Effects toolbars, in earlier lessons.

Open and then close the Common Task toolbar

1   In Slide view, move the pointer over any toolbar, and then click the right mouse button.

The toolbar shortcut menu appears. Notice that Standard, Formatting, and Drawing have check marks beside their names, indicating that the toolbars are currently open.

2   From the shortcut menu, click Common Task.

The Common Task toolbar opens.

3   On the View menu, point to Toolbars, and click Common Tasks.

The Common Tasks toolbar closes. You can also click the toolbar Close button to close the toolbar.

Create a new toolbar and add buttons to it

If you find that you use a particular command or button often, or another button infrequently, you can customize existing toolbars to make them work better for you or you can create new toolbars that contain only the buttons that you need to use. You can also move buttons around on your existing toolbars to make them easier to use, or move the entire toolbar to a new location.

1   On the Tools menu, click Customize.

The Customize dialog box appears with the Toolbars tab selected.

2   Click the New button.

The New dialog box appears.

3   In the Toolbar Name box, type **Special**, and then click the OK button.

An empty toolbar appears in the upper-left corner of the presentation window, as shown in the left margin.

4   Click the Commands tab.

5   In the Categories list box, click Slide Show.

Your Customize dialog box should look like the following illustration:

You can click a command and click the Description button to display a description of what each button does.

6   Drag the Custom Shows button to the Special toolbar you just created.

Arrange the buttons on your new toolbar

You can move buttons onto a toolbar or from one toolbar to another. With the Customize dialog box open, you can move a button by dragging it to a new location. Be careful not to drag the button off the toolbar and release the mouse button. If you do, you'll need to add it again.

1 In the Categories area, scroll down and click Slide Show.

2 Drag the Action Settings button on the Special toolbar.

A black insertion bar appears as you drag the button on the Special toolbar to indicate the new location of the button. The Action Settings button appears on the Special toolbar.

3 Drag the Custom Shows button to the other side of the Action Settings button.

You can move a toolbar button to another location on a different toolbar by dragging the button.

4 Scroll down and drag the Custom Animation button on the Special toolbar.

If you add the wrong button, you can remove it by dragging the button off the toolbar in a blank area of the window.

5 Drag the Custom Animation button off the toolbar.

The button is removed.

6 Click the Close button.

7 Click the Close button on the Special toolbar.

Customizing PowerPoint Defaults

Default settings are the initial attributes that are applied when creating an object. Some examples of PowerPoint default settings include: fill color, shadow, line style, and font style. To find out the current default settings for your presentation, draw an object or create a text object and check the object's attributes.

Change font defaults

1 Open any presentation and switch to Slide view.

2 On the Drawing toolbar, click the Text Box button.

Text Box

3 Click a blank area of the presentation window to create a text box.

4 On the Format menu, click Font.

The Font dialog box appears.

5 In the Font list, click Book Antiqua.

6 In the Size list, click 18.

7 Click the Default For New Objects check box to select the option.

Your Font dialog box should look similar to the following illustration:

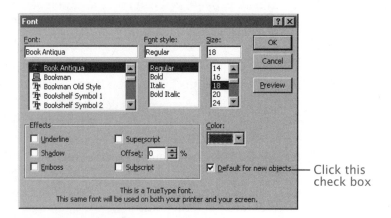

Click this check box

8 Click the OK button.

The text styles are applied to the text defaults.

9 Type **Book Antiqua, size 18, is now the default font**

10 Select the text object and press the DELETE key.

Change object attribute defaults

Oval

1 On the Drawing toolbar, click the Oval button (or any drawing tool button).

2 Drag an oval.

Notice the current default fill color, shadow, and line style settings.

3 On the Format menu, click AutoShape.

The Format AutoShape dialog box appears.

4 Click the Fill Color drop-down arrow and then change the fill color.

Make any changes you want to the object.

5 Click the Default For New Objects check box to select the option.

6 Click the OK button.

7 On the Drawing toolbar, click the Oval button.

Oval

8 Drag an oval.

Because you changed the object's styles to the object defaults, the original oval object has the same attributes as the new object.

9 Click the oval object and press the DELETE key.

Changing PowerPoint Options

You can customize PowerPoint operations by changing different options. You can view these options by clicking the Options command on the Tools menu. Then you click the tab corresponding to the options you want to change. For example, you can change how some dialog boxes display, change text editing options, and change undo settings.

View options

Click the View tab to change options that affect the status bar, ruler, and slide show.

General options

Click the General tab to change options that affect the PowerPoint Startup dialog box, New Slide dialog box, printing, recently used files, file properties, and full text search. For more information about a dialog box option, click the Help button on the title bar, and then click an option to get help.

Edit options

Click the Edit tab to change options that affect Smart Quotes, automatic word selection, Smart Cut, drag and drop editing, and spelling.

Print options

Click the Print tab to change options that affect printing the background, TrueType fonts, inserted object, and print button settings.

Save options

Click the Save tab to change options that affect the save AutoRecover information, file properties, full text search information, and default save option.

Spelling options

Click the Spelling tab to change options that affect the proofread as you type, suggest words, and ignore words in uppercase and words with numbers.

Advanced options

Click the Advanced tab to change options that affect the maximum number of undos, picture quality, and file location.

Simplifying Tasks with Macros

If you perform a task repeatedly, you can record a macro that will automate the task. A macro is a series of commands and functions—stored in a Visual Basic module—you can run whenever you need to perform a task. You can record a macro in PowerPoint to combine multiple commands into one, speed up routine editing and formatting tasks, or make a dialog box option more accessible.

Record a new macro

1   On the Tools menu, point to Macro, and then click Record New Macro.

The Record Macro dialog box appears.

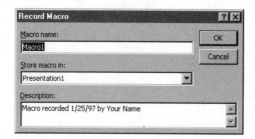

The default macro name appears selected in the Macro Name box. To give the macro a name, you can type a name without spaces.

2   Type **InsertTitleOnlySlide**

3   Click the OK button.

The Stop Recording toolbar appears with a Stop Recording button.

4   On the Standard toolbar, click the Insert New Slide button.

The New Slide dialog box appears.

5 Click the Title Only layout.

6 Click the OK button.

7 On the Stop Recording toolbar, click the Stop Recording button.

The macro is recorded and the Stop Recording toolbar closes.

Run a macro

Before you record or write a macro, you need to plan the steps and commands you want the macro to perform. If you make a mistake while recording, you can also record a correction.

1 On the Tools menu, point to Macro, and then click Macros.

The Macro dialog box appears.

2 In the Macro Name area, click InsertTitleOnlySlide, as shown in the following illustration:

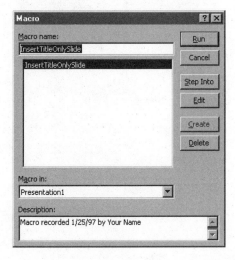

With the Macro dialog box, you can run a macro completely or step through one command at a time. You can also create, edit, or delete a macro.

3 Click the Run button.

The Macro dialog box closes and executes the macro.

> **TIP** You can create more advanced macros by entering Visual Basic commands in the Visual Basic Editor. To open the Visual Basic Editor, point to Macro and click Visual Basic Editor on the Tools menu. Click the Help button to learn how to use the product.

Expanding PowerPoint Functionality with Add-ins

Add-ins are supplemental programs that extend the capabilities of PowerPoint by adding custom commands and specialized features. You obtain add-ins from independent software vendors, or write your own using the PowerPoint Visual Basic Editor. To use an add-in, you must first install it on your computer and then load it into PowerPoint. PowerPoint add-ins have the file name extension .ppa. You can find PowerPoint add-ins on the Office 97 CD-ROM or on the Microsoft Web site at http://www.microsoft.com.

Load an add-in program

1   On the Tools menu, click Add-Ins.

    The Add-Ins dialog box appears.

2   Click the Add New button.

    The Add New PowerPoint Add-Ins dialog box appears.

3   In the Look In box, click the folder where you stored your PowerPoint add-in programs.

4   In the list of file and folder names, click a PowerPoint add-in program.

5   Click the Open button.

    The add-In program is loaded. To conserve memory and increase the speed of PowerPoint, it's smart to unload add-in programs you don't often use. When you unload an add-in, its features and commands are removed from PowerPoint. However, the program itself remains on your computer for easy reloading.

6   In the Available add-ins list, click the add-in you want to load, and then click the Load button.

    The add-in program is registered and a check mark appears.

7   Click the Close button.

    The add-in program is available for use.

Unload an add-in program

1   On the Tools menu, click Add-Ins.

    The Add-Ins dialog box appears.

2   Click the add-in you want to unload.

3   Click Unload to remove the add-in from memory but keep its name in the list or click Remove to remove the add-in from the list and from the registry file.

    When you unload or remove an add-in it remains on your computer.

4   Click the Close button.

3-D Settings toolbar A toolbar that contains tools for changing the attributes, such as lighting, depth, direction, surface and color, of a 3-D object.

accent colors Three colors in the color scheme designed to work as the colors for secondary features, hyperlinks, and visited hyperlinks on a slide.

active cell The currently selected cell of a datasheet, indicated by a heavy border.

add-in program A supplemental program that extends the capabilities of PowerPoint by adding custom commands and specialized features.

adjustment handle A diamond the size of a resize handle that you drag to adjust object dimensions.

anchor point The point that remains stable as the text grows and shrinks during editing; for example, a top anchor point with a left text alignment allows the text to grow right and down as it normally would when you type. A top center anchor point would allow the text to grow left, right, and down.

Animation Effects toolbar The tools on the Animation Effects toolbar are used for setting animation effects such as drive-in, typewriter text, laser text, and camera.

animation settings The dialog box controls for setting animation options and transition effects.

animation slide A slide that shows objects progressively (one after another) during a slide show as you click the mouse button or use slide timings.

application A piece of software, like Microsoft PowerPoint or Microsoft Excel.

attributes The features of an object, such as color, shadow, and pattern.

AutoCorrect A feature that replaces common misspellings as you type with the correct spelling.

AutoLayout Ready-made placeholders for titles, text, and objects such as clip art, graphs, and charts.

AutoLayout object area Object placeholders for text, graphs, tables, organizational charts, and clip art. Click to add text in a placeholder, or double-click to add the specified object.

automatic link A link to information that is updated whenever the information is changed.

automatic word selection A selection option that makes it easier to select multiple words. Place the pointer anywhere in a word and drag to select the entire word.

AutoShapes toolbar A toolbar that contains tools for drawing common shapes such as stars, banners, flowcharts, connectors, and action buttons.

axis A line that serves as a reference for plotting data (x,y, and z axes) in a graph.

Background color The underlying color in the color scheme. All colors added to your presentation are added over the background color. To change the background color, change the first color of the color scheme.

background objects Objects you add to the master slide so they will appear on each slide in a presentation. Any object on the masters other than the title or main text object is considered a background item.

Black and White view A toolbar button for viewing color slides in black and white.

browser Software, such as Microsoft Explorer, that interprets the markup of HTML files posted on the World Wide Web and displays them to the user.

bullet A mark, usually a round or square dot, used to emphasize or distinguish items in a list.

cell One rectangle of the datasheet where you enter data.

chart window The window within Microsoft Graph that displays your data graphically.

click To press and release a mouse button in one nonstop motion.

Clipboard A temporary storage area for cut or copied text or graphics. You can cut or copy contents from any application, such as PowerPoint or Word, to the Clipboard and then paste them into any application.

color scheme The basic set of eight colors provided for any slide. The color scheme consists of a background color, a color for lines and text, and six additional colors balanced to provide a professional look to your presentation. You can apply color schemes to slides and to notes pages.

column control box The box to the left of the column heading in a Microsoft Graph datasheet. Click this box to select a column; double-click it to exclude or include the data in the graph.

column heading The left column of the datasheet in Microsoft Graph where you enter column labels.

constrain keys Keys such as CTRL and SHIFT that when held down constrain how an object is drawn. Using these keys can constrain an object to expand from its center or its sides, top, or bottom.

control handle The square that appears at each vertex of arcs and freeform objects when you are editing them. Select and drag the control handle to change the dimensions of such objects.

Control Panel The Microsoft Windows application that adjusts operations and formats, such as the date, time, screen color, fonts, and printer settings. The settings affect both Windows and PowerPoint.

crop To trim away the parts of a graphic or picture you don't want to display.

cut To remove selected text or graphics from a slide that you can then place in another slide, presentation, or application. The information cut is placed on the Clipboard and stays there until another piece of information is cut or copied.

data series A row or column of a datasheet in Microsoft Graph used to draw one or more data markers on a graph.

datasheet window The window within Graph that contains the rows and columns of the datasheet in which you enter your data.

defaults Predefined settings such as the slide size, slide orientation, color settings, and fonts. Use appropriate dialog boxes and master views to change defaults.

dialog box A box that displays available command options that you review or change before issuing a command.

drag To hold down the mouse button while moving the mouse.

drawing object A single component of your drawing. Objects can be drawn using tools from the Drawing toolbar, which include AutoShapes, ovals, rectangles, freeform shapes, and arcs.

Drawing toolbar A toolbar that contains the tools to draw lines, circles, boxes, arcs, and freeforms, to modify object attributes such as the fill color and line width, and to rotate objects.

edit To add, delete, or change text, objects, and graphics.

embed To store information inside your PowerPoint presentation that was created using a different application. The information that was not a part of your presentation before embedding now becomes a part of your presentation.

embedded object An object that is created with another application but is stored in PowerPoint. To update an embedded object, you work with it within PowerPoint.

file A presentation that has been created and saved with a unique file name and location. PowerPoint stores all presentations as files.

File Transfer Protocol (FTP) A protocol that makes it possible for a user to transfer files from one location to another over the Internet.

Fills color A color in the color scheme used to fill objects that contrasts with the background and lines and text colors.

folder A container that allows you to group documents and files. Part of file organization structure—like a directory.

font A collection of symbols and alphabetic and numeric characters with a consistent design. Each font has a name with which you can apply the font to text.

Format Painter A feature that picks up an object's format and applies that format to another object.

Formatting toolbar A toolbar that contains tools to modify text attributes and is available in Slide view, Outline view, and Notes Pages view.

four-headed arrow The pointer you use to move text lines and paragraphs around in the main text.

frame The line that forms the object. The four lines of a rectangle are its frame, the three lines of a triangle are its frame, etc. You can change the style of the frame by changing the line style.

Graph tool The tool on the Standard toolbar that allows you to access Microsoft Graph.

Graph window The window in which you work with Microsoft Graph. It is similar to the PowerPoint window.

grid An invisible network of vertical and horizontal lines that covers the slide. The grid automatically aligns objects to the nearest intersection of the grid.

gridlines Optional lines in Microsoft Graph that extend from the tick marks on an axis across the plot area to make it easier to view data values.

group A multiple selection of objects that is treated as a single object when you use the Group command on the Draw menu.

guides Two straight edges, one horizontal and one vertical, used for visually aligning objects. You can align objects at the corner or the center depending upon which is closer.

hidden slide A slide that isn't automatically displayed during a slide show or printed.

home page The first page in an HTML document that appears in the browser.

hyperlink A "hot spot" or "jump" to a location in the same file, another file, or an HTML page represented by colored and underlined text, or by a graphic.

icon A graphical representation of a file-level object (for example, a disk drive, a directory, an application, or another object) that you can select and open.

Internet A worldwide network of thousands os smaller computer networks and millions of commercial, educational, and personal computers.

Intranet A network within an organization that uses Internet technologies to navigate between documents, pages, or objects using hyperlinks.

landscape A term used to refer to the horizontal page orientation; the opposite of portrait orientation.

legend The key that identifies the patterns, colors, or symbols associated with the markers of a data series in Microsoft Graph and shows the data series name that corresponds to each marker.

levels The different paragraph indentations at which paragraphs appear in an outline.

link To include information within your presentation that is stored outside your presentation. The information remains "attached" to the original source while you work on it in your PowerPoint presentation.

linked object An object created in another application that maintains a connection to its source. A linked object, unlike an embedded object, is stored in its source document, where it was created. PowerPoint stores only a representation of the original document and information about its location. You update a linked object within its source application.

macro A series of commands and functions stored in a Visual Basic module to perform a task.

main text object The main text on a slide.

main text placeholder The empty main text object that appears on a new slide.

master text The formatted placeholder for the main slide text on the Slide Master. The master text controls the font, color, size, and alignment of the main text object as well as its placement on the slide.

master title The formatted placeholder for slide titles on the Slide Master. The master title controls the font, color, size, and alignment of the title text as well as its object attributes (fill, line, and shadow) and its placement on the slide.

menu A list of commands that drop down from the menu bar. The menu bar appears across the top of the application window and lists the menu names (for example, File and Edit).

move up/move down To move a paragraph up or down to exchange it with the paragraph above or the paragraph below.

multiple selection Selecting more than one object by using the SHIFT+click method or by dragging the selection rectangle. When you flip, rotate, or resize a multiple selection, all objects in the multiple selection react together.

Office Assistant A help system that answers questions, offers tips, and provides help for a variety of Microsoft Office 97 program features.

other colors Non-scheme colors you can use for special purposes. Every color menu has a command on it so you can choose a special color. Other colors will not automatically change when you choose a different color scheme for a presentation.

outlining functions A set of functions on the Outlining toolbar you use to promote and demote paragraphs to different levels in the outline and move them up and down within your presentation. These functions work in any PowerPoint view.

Outlining toolbar A toolbar that contains tools to rearrange outline title and paragraph text.

Pack And Go A wizard that makes it easy to compress your presentation onto a disk. Use the Pack And Go wizard to prepare a presentation for use on another computer

paragraph Text that begins when you press ENTER and ends when you press ENTER again.

paste To insert cut or copied text or graphics into a slide from the Clipboard.

paste special To insert cut or copied text or graphics with a special format (for example, BMP and RTF for graphics and text, respectively).

picture An image from another application. A picture has object properties. You can resize it, move it, and recolor it; and some pictures can be ungrouped into component objects.

placeholder A reserved object to place information. Each placeholder is surrounded by a dotted line with a message telling you to click and type your text or to double-click to open an embedded application.

portrait A term used to refer to the vertical page orientation; the opposite of landscape orientation.

PowerPoint Animation Player A special application that is designed to display the full range of PowerPoint's special effects over the Internet. You can distribute the Player freely.

PowerPoint Viewer A special application that is designed to give electronic slide shows for those who are going to be running slide shows on computers without PowerPoint. You can distribute the Viewer freely.

Presentation Conference A wizard that makes it easy to present a slide show over a network or the Internet on two or more computer at the same time.

promote/demote To move lines of text or paragraphs out or in a level in the outline. Usually, when you promote text, it moves to the left; when you demote text, it moves to the right.

regular shape A perfectly proportioned shape that you can inscribe within a square. You can draw regular shapes by using the SHIFT key. The following shapes can be made regular by using the SHIFT key: circle, square, diamond, cross, star, hexagon, equilateral triangle, and octagon.

remaining colors The six additional colors in the color scheme.

resize handle The square at each corner of a selected object. Dragging a resize handle resizes an object.

row control box The box above a row heading. Click this box to select a row; double-click to exclude or include the data in the graph.

row heading The top row of the datasheet where row labels are entered in Microsoft Graph.

ruler A graphical bar displayed on the left and at the top of the PowerPoint window. From the ruler you can set tabs and indents to any text object.

scale To change an object's size by reducing or enlarging it by a constant percentage or to a specific size.

scroll bar A graphical device for moving vertically and horizontally through a presentation slide with the pointer. Scroll bars are located along the right and bottom edges of the presentation window.

selection box The gray slanted-line or dotted outline around an object that indicates it is selected. Selecting and dragging the selection box moves the object.

series names The names that identify each row or column of data.

Shadow color The color in a color scheme that PowerPoint applies to a shadowed object. The shadow color is often a darker shade of the Background color.

shape The form of an object, such as a rectangle, circle, or square. The shape is also an attribute because you can change the object's shape without redrawing the object. Arcs, freeforms, and lines are not considered shapes.

slide icon An icon that appears next to each slide title in the outline.

smart cut and paste A cut and paste feature that makes sure words are correctly spaced after using the Cut and Paste commands.

source The document that contains the original information in a linked object; the document to which you are linking.

stacking The placement of objects one on top of another. Use the Order commands to change the stacking order.

template A presentation whose format and color scheme you apply to another presentation. There are professionally designed templates that come with PowerPoint, but you can use any template or create your own.

Text and lines color A color in the color scheme, which contrasts with the background color for writing text and drawing lines on the slide. Together with the background color, the lines and text color sets the tone for the presentation.

text attributes Characteristics of text, including its font, type size, style, color, etc. You can change text attributes before or after you have typed the text.

text editing buttons Buttons on the Formatting and Standard toolbars used to change the attributes of text, including the font size, bold, italic, underline, shadow, and bullet attributes.

tick mark A small line that intersects an axis and marks off a category, scale, or data series. The tick mark label identifies the tick mark.

tick-mark labels The names that appear along the horizontal axis of an area, column, or line graph or along the vertical axis of a bar graph. When data series are in rows, the tick-mark labels are the column labels. When data series are in columns, the tick-mark labels are the row labels.

timing The amount of time a slide stays on the screen during a slide show. Each slide can have a different timing.

title object The title on the slide.

title placeholder The title box that appears on a new slide.

Title text color A color in a color scheme that, like the Lines and Text color, contrasts with the Background color.

toolbar A graphical bar in the presentation window with buttons that perform some of the common commands in PowerPoint. You can display or hide existing toolbars and create new ones. The toolbar changes in PowerPoint depending on the view, except for Slide and Notes Pages views, which use the same toolbar.

transitions The effects that move one slide off the screen and the next slide on during a slide show. Each slide can have its own transition effect.

view Different ways to display your presentation in PowerPoint. PowerPoint has four views—Slide, Outline, Notes Pages, and Slide Show.

window A rectangular area on your screen in which you view and work on presentations.

World Wide Web A system for navigating the Internet by using hyperlinks with a Web browser.

Index

Index

Index

Index

The
Step by Step
Practice Files Disk

The enclosed 3.5-inch disk contains timesaving, ready-to-use practice files that complement the lessons in this book. To use the practice files, you'll need PowerPoint 97 and either the Windows 95 operating system or version 3.51 Service Pack 5 or later of the Windows NT operating system.

Most of the *Step by Step* lessons use practice files from the disk. Before you begin the *Step by Step* lessons, read the "Installing and Using the Practice Files" section of the book. There you'll find a description of each practice file and easy instructions telling how to install the files on your computer's hard disk.

Please take a few moments to read the license agreement on the previous page before using the enclosed disk.